TAKIN

THE LEGACY OF SOMA WEISS, EUGENE STEAD, AND PAUL BEESON

William Hollingsworth, M.D.
Professor of Medicine, Emeritus
University of California, San Diego
and
Chief, Medical Service, Emeritus
VA Medical Center
San Diego, California

Library of Congress Catalog Number 94-65579

ISBN Number 1-57087-038-1

Production Design by Robin Ober

Professional Press
Chapel Hill, North Carolina 27515-4371

For: Medical Education and Research Foundation
      PO Box 81344
      San Diego, CA 92138

Manufactured in the United States of America
96 95 94 93 92   10 9 8 7 6 5 4 3 2 1

Contents

Francis Weld Peabody, M.D., *The Care of The Patient*,
1927, Harvard University Press:

> *Page 12:* "The treatment of a disease may be
> entirely impersonal; the care of a patient must be
> completely personal."

> *Page 10:* "The art of medicine and the science of
> medicine are not antagonistic but supplementary
> to each other."

> *Page 35:* "The treatment of disease -- takes its
> proper place in the larger problem of the care of
> the patient."

Russell Baker, about 1987, The New York Times:

> "It's important to strive, but absurd to strut."

Dedication

To Eugene Stead and Paul Beeson, two remarkable teachers and exemplary doctors, who gracefully encouraged my relationship to them to move from pupil to colleague to friend,

and

To Dorothy Reycroft Hollingsworth, spouse, friend, and collaborator in many things for more than 40 years, a skillful and patient but unofficial editor.

Acknowledgements

First, Eugene and Evelyn Stead and Paul and Barbara Beeson supplied the subject matter for this book, and spent endless hours giving information and answering my questions, and editing portions of the book. Soma Weiss's daughter Lucy and son Robert, and especially his widow Elizabeth Weiss Jones were helpful and gracious. Dr. Weiss's nephew, the neurosurgeon Dr. Ernest Sachs, Jr., provided me with a wonderful Sachs family tree, and reviewed the chapter on Dr. Weiss.

In Boston, many people were helpful but I am particularly indebted to Richard Wolfe, Director of the Countway Library at Harvard, for his assistance, and for the many pleasant hours spent browsing through the Soma Weiss shelf in the historical section.

Dr. John Romano, University of Rochester and a former colleague of Dr. Weiss, sent me a long letter about Weiss and his early days at the Brigham. The late Dr. William Castle and his wife Louise provided a helpful and memorable morning of reminiscences.

In Durham, Dr. Jerome Harris, Professor Emeritus of Pediatrics, recalled an interesting experience as a student with Dr. Weiss. Duke Medical School's historian and archivist, Professor James F. Gifford, Jr., spent a morning hearing about this project, learning about the three men and provoking me to clarify my perceptions and focus my goals for the book.

My secretary for a decade, Mrs. Susan Johnston cheerfully typed my endless drafts. As unofficial editor, my wife Dorothy shaped the manuscript for my friend and official editor, Mrs. Sherrie Epstein.

Finally, had Dr. Robert Glaser not encouraged me in the venture and suggested that I apply for a grant from the Commonwealth Fund, the book would not have materialized. I was continually encouraged by medical students, house officers, colleagues, and friends of mine and of Drs. Beeson and Stead, and I only hope the final product proves valuable.

Chapter I

THE SOMA WEISS LEGACY

Soma Weiss, Soma Weiss, Soma Weiss. No amount of conjecturing would have suggested to me that I would spend my sixty-second year (1988) repeating that unusual and somewhat exotic name, trying to comprehend the man, hoping to understand the unusual magic possessed by a Professor of Medicine who died in 1942 when I was just a teenager entering college. Even by the standards of that day, Soma Weiss was a young man, only 43 years old when he died. He left behind him an important body of medical scientific writing, but his power as a teacher was to remain his outstanding legacy.

William Osler left a legacy of wise orations delivered to various graduating classes and professional bodies, pithy exhortations that distilled the wisdom of a long life and vast experience. Soma Weiss died too young to have his incisive wisdom and philosophy of education left in writing, but the legacy of a magical teacher rests on the reminiscences of his students and colleagues. They continue to refer to Soma Weiss with respect and reverence, basking in memories, but his immediate colleagues and pupils are now growing older. However, the academic offspring of Soma Weiss continue to build the image, and they represent his lineage. Fifty years after his death, Soma Weiss remains alive.

I only became truly aware of Soma Weiss in 1987 when I had planned to begin a sabbatical year in Australia. I hoped to spend part of that year in Australia gathering data for a book about two remarkable men who had both been my mentors: Eugene A. Stead, Jr., at the beginning of my professional life and Paul B. Beeson later. During their careers, they had influenced not just me, but an astonishing number of physicians and professors of medicine. Both Stead and Beeson are alive and well in their eighties, with physical capacities undiminished and memories intact. I wanted to write something about my mentors, then, to try to capture the qualities of leadership which led them to be successful in guiding their students, residents, and faculty into academic careers, leadership roles, and into the competent and compassionate practice of medicine. After all, the Medical Schools of Duke and Yale Universities did not have large training programs in the days of Stead and Beeson. But, through the mechanism of the diaspora of their junior colleagues, Duke under Stead and Yale under Beeson have exerted an enormous influence on medical education. I hoped to capture, in a monograph or perhaps a series of articles, the unusual qualities of these two men who were contemporaries, worked together in Boston and at Emory University in Atlanta, and who begat so many fine doctors and outstanding medical educators. I knew that they had both worked in Boston in about 1940 under a young professor named Soma Weiss who died of a stroke while a very young man, but I had only a hazy idea of their debt to Dr. Weiss.

Stead and Beeson were most active in the 1950's and 1960's, when the discipline of academic internal medicine began its accelerating growth under the impetus of federal funding for research and subspecialty training through the National Institutes of Health (NIH). University Departments of Medicine expanded explosively in those years as subspecialties developed. The expansion reflected a burgeoning of medical research that provided internists with new tools to investigate, treat and cure disease.

As I remember my early years in training in the 1940's, affirmed by Lewis Thomas in his remembrance *"The Youngest Science,"* most treatment was surgical, with only a few specific medical therapies available, mostly related to hormonal replacement. The role of the internist was to arrive at a diagnosis, exclude some process that a surgeon could help, and function as a warm and empathetic physician to the patient and family until the patient's fate was decided by getting well or by dying. The internists were correctly called diagnosticians in those days; relatively few of them were essential and there was little need for them to become super-specialists. The discovery of the sulfonamides before World War II, and of penicillin during the war, began the era of scientific medicine that will lead, I believe, to the conquest of most diseases and heritable disorders within the first decades of the 21st century.

Stead and Beeson were key professors during that period of expansion of faculty and growth of research. By themselves, as heads of departments of medicine at two of a total of 72 medical schools, their influence would not have been overwhelming. They were unusual, however, in having a remarkable ability to stimulate young people to become teachers and researchers, prepared to accept responsibility as academic leaders and to create favorable environments for the growth of scholarship and research. They educated a remarkable number of well-trained, highly-compassionate young men and women physicians who would remember them and their teachings all the rest of their lives.

Table 1 is adapted from the book about Dr. Stead that was written in 1978 by Galen S. Wagner, Bess Cebe, and Marvin Rozear, and Table 2 is a similar compilation I composed for Dr. Beeson. From those Tables, I estimate that 10-15% of interns and residents in internal medicine today are being educated in departments headed by one of their progeny. Even more are being taught by faculty trained by that progeny.

TABLE 1 Academic Leaders Trained by Stead (from *E.A. Stead, Jr.*, by Galen S. Wagner, Bess Cebe, and Marvin Rozear)

Paul B. Beeson: Chairman, Medicine, Emory; to Chairman, Medicine, Yale; to Nuffield Professor, Oxford, England

Ivan Bennett: Chairman, Pathology, Hopkins; to

Vice-President, New York University Medical
School (Deceased)

Kenneth Blaylock: Chairman, Dermatology, University of Virginia

Morton D. Bogdonoff: Chairman, Medicine, University of Illinois; to Executive Associate Dean, Cornell

Stuart Bondurant: Chairman, Medicine, Albany; to
Dean, University of North Carolina

*   Rubin Bressler: Chairman, Pharmacology,
    Arizona; to Chairman, Medicine, Arizona

C. Hilmon Castle: Chairman, Family and Community Medicine, Utah

Leighton Cluff: Chairman, Medicine, Florida; to
Robert Wood Johnson Foundation

William P. Deiss: Chairman, Medicine, Texas at
Galveston

Richard V. Ebert: Chairman, Medicine, Arkansas;
to Chairman, Medicine, Minnesota

E. Harvey Estes: Chairman, Community Health
Sciences, Duke

Abner Golden: Chairman, Pathology, Georgetown;
to Chairman, Pathology, Kentucky (Deceased)

Sidney E. Grossberg: Chairman, Microbiology,
Medical College of Wisconsin

John B. Hickam: Chairman, Medicine, Indiana
(Deceased)

Bernard C. Holland: Chairman, Psychiatry, Emory

* J. William Hollingsworth: Chairman, Medicine, Kentucky; to Vice-Chairman, Medicine, University of California, San Diego

Wallace R. Jensen: Chairman, Medicine, George Washington; to Chairman, Medicine, Albany

David Kipnis: Chairman, Medicine, Washington University

William H. Knisely: Vice-Chancellor, Texas; to President, Medical University of South Carolina

Peter O. Kohler: Chairman, Medicine, Arkansas; to President, Oregon Health Sciences University

James Leonard: Chairman, Medicine, Pittsburgh; to Chairman, Medicine, Armed Forces Medical School

Samuel P. Martin: Chairman, Medicine, Florida; to Wharton School of Finance, Pennsylvania

Henry McIntosh: Chairman, Medicine, Baylor

Charles E. Mengel: Chairman, Medicine, Missouri

A. Donald Merritt: Chairman, Genetics, Indiana (Deceased)

Jack D. Myers: Chairman, Medicine, Pittsburgh

Joseph C. Ross: Chairman, Medicine, South Carolina

Peritz Scheinberg: Chairman, Neurology, South

Carolina

Theodore B. Schwartz: Chairman, Medicine, Rush-Presbyterian

James V. Warren: Chairman, Medicine, Texas at Galveston; to Chairman, Medicine, Ohio State (Deceased)

Arnold M. Weissler: Chairman, Medicine, Wayne State

James B. Wyngaarden: Chairman, Medicine, Duke; to Director, National Institutes of Health

*   Also trained with Beeson

TABLE 2 Academic Leaders Trained by Beeson as Defined by Membership in The Association of American Physicians (* Holds, or has held, chairmanship, deanship, or other major administrative position; + Deceased)

Louis Avioli, Washington University

*+ Ivan Bennett, New York University

Joseph Bertino, Sloan-Kettering

*   Philip Bondy, Yale

Paul Bornstein, University of Washington

*   Rubin Bressler, University of Arizona

Ward Bullock, University of Cincinnati

* Gerard Burrow, Yale
* Paul Calabresi, Brown
  Harold Conn, Yale
* Robert Couch, Baylor
  Louis J. Elsas, II, Emory
* Franklin Epstein, Harvard
* Harold Fallon, Medical College of Virginia
  Douglas Fearon, Hopkins
  Alvan R. Feinstein, Yale
  Philip Felig, Yale/Columbia
* Thomas Ferris, Minnesota
* Stuart Finch, Rutgers
  Harry Fozzard, University of Chicago
* Lawrence Freedman, University of California, Los Angeles
* Lawrence Frohman, University of Illinois, Chicago
  Gordon Gill, University of California, San Diego
* Phillip Gorden, National Institutes of Health
  Paul Hoeprich, University of California, Davis
* J. William Hollingsworth, University of California, San Diego
* Edward Hook, University of Virginia
* Willis Hurst, Emory
* Roland Ingram, Minnesota
  Fred Kantor, Yale
* Charles Kleeman, University of California, Los Angeles
  Francis Klocke, Buffalo
* Lewis Landsberg, Northwestern
* Aaron Lerner, Yale
* Robert J. Levy, Columbia

* Robert Luke, University of Cincinnati
  Steven Malawista, Yale
* Patrick Mulrow, Medical College of Ohio, Toledo
  Yale Nemerson, Mt. Sinai, New York
* James Nolan, Buffalo
  Joseph Pagano, University of North Carolina
  John Parker, University of North Carolina
  Ira Pastan, National Institutes of Health
* Robert Petersdorf, President, AAMC
* Leon Rosenberg, Yale
  Robert Schwartz, Boston University
  Kenneth Sterling, Bronx VA Medical Center
* Robert Wagner, University of Virginia

I hoped to be able not only to praise the men themselves, but to express in some way that their values and standards are just as important in teaching students of medicine today as they were in the 1950's. Perhaps those values are more important today, because growth and indeed the success of the overall medical endeavors has resulted in so many researchers vying for a static amount of federal funds that discord and discontent has arisen among academic physicians, creating cynicism among students. We need to be reminded of how far we have come in the practice of medicine, yet how far we still have to go. The profession of medicine as a venture remains exciting, even noble if we can tolerate such an old-fashioned expression, and provides remarkable personal satisfaction for most physicians.

Filled with these rather nebulous and perhaps disconnected ideas of what I wanted to do and to say in this book, I began to talk to Paul Beeson and Eugene Stead about their careers. I knew how interwoven their teaching and research endeavors had been, and how many honors they had received. From their curricula vitae I constructed a table (Table 3) showing certain milestones and honors that each received. The collection of honors, however, was not what I wanted to write about. Honors do, however, confirm their recognition as leaders in the academic community as a whole and from their peers and medical descendants. The Kober Medal, for example, is the highest honor that academic internal medicine can bestow on one of its members, awarded at the end of an outstanding career. The Flexner Award from the Association of American Medical Colleges (AAMC) rewards outstanding contribution to medical education. Both men received both honors. Beeson, the continuing active scientist, was elected to the National Academy of Science.

TABLE 3 Life Events and a Partial List of Honors, Eugene A. Stead and Paul B. Beeson

STEAD

Age

0   Born, Atlanta, Georgia

24   Intern, Peter Bent Brigham Hospital

34   Chairman, Department of Medicine, Emory University

39   Chairman, Department of Medicine, Duke University

62   Abraham Flexner Award for outstanding contribu-

tions to medical education of the Association of American Medical Colleges

64   President, Association of American Physicians

70   Distinguished Physician, Veterans Administration

72   Kober Medal for a distinguished career in academic medicine, Association of American Physicians

BEESON

Age

0   Born, Livingston, Montana

25   Intern, University of Pennsylvania

38   Chairman, Department Medicine, of Medicine, Emory University

44   Chairman, Department of Medicine, Yale University

55   Nuffield Professor, Oxford, England

59   President, Association of American Physicians

60   Member, National Academy of Sciences

65   Kober Medal for a distinguished career in academic medicine Association of American Physicians

66   Distinguished Physician Veterans Administration

69   Abraham Flexner Award for outstanding contributions to medical education of the Association of American Medical Colleges

I visited an old acquaintance, Dr. Robert Glaser, in 1987, as I contemplated the writing of this book. In his long academic career as dean of several medical schools and director of several medical philanthropic foundations, Glaser, of course, knew Paul Beeson and Gene

Stead and believed, as I did, that they had had an unusually strong influence on medical education from the middle of this century to the present. Because he had been a Harvard medical student in the early 1940's, he also had known Soma Weiss and felt that Weiss had had a profound and lasting influence on his young colleagues from the 1930's and 40's. Glaser, in another role as editor of the periodical *Pharos*, journal of the AOA medical student honorary society, knew that Stead had recently written an appreciation of Soma Weiss for that journal. It was partly Glaser's enthusiasm for a project that involved Stead, Beeson, and probably Soma Weiss that I decided to pursue my sabbatical in Australia and to put emphasis on preparing this monograph.

As I talked further with Paul Beeson, I realized that he had been heavily imprinted during his brief time with Soma Weiss (eighteen months as his chief resident in 1939-40). In the spring of 1988, I invited myself for a long weekend with Gene and Evelyn Stead at their home on a lake outside Durham, North Carolina. There, during a wonderful couple of days of relaxing and talking, I learned more about Soma Weiss. Gene and Evelyn, one night, produced a beautiful leatherbound volume of the eulogies about Dr. Weiss, delivered in Boston a few weeks after his death in 1942. That night I devoured the contents of the volume, and Soma Weiss became alive for me, magnetically alive. That slim volume, *In Memoriam to Soma Weiss*, is reproduced in the appendix of this monograph. Soma Weiss captured my imagination, and he continues to enter my life and work in unexpected ways.

No doubt Soma Weiss's personality had an enormous impact on all who came in contact with him. To the extent that like attracts like, his group in Boston in the late 1930's may also have reflected a group of people who thought and acted in a similar manner on many issues, but particularly on critical aspects of medical education. To Weiss and his colleagues, the patient was the center of the educational process, and a careful history from the patient and a complete physical examination constituted the main tools for understanding the patient. Once this fundamental information was obtained, they attempted to define and understand how the disease resulted in abnormalities of body chemistry and physiology. Expressed in a more pragmatic way, Soma Weiss and his colleagues represented the genesis of the modern clinical investigator who must be a doctor with proven excellence in both science and in medicine, striving to enhance the content of clinical knowledge. Weiss and his group were, of course, not the only clinical investigators of that time, but they were often ahead of their colleagues in breaking the fetters of past clinical dogma to apply the new sciences of physiology, biochemistry, and pharmacology to solving clinical problems at the bedside. As John Romano, one of the young physicians in training with Dr. Weiss, who later became Chairman of the Department of Psychiatry at the University of Rochester, recently expressed it: "We had so much hope for the future."

To a considerable extent, the spread of Soma Weiss's influence on his colleagues, and the dispersion of that group and their medical offspring throughout the medical schools of the United States, represents a spread in the belief that scientific investigation based on the patient is the cornerstone of modern medical education and clinical care. Why were Eugene Stead and Paul Beeson, and before them Soma Weiss in his tragically short career, so successful in reproducing clinical investigators who were educators and leaders? I hope this book will help to define responsible leadership.

Chapter II

Medical Education and Health Care in the Late 19th and Early 20th Centuries[1]

The careers of Soma Weiss, Eugene Stead, and Paul Beeson as medical educators and chiefs of medical services spanned half a century, from the early 1920's into the 1970's. These 50 years encompassed a period of rapid change in medical science and in medical care, with associated evolutionary changes in the education of physicians. To understand the work of these three medical educators, it seems important to appreciate the evolution in medical care during the late 19th century and early 20th century. In essence, modern medicine as we know it was just emerging when these three men began their careers.

---

[1] Much of the information in this chapter represents generally acquired information, but the following books provided specific help: Lewis Thomas, *The Youngest Science. Notes of a Medicine-Watcher*, 1983, Viking Press, New York, NY; Paul Starr, *The Social Transformation of American Medicine*, 1982, Basic Books, Inc., New York, NY; Rosemary Stevens, *In Sickness and in Wealth, American Hospitals in the Twentieth Century*, 1989, Basic Books, Inc., New York, NY; A.L., Lyons and J.R. Petrucelli, II, *Medicine. An Illustrated History*, 1987, Avondale Press, New York, NY; and G. C. Ward, *The Civil War*, 1990, Alfred A. Knopf, New York, NY.

A. Medical Care During the American Civil War (1861-1865)

The Civil War was such a cataclysmic event in the history of the United States, as well as a defining point in the industrial revolution in this country, that we tend to date important happenings or changes from before or after this devastating conflict. The War had a similar defining point in medical history: the Civil War highlighted the inadequacy of medical care as the newly invented camera provided startling photographic examples of the wounded and dead lying in large depots where medical facilities were nearly absent. The photographs plainly showed the tragedy of war and the virtual inability of physicians and surgeons to mitigate the suffering of the wounded.

Medical education was woefully deficient in Civil War physicians. Most doctors had been educated in proprietary medical schools that usually required no preliminary general education for admission. A typical medical curriculum consisted of lectures given for only three months by a faculty of three or four practitioners. Knowledge of physiology was almost non-existent, and surgical teaching represented most of the didactic lectures. By about 1850, anesthesia had been discovered (ether, chloroform, and nitrous oxide), so that painless surgery could be performed. Although doctors could perform surgery technically, the critical importance of sterile technique was only vaguely appreciated at the time, and there was no concept of bacterial or viral illnesses. Various humours or miasmas were felt to cause diseases.

The Civil War brought casualties in unprecedented numbers. A total of 660,000 men died (2% of the total population), compared with 50,000 out of a population of 240 million dead in the Vietnam War, and for every one killed in battle, two died of the raging pestilences associated with poor sanitation and the bringing together in crowded circumstances of men previously unexposed to many diseases. The recruits were largely farm laborers who had lived in sparsely settled areas in the large agrarian young nation. Contagious diseases had catastrophic effects. Chicken pox and measles epidemics caused suffering and death, and typhoid and flea-borne typhus were devastating.

In early battles, casualties were enormous. For example, the first Battle of Bull Run resulted in 5,000 casualties. The Union and the Confederate Armies attempted to organize medical corps and to provide field hospitals where the wounded could be treated. These primitive efforts did help in organizing rescue and emergency care, but as one Union soldier put it, "If a fellow has to go to the hospital, you might as well say good-bye."

The Civil War also brought out the marked differences in the general education of doctors, as well as differences in their medical abilities and experience. The best doctors were educated in colleges, mostly in the East, Yale, Harvard, Princeton, Columbia, and Pennsylvania and a few similar institutions scattered elsewhere in the United States. Their medical training was likely to have been obtained under the auspices of one of those colleges, or perhaps in Europe or supplemented by a European stay: London, Scotland, and Germany were places of medical excellence. These doctors, obviously members of the upper class, were relatively few compared with those trained in what could, at best, be described as apprentice medical schools. The *Illustrated History of the Civil War* records this comment from an Alabama private, "I believe the doctors kill more than they cure. Doctor's hain't got half sense." The soldier was probably correct. Wound infections, in this era before bacteria were known and antisepsis practiced, caused surgical mortality of about 50%. Because half their patients died, it was understandable that surgery was not performed electively, and that only severely wounded or extremely sick patients would opt for surgery.

One important reform was initiated during the Civil War, the founding of the United States Sanitary Commission, which urged cleanliness, proper disposal of human waste, and clean water supplies. This group, made up mostly of women untrained in medical care but with good common sense, urged sanitary principles on the surgeons during the War, came to the camps and washed clothes, boiled water, cooked, and distributed food and supplies. From this Union effort during the War, the concepts of sanitation and hygiene carried out by the modern public health service would emerge.

B. Changes in Medicine from the Civil War to the Early Twentieth Century

A Union surgeon general, looking back at the Civil War and medical practice, remarked that the War was fought "at the end of the medical Middle Ages." A better understanding of illness and trauma would, indeed, advance rapidly as a result of scientific and technical

progress. These achievements, in turn, would profound-
ly affect the practice of medicine, its organizational
structure, and the education of doctors and other health
professionals.

Growth of Science in Medicine

Before the Civil War, the practice of medicine reflected the meager scientific base for the profession. A
few empiric observations provided valuable drugs: opium
from poppies for severe pain, quinine from a South
American tree for cure of malaria, and digitalis from the
fox-glove plant for heart failure. These few useful drugs
were almost buried under a large pharmacopeia of useless or even dangerous concoctions.

Pasteur after 1860 and Koch in the 1880's proved
that most of the humours and miasmas thought to cause
disease were indeed bacteria, visible under the microscope and cultured on artificial media designed
to support the growth and metabolism of these small
organisms. Remarkable clinical advances followed as
bacteriology evolved into a science. Diphtheria provided
a striking example. It had been a dreaded scourge of
young children, initiated by a sore throat leading to black
gangrene-like occlusion of the pharynx and the trachea.
Diphtheria organisms produce a toxin which causes the
black gangrene and enters the bloodstream to cause
heart muscle damage and skeletal muscle paralysis.
In 1901, von Behring was awarded the first Nobel Prize
in Medicine for his work on diphtheria. He injected
the diphtheria toxin into animals and produced a protective antibody against the harmful agent. The relief of

severe respiratory strangulation in a diphtheritic infant by infusion of the antitoxin was one of the dramatic and gratifying therapies of the early 20th century. Vaccination with killed diphtheria bacteria produced protection against the disease and immunized the children, so that diphtheria became an almost extinct scourge.

Even more dramatic had been Pasteur's conquest of rabies late in the 19th century. When a rabid dog ("mad dog") bit people, mostly children, each person bitten would die, weeks or months later, of a terrible madness with fever and convulsions. The disease was called hydrophobia because the sight of water often caused patients to have convulsions. This illness turned out to be caused by a virus (unlike Koch's bacteria, not visible under the microscope) that worked its way up the nerves to the brain and caused diffuse brain infection. Pasteur only knew that the children all died, and he presumed that the rabid dog's nerve tissues contained the agent which caused the disease. He took tissue from experimentally infected animals, treated it with formaldehyde to kill an infectious agent, and injected children who had been bitten with a crude extract of the tissue containing the virus. The treatment was long and difficult, but the children lived.

Cure of rabies was a dramatic demonstration to the general public of the power of medical science, but the most significant, widely applicable medical advance from the studies of Pasteur and Koch was the control of infections during and after surgery and trauma. The American public became aware of the European advances in medicine, as names like Louis Pasteur, Marie

and Pierre Curie, and Robert Koch became internationally famous.

Surgery and the Growth of Hospitals as the Center for
Medical Education and Patient Care

Civilian hospitals during the Civil War were hor-
rors. Not much better than the military hospitals, patients
languished, many of the doctors were overworked or
incompetent, and the hospitals were run with no appreciation of cleanliness. Although military hospitals
improved during the course of the War, civilian hospitals
remained until the latter part of the 19th century primarily a place for terminal care of indigent patients, or,
during epidemics, for control of infections such as typhoid
fever and cholera. The names of Victorian-era hospitals
mirrored their function. In England, the hospital in which
the modern hospice movement (for care of terminally ill
patients) in the 1950's began bore the appropriate title
(in a wrought-iron semi-circle over its gate), Hospital for
the Sick and Dying. One of our American hospitals was
called, well into the 20th century, Hospital for the Ruptured and Crippled.

Most well-to-do patients were cared for in their
homes, with the doctor making house calls. In the late
19th century, doctors began to have offices, and, to ac-
commodate surgical patients, began to perform surgery
in their homes. It was a small step from the addition of
a surgical suite to a doctor's house to the construction of
private hospitals, most of them small and owned by one
surgeon. The number of these proprietary hospitals grew,
and in the early 20th century were augmented by munic-

ipal or county hospitals built to care for the needs of the poor as immigration swelled the population.

Hospitals were dominated by surgery in the last half of the 19th century, and the improvement in methods of administering anesthesia made more surgical procedures technically possible, although surgical progress was slow. As autopsy became more acceptable, examination of tissues by microscopy provided a better understanding of the nature of disease. A principal reason for the slow growth of surgery, and the concomitant slow emergence of hospitals as the cornerstone of the medical system, was the continued problem of wound infection. John Lister in England from 1870-1880 seized on the discoveries of Pasteur and Koch and began to use antiseptics on the skin. In addition, Lister pioneered in the use of aseptic surgical techniques. By the beginning of the 20th century, many hospitals had been established in the United States. They provided, as before, care of the dying, but with aseptic surgery and supporting laboratories of pathology and bacteriology, hospitals at least became for their patients places not to approach in fear and dread, but in hope for a cure.

What Makes a Doctor?

Medicine has always been a profession devoted to the care of the ill and injured, but this mission was poorly defined in the 19th century. In a learned profession, the practitioner might be expected to possess a relatively clearly defined body of knowledge. In the 19th century, however, medicine could not meet this expectation. No educational standards existed for a doctor of medicine.

Medical schools had negligible educational requirements for admission. Many of the institutions were simply diploma mills, operated by selfprofessed doctors for their own personal financial gain. As late as 1906, the fledgling medical organization, the American Medical Association, inspected 160 medical schools and found only half of them to be of acceptable quality. Practitioners, obviously, were a polyglot lot, and their behavior, although most often altruistic and well-meaning, was sometimes reprehensible. Surgery was the definitive therapeutic intervention. Nothing prevented a practitioner from performing surgery except the patient's innate distrust or refusal. Non-surgical interventions were few and generally ineffective. Disciplines such as Christian Science, in this era, vied with medical science for the care of sick people, and non-interventional medical subspecialties such as homeopathy, a system of medical practice that administered only minute doses of a remedy, flourished.

Among this disparate group there were well-educated men and some women who had graduated from good colleges and medical schools. Many were making a plea for the profession to discipline itself. The American Medical Association (AMA) was formed in 1846 in an attempt to improve and standardize medical care and medical education, but it would be another 50 years before it was a substantial force in medical affairs. The lay public was beginning to ask for standards in the profession, and this trend accelerated when the press reported gross examples of incompetence. In 1904, the AMA set up a Council on Medical Education, which inspected medical schools and divided them into grades

A, B, and C; after this, the B's and C's tended to disappear. By 1922, the number of medical schools had been reduced to 82, about half the number present when the first survey was completed in 1906. The AMA Council on Medical Education became a respected organization, and decreed in 1915 that at least one year of college be required before entrance to medical school. By 1929, the minimal standard was two years of college and most medical schools urged or required a full-fledged Bachelor's degree before matriculation into medical school.

At the same time that educational reform was improving the professional quality, or at least the academic background, of doctors, some states proposed and implemented the concept of medical licensure. Although state laws and regulations were quite variable, the concept of licensure as a minimal guarantor of competence was supported by the people and their legislators, as well as by responsible doctors.

As the century turned, pressure for reasonable conformity in medical training, and pressure for standards of practice, was having an effect. By 1910, when the famous Carnegie Foundation Report on Medical Education (the Abraham Flexner Report) recommended sweeping changes in medical education, many of the changes had already been set in motion. Medicine was becoming a responsible profession.

Medical Education in Late 19th-Early 20th Centuries
        The previous lack of formal medical education in this country had been a response to our pragmatic nature

as a young and robust nation. Why a physician need be a broadly educated person was not readily perceived. He was seen as a tradesman, practicing a skill. Apprenticeship with a practicing doctor represented one method of becoming a physician. Mostly, however, students had enrolled in proprietary medical schools that operated for profit. The schools provided them with lectures and demonstrations, but little or no laboratory teaching, and little direct contact with patients.

Gradually this system changed. By 1870, Harvard Medical School, which had previously been independent, was incorporated into the university, and premedical educational requirements were established. A Department of Physiology was established in 1873 and a three-year graduate medical curriculum was put in place. Other large Eastern and Midwestern universities followed, so that by 1900 most reputable schools required some college education before enrollment and provided a well-defined curriculum.

The establishment of Johns Hopkins University in 1873 and its medical school and hospital in 1889 radically and abruptly improved medical education. Johns Hopkins University controlled its own hospital and used it as a vital and primary teaching site. Teaching was not an independent activity carried out only in lecture halls; students were incorporated into the daily care of patients at the bedside. The radical effect of the Johns Hopkins method was, to considerable extent, determined by the foresight of Mr. Hopkins and by the remarkable talent of the founding faculty: William Welch in Pathology, who also served as Dean; William Osler in Medicine; William

S. Halsted in Surgery; and Howard D. Kelly in Obstetrics. By 1910, when the Flexner Report was released, Johns Hopkins was clearly considered the template for a modern medical school. Most of the changes recommended in the Flexner Report were a strong affirmation of the Hopkins system: The requirement for solid basic premedical education (usually a Bachelor of Arts or Science degree), teaching of the basic sciences pertinent to medicine with active student participation, and the active involvement of students in patient care. Because Hopkins owned its hospital, none of the conflicts common between proprietary schools and hospitals arose.

Interestingly, Harvard Medical School, impressed with the pertinence of the Hopkins model, brought Henry Christian from Baltimore to Boston to become Dean of the Harvard Medical School before he assumed, in 1913, his position as Chief of Medicine at the new Peter Bent Brigham Hospital. The brief deanship of Henry Christian at Harvard was followed by many stable years of building and regrouping under Dean David Edsall, in conjunction with Henry Christian at the Brigham and James H. Means of the Massachusetts General Hospital as outstanding Professors of Medicine and heads of the respective medical services of the two hospitals.

Before the turn of the century, medical professors cared for their private patients and taught students in their spare time, usually as a volunteered activity. By 1900, a few institutions were considering providing full-time clinician-teachers, and by the early part of the 20th century the concept of a few key full-time faculty members in clinical departments was becoming accepted.

Even then, most of the teaching was done by faculty-prac-
titioners who volunteered their time to the medical
school. It was not until after World War II that subspecialization dictated a larger full-time faculty, aided in
their teaching by practitioners.

As explained, medical postgraduate education
began in the 19th century and, even earlier, by the
simple process of a young medical graduate being
apprenticed to a more experienced doctor and working
with him. When hospitals became centers of medical
education, individual apprenticeships were replaced by
full-time work in these settings. The need for this additional hospital-based training was particularly relevant to
the evolving specialty of surgery and its various subspecialties. Young medical school graduates became house
officers and lived in the house (hospital) on a full-time
basis. Pay consisted of room and board and uniforms.
Beginning house officers were called interns for a year or
two. As their training was extended to additional years,
they were referred to as residents, or resident physicians.
The usage of these titles reflected the hospital-based nature of their work. Internship for a one- or two-year
period became common among graduates of the better
medical schools, sometimes followed by a residency for
two or three more years. As surgical specialization
evolved, the duration of the residency period grew longer. In the non-surgical disciplines, research fellowships
were sometimes interspersed with or followed residencies. Internship was thought desirable in the early part of
the 20th century, but was not mandated by law in all
states until after World War II. House officers provided

an important complement to patient care, as well as contributing greatly to education of medical students.

Medical Education and Training in the 1920's

By the time Soma Weiss arrived in this country in 1920, subsequently graduated from medical school, and embarked on his residency training at Bellevue Hospital in New York City, the chaotic state of medical education in the 19th century had largely subsided. The medical school curriculum consisted of two years of basic medical sciences followed by two years of clinical clerkships in medicine, surgery, pediatrics, and obstetrics. Even today, that basic format has not changed in most medical schools, although the content has, of course, been radically altered by scientific medical advances. The two-year internship had become widespread by 1920, with some teaching hospitals offering residencies as well.

The profession had largely policed itself and had established standards of practice. The poorly trained doctors of the 1870's had been replaced by generally admired and respected professional physicians. The American Medical Association, the Association of American Medical Colleges, the American College of Surgeons, the Association of American Physicians, and the American Hospital Association had become powerful organizations that had helped restore order and discipline to the profession.

Hospitals were now clearly the centers of education and patient care, and many an individual hospital had acquired a mystique and personality of its own. In Boston, the Massachusetts General Hospital, the Boston

City Hospital, and the Peter Bent Brigham Hospital reflected the eminence of Harvard Medical School, but acquired their own special flavors. In New York, the Presbyterian Hospital and Columbia University College of Physicians and Surgeons were almost synonymous. The huge and famous city hospital, Bellevue, was vital for teaching by Cornell, New York University, and Columbia University. Although Hopkins remained one of the few medical schools with a totally controlled hospital, other schools managed to develop a sort of hegemony over their affiliated hospitals by controlling the appointments of significant staff members.

As laboratory sciences provided more and more information for diagnosis and treatment of patients, clinical laboratories emerged within hospitals. It became standard practice for each hospital to have its own bacteriology, hematology, and blood chemistry laboratories. Other laboratories developed as faculty or staff devised new diagnostic procedures. As surgery became more complicated, there was an expansion of knowledge of gross anatomic and microscopic pathology of tissues and organs. Roentgen reported in 1895 on his invisible rays that could "photograph" bones and tissues, and within ten years the technique of roentgenography (x-ray) spread throughout the world. Departments of Radiology (including radiation therapy) became an indispensable part of the hospital-based diagnostic technology for all physicians and surgeons.

By 1920, many medical schools had three to ten full-time faculty members in their Departments of Medicine who both taught and published reports based on their clinical (patient care) experience. Clinical research became more sophisticated as researchers incorporated components of what they were learning about physiology, pharmacology, and biochemistry, into their observations of illness. Most research was performed by full-time faculty, but scholarly practitioners still played an important role in both research and education. Few clinical physicians had been trained as medical scientists, and even those who had achieved success as clinical investigators continued to view themselves primarily as physicians. Young doctors interested in clinical research were likely to train by going to work with a full-time faculty member. A few had specific training in physiology or biochemistry, and quite a number had had a year or two of experience in pathology, studying the tissues of patients who had succumbed to disease. Medical subspecialization was beginning in response to individual interests. This trend set the stage for the more formal medical subspecialization that was to flower after World War II.

Chapter III

SOMA WEISS

I n the Autumn of 1941, a patient with subarachnoid hemorrhage secondary to a ruptured berry aneurysm entered the Peter Bent Brigham Hospital in Boston. Dr. Soma Weiss, with his intense interest in vascular disease, studied the patient well, brought expert consultants by to see him, and conducted a conference on this unusual cause of brain hemorrhage in a young person. In late-December of 1941, when returning to Boston on the train from a war-related meeting in Washington, D.C., Dr. Weiss experienced a sudden blinding headache followed by vomiting and stiffness and pain in the neck. He made his own diagnosis of ruptured aneurysm with hemorrhage, confirmed by his physicians. These aneurysms, a congenital defect in the walls of the large blood vessels at the base of the brain, result from weakening of the wall and ballooning out of the defective segment, often with total rupture and rapid death of the patient secondary to a massive stroke.

In Dr. Weiss's illness, the aneurysm bled a little, clotted, and healed, and then bled again. In such "leaking" aneurysms, the hope is that the aneurysmal balloon will clot, scar, and heal, and that the patient will recover; a few do so. Dr. Weiss, after two or three small secondary hemorrhages, seemed to be stabilizing at home, and by mid-January the constant bedside vigil of his two young colleagues, Drs. Charles Janeway and John Romano, was relaxed somewhat. He felt well enough to attend to some business, and his secretary, Evelyn Stead, had twice been to the bedroom in the family home on Bryant Street to take dictation and to bring important correspondence from the office. A letter written on January 26, 1942 offered Paul Beeson, his former Chief Resident, a position back at the Brigham on his return from volunteer service in a hospital in war-time England.

On the last day of January in 1942, Dr. Romano reported that Dr. Weiss had been restive during the night when Dr. Romano had been with him. The next morning, as Dr. Janeway took over attendance of the patient, another extensive hemorrhage occurred and the patient died quickly. An autopsy was performed by Dr. S. Bert Wolbach, Chief of Pathology at the Brigham. The aneurysm had been located on the anterior communicating artery, and with the final hemorrhage blood dissected into the brain. Had he lived, says Dr. Romano, he would have lost the frontal lobes of his brain, the part that governs intellect. It was fortunate perhaps that the January 31st hemorrhage proved fatal.

By 1942, neurosurgeons were beginning to operate on aneurysms, successfully in some circumstances, and doctors have wondered, since, why surgery was not attempted on Dr. Weiss. No one really knows, but Dr.

Weiss was seen on several occasions by his personal physician, Richard Stetson, and by his colleague, the famous neurologist, Houston Merritt. His nephew, Ernest Sachs, now a distinguished Emeritus Professor of Neurosurgery at Dartmouth and then a fourth year medical student at Harvard, recalls Dr. Weiss staying in bed after the first episode and reading extensively about subarrachnoid hemorrhage. My guess is that Dr. Weiss himself decided against surgery, with the concurrence of his doctors, because he feared that surgery would damage his brain and his intellect.

Dr. Romano, in a letter in 1987, talks of the effects of Dr. Weiss's death on interns and staff at the Brigham: "I clearly remember the shock and disbelief of most of the interns and staff as we were to conduct weekly Grand Rounds without Soma Weiss. It was my first experience with the fact of denial. So many people found the fact of his death difficult to believe. That evening my wife, Miriam, and I held open house at our flat on Netherlands Road. We had invited all of the house staff to be with us. We drank beer and talked and talked. We grieved, but we also laughed, particularly in remembering Soma's many *lapsus linguae*. He was an unusual person—energetic, enthusiastic, intelligent, charming, and yet truly generative in giving of himself unstintingly to teach the young."

The Early Years in Hungary

The talented young man who died of a ruptured cerebral aneurysm in Boston on January 31, 1942, began life in Hungary, in the mountain town of Bestercze. Father Weiss was a civil engineer who was responsible for building many of the roads and bridges in the mountains of his native country. In the solid and perhaps stolid world of the dual kingdom of Austria-Hungary under Emperor Franz Josef, Mr. Weiss was a substantial citizen of Bestercze and had been knighted by the Emperor.

We know little of young Soma during his childhood years in Bestercze. He must have been an outstanding student because he was able to persuade his parents to rent him a room in the village so that he could study in peace and quiet, away from the other children in the Weiss household. His adolescence coincided with the Great War of 1914-1918. Most of those years must have been spent in Budapest as a student at the Royal Hungarian University, because by age 17 (1916) he was already at work with a well-known physiologist, Professor Hari, on research related to the respiratory quotient and muscle work. This research, published in 1919 in a major German biochemical journal, cited only one author, Soma Weiss (see C.V. in Appendix). His talent must have shown itself early.

The circumstances surrounding Soma Weiss's departure from the Old World to the New are not entirely clear. For 50 years his homeland had been a province of Hungary in the Austria-Hungary Empire, which had prospered in peace under Franz Josef's long and benign reign. World War I brought an end to this era as Franz Josef found himself aligned with Germany during that ferocious conflict in which many of the finest young men of Europe perished. The aged Emperor died during the war, and the end of the war brought chaos to his country as the monarchy collapsed. In 1919, a republic had been established in Hungary, superseded rapidly by a militant communist regime under a man named Bela Kun. There is vague talk of atrocities in the Weiss family, but it is certain that a prominent and wealthy family in Hungary would be caught up, in some way, in the turbulent politics of the time. By 1920 and the Treaty of Trianon, which formally ended World War I, the ancient Magyar Kingdom of Hungary, with its separate language and culture, was stripped of most of its land. Bestercze, a town that lies due north of Budapest, is now the little city of Banska Bystrica in Czechoslovakia.

We do not know exactly how these events affected the young medical student in Budapest. What is clear, however, is that Soma Weiss had developed a fierce belief in freedom, and by 1920 left Europe with his face firmly turned to the freedom of opportunity embodied by the United States. He wanted to be an American and was accepted as one almost as soon as he stepped off the boat. His irrepressible vibrant spirit and that of his new country were interlocked from the very beginning.

New York, 1920-1925

The tall young man from Hungary disembarked in New York and filed his United States citizenship papers that first morning. Dr. Graham Lusk at Cornell Medical School was a friend of Professor Hari, with whom Weiss had worked in Budapest. Later that first day, the young Soma Weiss applied to Dr. Lusk seeking to complete medical school at Cornell. He also found time that day to talk with Cornell medical students about respiratory quotients in relationship to clinical medicine.

Dr. Lusk found young Weiss a position as an assistant to Dr. Robert A. Hatcher, Professor of Pharmacology at Cornell, where he worked on a study of why the drug digitalis produced side-effects of nausea and vomiting when given in relatively high doses. That work with Professor Hatcher was widely recognized as showing that digitalis (and other drugs and disease processes) worked centrally on the brain to induce nausea and vomiting, rather than producing these symptoms by irritating the stomach. Dr. Weiss later recognized the central nervous system mechanism in the vomiting that accompanied his own first subarrachnoid hemorrhage. Drs. Weiss and Hatcher were to remain close friends and colleagues throughout their lives, and Soma Weiss's second child is Robert Hatcher Weiss.

Those early encounters in New York clearly establish that Soma Weiss, even as a young man, had some sort of magnetism about him. Everyone like him, wanted to know him, and wanted to help him reach his goals, whatever they were. Drs. Lusk and Hatcher were immediately enlisted to his cause, soon to be joined by Cornell's paramount leader and Chairman of Medicine, Eugene F. DuBois. Dr. DuBois, in his recounting in the *Memoriam* (see Appendix) of his contact with Dr. Weiss at Cornell, recognized this remarkable magnetism of Soma Weiss's personality, and one quote seems worth recording here: "There came to the wards of Bellevue all sorts and conditions of men; minor gangsters, major politicians, the black sheep of the best families, the humblest of hoboes. He treated them all with equal kindness and they all trusted him. Soma could become the friend and advisor of the stern hospital superintendent, the crusty medical examiner, the exasperating head nurse, and even the floor polisher whose buzz machine would nullify all efforts toward auscultation."

Between 1920 and 1923, the young emigre from Hungary obtained a B.A. degree from Columbia University in order to qualify for medical licensure. During medical school he and Professor Hatcher completed several major papers on the metabolism and toxicity of digitalis, and by the time he had completed medical school he was author of a dozen publications. Although Dr. DuBois felt that Soma Weiss was Cornell University's brightest medical graduate, he admitted that the official transcript recorded less than brilliant grades in some subjects. One suspects that Soma Weiss was having more fun learning new facts and doing research than he was in memorizing some of the useless material that filled a curriculum, then and now.

In any event, enough people at Cornell thought Weiss outstanding so that he received the two-year internship at Bellevue Hospital (Cornell University Service) which he coveted. Bellevue was then, and remains today, the legendary public hospital for the poor and homeless when they are stricken with terrible illnesses. This was the hospital whose patients had the biggest spleens, the largest hearts, and all the other medical Guinness records. Bellevue provided the young Soma Weiss with a vast array of patients with all sorts of physiological and chemical defects, patients to learn from and to study, but also patients to love, to nourish, and to encourage. The hospital population represented America's melting pot of people and Soma Weiss, as a young, self-confident, and optimistic emigre physician, must have reflected the hope for future success that America represented to those sick people. At Bellevue, Soma Weiss had already started his collection of notes on cards about unusual patients, cards that would be called forth to bolster an argument or cement a fact for the rest of his life.

The Boston City Hospital and the Thorndike
In 1925, a remarkable man with a powerful vision was drawing together a group of young doctors who were strongly motivated by the spirit of inquiry. They were to form the staff of the new Thorndike Memorial Laboratory, a recently endowed research unit to be constructed physically and emotionally into a great facility for the poor, the Boston City Hospital. Dr. Francis Peabody, a true Bostonian, had already shown his creative and independent streak by combining impeccable research training and clinical expertise with a stint at the Peking Union Medical School (PUMC), an institution where so many imaginative young American doctors would work for a time to bring modern medical science to the ancient kingdom of China, later transformed as the Republic of China under the leadership of Sun Yat Sen.

Francis Peabody's vision of clinical research embedded within a city hospital was new and powerful, and his mandate for the Thorndike was derived both from Harvard University and from the city of Boston. The building was completed in 1924, and Peabody had already recruited his few permanent staff.

Peabody obviously was gifted with good taste in

young people, because along with Soma Weiss in September, 1925, arrived another 26year-old man named William Castle, who, like Weiss, was destined for a lofty place in American medicine. Those two young men must have seemed both similar and contrasting. Castle, a born and bred Harvardian, son of a professor and raised and educated in Cambridge, was reserved and thoughtful. Soma Weiss was more outgoing, exuberant, and talkative. Both were over six feet tall, both dark and handsome, and both were impressive in their intellect. They liked one another instantly and remained close friends for life. Castle and Weiss, over the next dozen years, were to play a major role in setting the ambience and defining the unique role of the Thorndike Laboratory and the Boston City Hospital in American medicine.

Dr. Peabody had assembled, in a short time, a remarkable group of clinical investigators. His first group of appointees, in 1923, included Henry Jackson, Robert Nye, and Joseph Wearn; in 1924, Herrmann Blumgart, Charles Doan, Perrin H. Long, and Gulli Linda Muller (reputed to be the first woman medical graduate of Columbia); followed by Castle and Weiss in 1925. All of these individuals became leaders and many migrated out of Boston for distinguished careers. Wearn, for example, went to Western Reserve in Cleveland as Professor of Medicine, and, later, Dean. Charles Doan played a similar major role at Ohio State for many decades. Herrmann Blumgart migrated a few blocks away in Boston to the Beth Israel Hospital.

Francis Peabody's Thorndike Lab at
Boston City Hospital

Francis Peabody was an impressive leader who set the pattern of excellence as Director of the Thorndike and as Physician-in-Chief of Harvard's Fourth Medical Service at Boston City Hospital. Harvard, Boston University, and Tufts each had two 40-bed services at Boston City; services II and IV were the Harvard services. The Thorndike had its own staff and patients, but interacted closely with the II-IV Medical Services.

Peabody believed and practiced the dictum that both excellent teaching and excellent patient care are essential ingredients for the achievement of research of high quality. One quote from Dr. Peabody amplifies this belief: "The treatment of disease may be entirely impersonal; the care of the patient must be completely personal." He was a low-keyed but inspiring leader, spending long hours caring for his patients while teaching by example at the bedside, and at the same time guiding his younger colleagues in meaningful research. Within only two or three years, he had created an environment in which bright young doctors flourished. Such unique environments arise when a leader with clear vision recruits a group to share his vision and work toward common goals. Peabody's vision is well-delineated in his writings, collected in his little book *Doctor and Patient* (New York, the Macmillan Company, 1930). The goal was excellence in patient care, providing insight into meaningful research on mechanisms of disease. In this enlightened environment blessed by a creative, unselfish leader, young doctors were happy and worked hard, converted obstacles into opportunities, and formed strong interpersonal bonds. In this atmosphere, morale is high, and group ego is strong but individual egos are dampened. At Boston City there were plenty of obstacles in the form of inadequate funding, political interference, and patients with little hope or prospect for the future. The doctors, in various accounts in the Maxwell Finland-William Castle three volume history *The Harvard Medical Unit at Boston City Hospital* (University of Virginia Press for the Countway Library, 1982) had wonderful tales of these obstacles and their individual attempts to overcome the problems. An esprit de corps develops in such an environment that tends to heighten egalitarianism; at Boston City Hospital the floorsweepers, technicians, clerks, nurses, and administrators were considered integral parts of the endeavor.

Francis Peabody came to Boston City in 1922 as Head of the IV Medical Service, supervised the opening of the Thorndike Laboratories and research beds in 1924, but unfortunately developed gastric cancer (an unusual one, a leiomyosarcoma) in 1926, and died in 1927 at age 45. Yet the spirit and fervor for learning with which he imbued this medical institution persisted for decades, in part because the memory of him persisted, but also because he had already recruited several intelligent and humanistic young men (and one young woman) as his academic medical team. They did not represent a personality cult, but did embrace a devotion to his principles and ideals. First-class young people kept coming to the Boston City, attracted by the aura. The permanent medical staff also increased, with physicians like Maxwell Finland

and Chester Keefer in Infectious Diseases, for example. The Cardiovascular group under Weiss and the Hematology group under Castle (and later George Minot) expanded, and both guided young doctors who would become famous names in American medicine. Perhaps the appointment of George Minot in 1928 as the Second Director of the Thorndike and Head of the Harvard Medical Unit helped to keep the flame lit by Francis Peabody alive. Minot was a superb clinical investigator and had won the Nobel Prize in 1925 for his demonstration that a diet high in liver cured pernicious anemia. Like Peabody, Minot was a Bostonian, quite unassuming and democratic in manner. There the similarities of the two men end. Minot did not roam the wards seeing patients, and, indeed, he often turned over his rounds to his resident or fellow. He was, on the surface, an erratic administrator, but his attributes included a humanistic respect for patients, a warm regard for housestaff and junior colleagues, and a strong sense of right and wrong. He had a wonderful ability to edit manuscripts, which he did for his junior colleagues, in the process teaching them to write and to think well. For fifty years the Harvard Medical Unit and the Thorndike Memorial Unit at Boston City were to maintain the remarkable esprit and dedication to excellence of the Peabody-Minot years.

The Weiss Years at Boston City

It was evident almost from the beginning, when they both arrived as research fellows in 1925, that William Castle and Soma Weiss were going to be significant members of the Thorndike staff. From 1925 until his appointment as Hersey Professor of the Theory and Practice of Physic and Physician-in-Chief at the Brigham Hospital in 1939, Soma Weiss's clinical skills and research abilities were so outstanding that, by 1939, he was a logical candidate to succeed the renowned physician, Henry Christian, who had held the professorship for many years. By 1932, at age 33, Soma Weiss had become Director of the Second and Fourth Medical Services and Associate Professor at Harvard. Dr. Minot had turned over the actual running of the clinical services to Dr. Weiss, giving him an extended opportunity to exercise his leadership skills and his talent for teaching, as Dr. Minot retained and expanded his own unique role as a thoughtful, beloved Director of the Thorndike. His appointment as Chief of Service documents Soma Weiss's maturity, but not the full scope of the intellectual accomplishments that led to the appointment. It seems worthwhile to examine those accomplishments in their separate but inter-related activities of research, teaching, administrative skills and leadership.

Soma Weiss as Investigator

Because Dr. Weiss was fascinated by every aspect of human health and disease, his research achievements have sometimes been said to be secondary to his other abilities. He has been compared to his friend William Castle, known primarily for his lifelong research on blood diseases and specifically on the problem of pernicious anemia. Castle did, in a series of lucid classical experiments, unveil the entire problem of pernicious anemia and eventually found the active vitamin, B12, that prevents the disease. To this day, Castle's experiments are used as a teaching model of clinical investigation that demonstrates the way careful clinical observation combined with sound, critical thinking can lead to elegant and definitive experiments. Some tend to emphasize Dr. Weiss's spectacular talents as a teacher and suggest that his research was less spectacular than Dr. Castle's.

I believe this is incorrect. Even a cursory look at his publications (see Appendix) indicates a man of incredible breadth of vision at a time (the early 1930's) when clinical science was rudimentary and truth tended to be veiled in a mist of accepted dogma. Soma Weiss understood with remarkable clarity the physiology of the circulation. He recognized early in his career, during experiments with Herrmann Blumgart, the striking dynamic nature of blood flow. He understood that small arterial vessels sustained blood pressure, and that those vessels lost their tone in shock from hemorrhage or severe bloodstream infection. He knew that the veins of the body could serve as a reservoir for blood, and that they did so when the heart was diseased and fell behind in its basic task of pumping blood around the circulatory system to supply oxygen to tissues. Soma Weiss came tantalizingly close to understanding the cause of edema in heart failure: the kidney retains salt and water in the body in an attempt to bolster the circulation when the heart's pumping is insufficient to do it normally. Later, just two or three years after Dr. Weiss died, his trainees James Warren and Eugene Stead were to unravel the mystery of the connection between heart failure and the action of the kidneys.

Weiss and his young colleagues became experts in the causes of fainting. They knew that fainting in most instances resulted from inadequate blood flow to the brain secondary to other transient problems. One of the best known of Soma Weiss's clinical observations involved a patient who fainted when he turned his head. Careful examination revealed that a high collar compressed his carotid artery and elicited a reflex from the carotid sinus. This was the first description of the hypersensitive carotid reflex syndrome. Other patients were noted to have heart block that caused fainting when the heart rate fell from a normal rate of 80 beats/minute to less than 50 beats/minute. His interest in fainting led to a better understanding of the related symptoms of dizziness and vertigo.

Dr. Weiss's research in heart failure led to an understanding of the mechanism of shock associated with low blood pressure. The investigation of this pathophysiological condition was later particularly important in managing war casualties and shock from blood loss during World War II. Weiss's interests would become the basis for the work of Stead and Warren, who studied the effects of shock on patients admitted to the Grady Hospital emergency room in Atlanta on Saturday nights, when knife and gunshot wounds simulated the trauma of war.

It was natural, with his interest in circulatory dynamics, that Weiss would describe unusual causes of heart failure. He defined the concept of high output heart failure, in which the heart worked hard and efficiently but blood was shunted away from tissues needing oxygen and returned to the veins of the lungs and heart for repumping. The presence of an arterio-venous communicating fistula was one example of this phenomenon in which a large artery became directly attached to a vein (usually because of trauma) and blood pumped by the heart followed a path of least resistance from artery to vein without passing through tiny capillaries. Application of pressure to the vein temporarily corrected the physiologic abnormality. Dr. Weiss and his colleagues made classic observations by their measurements of blood flow and pressures in arterial venous fistulas.

Vitamin deficiencies had been described in the 1930's, and Weiss recognized that in beriberi (vitamin B1 deficiency) small blood vessels were wide open and therefore functioned like an arterial venous fistula. In studies of patients with this problem, he defined the syndrome of beriberi heart disease and cured it by correcting the dietary deficiency.

He made a further clinical observation in patients afflicted with a poorly understood skin disease characterized by excessive scar-like tissue (scleroderma). He noted similar scarring of the heart in some individuals and was the first to describe scleroderma as a cause of heart failure.

Dr. Weiss understood that constriction of the arterial blood vessels resulted in hypertension. He knew that to enable the circulation to flow normally in hypertensive patients, the heart had to pump harder and harder to force the blood through constricted vessels. The force required for this additional pumping caused the heart to enlarge and subsequently to fail. During the last two or three years of his life, Dr. Weiss devoted much of his effort to hypertension. He helped delineate normal blood pressure levels, and to associate elevated blood pressure with the disease hypertension. His clinical observations on the effects of hypertension on the heart, kidneys, and brain (including the vessels of the eye) represented important studies in our concept of hypertension as a disease. He initiated experiments that would eventually lead to the role of hormones and the kidney in causing elevated blood pressure.

Dr. Weiss's study of factors in blood that might cause veins to constrict was exemplified and augmented by his intense interest in a disease known as toxemia of pregnancy. In its classical and severe form, a young woman (usually in her first pregnancy) becomes severely ill during the last three months of pregnancy. She begins to urinate less and to retain water in her body. Acute swelling (edema) of the legs develops, more marked than the swelling in normal pregnancy. She complains of progressively severe headaches, blurring of vision, and may develop generalized seizures (fits) that are life-threatening. Examination reveals acute and severe elevation of blood pressure, cool hands (indicative of intense constriction of arteries), and swelling of the legs, the face and body. The most revealing physical findings come when the eyes are examined with an ophthalmoscope, permitting visualization of the small vessels of the retina of the eye. The arteries are seen to be particularly constricted, and the entire retina is glistening and water-logged with edema.

Toxemia of pregnancy is treated, in the 1930's and today, by advising that the patient lie flat in bed. Her fluid and salt intake are restricted, and if the hyperten-

sion and headaches seem worse and are leading to seizures, she is given injections of magnesium sulfate which,
for some reason, specifically helps relieve the severe and
acute hypertension of toxemia of pregnancy (now called
eclampsia). The syndrome is, however, a true toxemia or
poisoning by pregnancy, and definitive treatment, then
and now, is expeditious delivery of the infant by natural
means, or, if necessary, by surgical delivery.

Soma Weiss's approach to toxemia of pregnancy
is characteristic of the man's genius. First, he saw the
problem during his years as Consultant in Obstetrics at
Boston City Hospital, and he enlisted an able and exciting younger colleague, Dr. Lewis Dexter, to study the
problem. Their common research products included a
discussion of toxemia of pregnancy before senior academic medical colleagues at the annual meeting of the
Association of American Physicians in 1940, and publication (Dexter and Weiss) of a monograph *Preeclamptic and
Eclamptic Toxemia of Pregnancy*. This effort brought the
fascinating syndrome of toxemia to the attention of physicians other than obstetricians. Dexter and Weiss did not
find all the answers, but they looked for toxic substances in the urine, speculated about generation of such
substances by the kidney, by the pregnant uterus, or by
the placenta from the fetal side of the maternal-fetal
junction. Their investigations emphasized the need for
understanding the physiological and chemical alterations
brought on by the pregnant state.

Dr. Lewis Dexter, now retired as Chief of Cardiology at the Brigham, recalls that as a junior person under
Dr. Weiss, he reviewed the extensive clinical experience

with toxemia at the Boston City and did experiments in animals looking for pressor substances in the placenta. Dr. Dexter prepared four papers on these aspects of toxemia of pregnancy and gave them to Dr. Weiss. Dexter was surprised when those manuscripts returned as a full monograph on the subject!

Dr. Jerome Harris, Professor Emeritus of Pediatrics at Duke University Medical School, was an intern at Boston Children's Hospital in the 1930's when Dr. Weiss was still at Boston City Hospital. A seven-year-old boy with severe hypertension was a patient on Dr. Harris's ward. Examination by x-ray revealed that the child also had a stone that was blocking the flow of urine from the right kidney. Harris was aware of early research that showed that impaired arterial blood flow to a kidney caused hypertension. These were the famous experiments of Goldblatt who caused hypertension to develop in rats by partially clamping their renal arteries. With these experiments in mind, Harris urged the staff at Children's Hospital to remove surgically the child's damaged kidney. Doctors at Children's Hospital were unconvinced. Frustrated by their inaction, Dr. Harris went to his former teacher, Soma Weiss, told him about the patient, and managed to have Dr. Weiss invited to Children's Hospital to discuss the problem. Dr. Weiss gave a brilliant discussion and suggested that the kidney be removed. The operation took place and the child recovered. This patient (Case 5) became one of the subjects of the first report describing cure of hypertension by removal of a single diseased kidney (Butler, A.M., Chronic Pyelonephritis and Arterial Hypertension, 1937, Journal of Clinical Investigation 16:889).

The story illustrates Weiss's interest in and the start of his investigation into pressor substances generated by kidneys that cause generalized hypertension. It also illustrates Weiss's openness to his students and young colleagues and his sensitivity and diplomacy in reversing the decision of the senior physicians at Children's Hospital.

Most physicians today know Soma Weiss (if at all) by the Mallory-Weiss Syndrome, a condition contemporary doctors diagnose frequently. They usually have no idea who Weiss was, and are probably not aware that two Mallorys, father and son, were famous Boston pathologists. The syndrome is a common condition in patients who vomit and retch severely enough to tear tissues in the lower end of the esophagus or the upper stomach, leading to hemorrhage and occasionally death from blood loss.

It is clear that Dr. Weiss was a remarkably broad-based physician, functioning most of the time as a cardiovascular physiologist and pharmacologist, but not inhibited from writing about any topic that interested him. It would not have been in his character to concentrate only in one limited area. His contributions in about a dozen years of research provide significant and permanent additions to our information about such topics as toxicity caused by digitalis, heart failure, hypertension and its relationship to kidney disease, arterial venous fistula, beriberi heart disease, fainting secondary to several basic mechanisms or disease, toxemia of pregnancy, and, almost as an afterthought, the syndrome that bears his name, the Mallory-Weiss esophageal tear.

Soma Weiss as Teacher

All his colleagues and students agreed that Soma Weiss was a truly great teacher and that his ability as a teacher was the feature that set him apart from all others. This special talent, I believe, brought him the coveted position as Hersey Professor. As is so often true in a great teacher, his research and teaching were inseparable because his enthusiastic probing into the mysteries of clinical medicine contributed to the immediacy of his teaching and stimulated his research ideas. Much of his greatness as a teacher stemmed from his personality; he was hardworking, energetic, incredibly knowledgeable of the literature, and had an excellent memory. He could make almost any medical problem interesting because he related the problem to a patient. Dr. Weiss's respect for and interest in people transcended their strictly medical problems. His sunny good nature and mild humor helped create an atmosphere for learning.

Weiss's teaching was particularly effective because he avoided adherence to hierarchy. A professor, or a student or an intern might have an equally good contribution to make to understanding a patient. This egalitarianism, remarkable for that era, is described by Norman Roberg in a recent reminiscence in the *Journal of the American Medical Association* (260:3645-3646, 1988). Soma Weiss liked, trusted, and respected young people, and that attitude must have been appreciated and reciprocated. Finally, there was a rigid intellectual honesty about Dr. Weiss, causing him to purposely separate his information into facts that were known, those that made sense but were not proved, and those that had simply been stated as dogma. It required a lot of intellectual effort in the 1930's to sort out one's information into such categories (it would be almost as hard in the 1990's); indeed, the success in sorting fact from supposition remains one measure of a good doctor.

Some of Dr. Weiss's success as a teacher ironically may have derived from his mispronunciation (W's tended to be V's) and also his correct but different and intriguing use of the English language. In a letter to me dated October 31, 1988, Dr. John Romano, Professor Emeritus of Psychiatry at Rochester University and one of the young doctors who helped care for Dr. Weiss during his fatal illness, reminisced about Soma Weiss's use of words. In the letter, Dr. Romano said, "Many people would make jokes about his lapsus linguae, or if you wish, malapropisms. When excited, I have heard him say, 'That fella is neither fish nor fry.'" Later in the same letter: "Lewis Thomas, then a fellow at the Thorndike, an undeclared poet-laureate of the housestaff, once said, 'There are two great men here at Boston City. One is Houston Merritt and the other is Soma Weiss, but I am getting suspicious of Soma because his accent is getting worse.' I don't think there is any question that Soma would from time to time purposely exploit his accent and his malapropisms." I agree with Dr. Romano. A great man and a great teacher will (and should) use all his assets, and the slight language variations enhanced his teaching.

In addition to his general teaching, Dr. Weiss involved himself in highly popular and effective biweekly conferences on clinical pharmacology and the traditional but effective clinical-pathological conferences, where pathologists's postmortem findings reinforce or confound the diagnosis of the clinician, which he shared with his close collaborator, the pathologist Frederick Parker.

Dr. Weiss achieved true eminence, however, for his examination of patients and subsequent discussion of their problems with the housestaff late each Thursday afternoon at the Boston City. These "rounds" as they are called, began when he became Chief of Service of the Harvard Unit at the City Hospital. Everyone who attended one of those rounds seems to remember the experience. If asked, Weiss saw patients anywhere in the hospital, beginning on the eighth floor and coming down floor by floor. He included several disciplines (surgery, obstetrics, neurology, as well as medicine) and patients from the other services (Tufts, Boston University). (Three universities shared the responsibility for what was then a very large public hospital.) Dr. Weiss had a remarkable capacity to integrate the example of a particular patient and his or her special circumstance and individual personality into a wide-ranging discussion of general medical and social problems. His medical knowledge was enormous and perhaps his European background helped him identify with the patients, many of whom were recent emigres. The rounds became celebrated in Boston, and from local acclamation their fame spread country-wide and world-wide.

Jack Myers wrote to me recently that he and others (housestaff at the Brigham in the 1930's under Henry Christian) regularly attended those rounds at Boston City despite the distance and inconvenience of getting there. Stead says that the rounds became so renowned that many physicians visiting in Boston on a Thursday evening made a point of joining Weiss. In 1939, by the time he was 40 years old, Soma Weiss had acquired an international reputation as a physician and as a clinical investigator, but especially as a master teacher.

Soma Weiss as Leader and Administrator

Soma Weiss's inherent leadership qualities were evident in his personality, his work habits, and his attitudes. He turned those qualities to good purpose as an administrator because his outgoing nature and interest in people made him known by all, and similarly he knew everyone in his environment. He was by nature a giver and not a taker in his basic approach to life, and thus when he needed something from others he was likely to get it as a return for past help and support. He was, of course, articulate in stating his needs but also modest in his requests. Even in his Bellevue days, his colleagues recognized his leadership qualities in his ability to get things done, and he was often designated by the hospital administration to do so. At Boston City, it is likely that George Minot's diffident, almost eccentric approach to management left Weiss as the person to whom the administration often turned for solutions to any problems with the medical staff; in turn, Weiss represented staff and housestaff needs to the administration. Gene Stead in his *Pharos* article (1987) tells of Weiss's remarkable skill in dealing with the Irish politicians who ran Boston City Hospital. What did the Irish politician and the young Hungarian emigrant physician have in common? I suspect that both respected the other's professionalism and understood the difficulties each had surmounted in coping with life in a new country.

Soma Weiss and Elizabeth Sachs

As Dr. Soma Weiss, the physician, was building his remarkable career at the Thorndike Laboratory and Boston City Hospital, the young Hungarian refugee, Soma Weiss, was busy courting a lovely young woman named Elizabeth Sachs, marrying her, starting his own family, and being enfolded into the large and important Sachs family of Boston and New York.

The marriage of Elizabeth Sachs and Soma Weiss amalgamated two remarkable families. Although our knowledge about the Weiss family is sketchy, those who met them reported them to be charming and impressive people during their visits to the United States on two or three occasions in the 1930's; the last visit ended not long before World War II began. The Sachs family in Boston represented one branch of the remarkable Goldman-Sachs family of financiers. Elizabeth's father, Paul, had started his professional life in the Goldman-Sachs financial empire in New York where he performed very well for ten years, even though disliking the work. During this time, Paul Sachs developed a remarkable talent for judging and criticizing art, and his family wealth permitted him to indulge his penchant for collecting. He was so successful as an art collector-historian that Harvard offered him a Professorship of Art and Co-directorship of Harvard's Fogg Museum. His genius was in teaching art, and more particularly in educating students who became directors of museums throughout the country. Paul Sachs was so well-regarded as a faculty member that, on his retirement, Harvard awarded him an honorary degree. Elizabeth's mother, Meta Pollock Sachs, was daughter of a distinguished jurist, and a vivacious and energetic woman.

The Weiss home on Bryant Street was back-to-back with Shady Hill, the estate of Paul and Meta Sachs. The Weiss children (Paul, Robert, and Lucy) grew up in what was essentially a family complex as their activities flowed back and forth between the two adjacent homes. (Shady Hill was donated by the Sachs family to Harvard University and now houses the American Academy of Arts and Sciences.)

Soma Weiss's correspondence on file in the Countway Library at Harvard Medical School includes many letters from medical colleagues offering warm thanks for a lovely dinner with the family in the Bryant Street house. Similarly, medical students and house officers were entertained by the Weiss family, and recalled those evenings with warmth and gratitude. Eugene Stead says that because Dr. and Mrs. Weiss set a pattern of sharing their home with younger colleagues, the Steads naturally adopted that pattern at Emory and Duke, even though it was not easy to do so on their income. In those days, departmental resources did not include an entertainment budget!

In the summer, both the Sachs and Weiss households left sweltering Boston for Keene Valley in the Adirondacks of New York. Keene Valley had been the summer resort for several Goldmans and Sachs, and Soma Weiss was quickly incorporated into the place and the family, and loved it. The Weiss home was close to that of Paul and Meta Sachs, and the two men shared an office-cottage. Paul Sachs and Soma Weiss would often finish their breakfasts and retreat to their little cottage to work on their separate writing projects. I suspect that much of Soma Weiss's most creative work was done at Keene Valley, working with father-in-law Paul Sachs in that little cottage. In addition, Weiss seems to have enjoyed his immediate family and the extended Goldman-Sachs clan. The atmosphere was both physically relaxing and intellectually stimulating as the families entertained distinguished guests. At different times, such people as William and Henry James and the artist Winslow Homer spent leisurely summer weeks at Keene Valley.

The Appointment as Hersey Professor of the Theory and Practice of Physic

In 1939, the 40-year-old Soma Weiss was appointed to the legendary position bearing the title of Hersey Professor of the Theory and Practice of Physic at Harvard. This was one of Harvard's most prestigious professorships and an outstanding tribute to the special genius of Soma Weiss. It was clearly unusual for a 40-year-old Hungarian Jewish physician to have been chosen to fill such a position. There were other Jewish professors at Harvard (father-in-law Paul Sachs was one), but such recognition was rare, and a strict Jewish percentile quota existed for admission to Harvard College and Medical School. Harvard brushed aside these prejudices in order to get the man they wanted to replace the venerable Henry Christian at the Brigham Hospital.

There were certainly other remarkable internists in Boston, including two men who had worked with Soma Weiss at the Boston City. William Castle had already achieved fame as a scientist and hematologist, and had an ideal personal and professional pedigree. In 1948 he would succeed Minot as the Director at the Thorndike and would become a revered professor at Harvard. Chester Keefer, with a worldwide reputation as an expert in infectious diseases, was also at the Boston City in 1939. Within two years of Weiss's move to the Brigham, Dr. Keefer would become Professor and Chairman of Medicine at Boston University, and would lure a talented group of young people from Boston City Hospital to his service.

From my vantage point, looking back 50 years, I wondered whether the choice between Soma Weiss, Chester Keefer, and William Castle wasn't a difficult one. During a visit with Dr. Castle in 1989, I posed that question to him and he seemed surprised. "Oh no," he said, "Soma was our leader." Louise Castle, his wife, contributed one important insight for me, in saying, "You could feel Soma when he entered the room. He exuded energy, not power." Chester Keefer was reported to be enormously knowledgeable about medicine, and William Castle offered this wry comment: "Chester knew everything cold, but Soma knew *almost* everything and warm."

Thirty Months at the Brigham
Soma Weiss was at the height of his professional

powers when he arrived at the Brigham in the summer
of 1939. All of his skills acquired at the City were ready
to be used on his own service, where he would be undis-
puted leader and chief.

The Brigham had begun life in 1912 as a public,
nonprofit hospital primarily for the poor. Henry Christian,
who had been its first and only Chief of Medicine, was one
of the outstanding internists of his time, and a founding
father of the Federation for Clinical Research, one of the
three major organizations of medical researchers in the
United States. While Christian was Chief of Medicine, the
world renowned neurosurgeon, Harvey Cushing, was his
counterpart in Surgery. But the Brigham of that day had
more pride than money, and the trustees worked hard
just to keep things going. Eugene Stead was Acting Chief
for a few months after Dr. Weiss died, and he said the experience was invaluable to him in teaching him how hard
it is to obtain money for worthy causes.

When Dr. Soma Weiss arrived at the Brigham
with his bright young team of physician-scientists, the air
became charged with excitement. John Romano tells of
that first day at the Brigham, on September 1, 1939, as
the bombs fell on Warsaw and World War II had truly begun. A proud Soma Weiss took his three young colleagues
(Stead, Romano, and Janeway) on a tour of the Brigham,
introducing them particularly to the older faculty, including such eminent physicians as the cardiologist Samuel
Levine. Each introduction included this comment: "I hope
you will allow these young men to earn your respect."
This remembrance illustrates Dr. Weiss's innate sensibil-
ity, and personal charm.

Soma Weiss's enthusiasm infected the staff, old and new alike. His curiosity continued to unearth new and exciting medical problems for study and for teaching. His legendary Tuesday night rounds at the Boston City Hospital became the Saturday morning rounds at the Brigham.

Paul Beeson, as Chief Resident for Dr. Weiss, had overall responsibility for the rounds. Beeson recalls that about 100 people participated in the teaching rounds, with perhaps half the group comprising students, housestaff, and full-time faculty of the Brigham. The others were practitioners in the area, many of whom were European immigrant physicians. Certainly, the rounds were crowded as patients were presented to Soma Weiss. Beeson recalls Dr. Weiss's fresh observations, his inventive curiosity, and his interest in each patient. Both Beeson and Stead were enormously impressed by Weiss's patience, tact, and courtesy in dealing with the private physicians in practice in nearby Brookline. Should a patient referred by one of those doctors be the subject for rounds, that doctor would be asked by Dr. Weiss to participate in the discussion of his patient.

In only 2-1/2 years, Soma Weiss left most of his imprint on the Brigham in things spiritual, and not in concrete projects. Therefore, it seems appropriate to close these remarks with direct quotations about Dr. Weiss, mostly from *In Memoriam*. One letter in Dr. Weiss's papers in the Countway Library, however, may serve as a summary of his work at the Brigham. Dr. Robert T. Monroe wrote a thank-you note for a dinner party, and concluded in a letter dated October 1, 1940, a year after Dr. Weiss began at the Brigham: "The Brigham worked under Dr. Christian because we believed in him; the Brigham will go forward in the next 20 years because we now believe in you."

From the *Memoriam* (see Appendix):

From Dr. Euqene DuBois, Professor of Medicine at Cornell (discussing the relationship of Dr. Weiss to his friend and American mentor, Dr. Hatcher) "Hatcher's profound respect and admiration for Soma influenced both men greatly. In our profession, the respect of pupil for master is no more important than respect of master for pupil."

"Teaching at times is a most discouraging vocation — Then there appears a young man like Soma Weiss — in such a student we can vicariously fulfill our own ambitions of younger days."

"Forces of evil can take the ascendancy, and we forget the vast stores of latent goodness. Then come the memories of young men that we have known, men whose idealism has lifted us to higher planes. Men like Soma who with deep sympathies, constant cheerfulness, and unfailing kindness have helped all with whom they come in contact. Men like Soma who, by their devoted labors, have helped physicians and patients in all civilized countries. Such men prove that, after all, this is a good world."

From Dr. George Minot, Nobel Laureate and Director of the Thorndike Memorial Laboratory at Boston City Hospital

"He was not swayed by the pressure of the moment and he never succumbed to the fads which agitate medicine. Indefatigable energy and enthusiasm contributed to every stroke he took."

"One of his greatest contributions was that of a person who gave freely of the love of mankind."

"No appraisal of his character would be complete without mention of his kindness and thoughtfulness for others and his agreeable and charming manner which endeared him to all."

Dr. Eugene B. Ferris, then a Research Fellow and later Chairman of the Department of Medicine at Emory University

"As time passed, those who worked closely with Soma began to recognize the finer qualities by which he exerted such a marked influence and to realize that his many talents were not inborn but were attained by the familiar process of hard work and selfdiscipline."

"The relationships which Soma maintained between himself and his young associates was to develop in them both independence of thought and energy output. He accepted each as an equal partner in the search for knowledge—. His youthful and humorous spirit made him a delightful as well as inspiring companion—. And with all he maintained a great dignity, based on the example which he set, the visible growth of understanding which he attained thereby, and his ever active interest in the intellectual development and personal happiness of each of us."

From Dr. Elliott C. Cutler, Chief of Surgery at Peter Bent Brigham

"His modesty and unselfishness led always to his putting others first; his gracious manner avoided all possibility of conflict... Moreover, there was firmness when necessity arose... Intellectually he combined... the analytical powers of the scientist with the integrative faculty of a philosopher."

"Soma Weiss bound men to his side with hoops of steel. His frank, generous, and cheerful spirit dissolved worries, set aside difficulties, and pointed the new and possible way ahead."

"He seemed fitted in every way to the place [the Brigham], and he appeared to glow with the response which he so affectionately provoked."

From Dr. Walter Cannon, Professor of Physiology at Harvard

"A survey of Soma Weiss's brilliant career after his arrival in the United States proves that he rose to eminence in his profession and enjoyed the respect and affection of all who knew him, solely because of the golden qualities of his unique personality and his unselfish devotion to the highest standards of medical service. In making his own way upward he became accustomed to independence and self-reliance. An inner core of firmly established integrity and idealism in his character assured him steadiness and poise. In discussions — at faculty meetings, for example — he was frank and courageous in expressing his views, an attitude emerging directly from large experience, clear thinking, and well-tried convictions. A quick appreciation of humor, and a readiness to use it on appropriate occasions, flashed moments of lightness into his remarks, whether in debate or in conversation."

"It has been said that a teacher affects eternity, for no one can ever tell where his influence will stop. When a great teacher is also a great physician he affects eternity to a magnified degree; his influences reach onward through his disciples whom he has inspired and also through the useful lives he has prolonged. The years of Soma Weiss reached scarcely beyond two score, only half of them spent with us in our land. But calmly estimating his career who would deny that in passing from us he is one of the immortal dead who lives again in the men and women who have felt the 'beauty and the strength of his spirit and who will pass it on to others through unnumbered years to come.'"

From Mary Koves Sachs, Family Friend and Mother of then Harvard Medical Student (Later Prominent Neurosurgeon), Ernest Sachs, Jr.

"He has not gone from us! Not when these halls
Throb with his presence! When continually
We seem to breathe in from the very walls
The essence of his rich vitality!
Forever in our hearts he is "The Chief,"
The Great Physician, teacher, guide and friend.
A gay blithe Spirit poised in bright relief
Against a world of pain. He could transcend
The narrow bounds of earth in daring flight.

And give us wings for pathless space above
Where we might soar in searching for the light
Of greater learning through our greater love;
But, of all the gifts that crowned his healing art,
The rarest was his understanding heart."

Postscript

I believe Soma Weiss accomplished a renewal of the Brigham Hospital in his brief tenure of only 2-1/2 years. He arrived there in September, 1939, on the day that World War II began with the bombing of Warsaw by Hitler's air force. Arriving with him were three young faculty: Eugene Stead, the subject of the next chapter in this book and future Professor of Medicine at Emory and at Duke; Charles Janeway, who would become Professor of Pediatrics at Harvard; and John Romano, later Professor of Psychiatry at Cincinnati and at Rochester. New residents included Jack Myers and Richard Ebert and interns included James Warren, Max Michael, and Louis Hempelmann — all to become professors of medicine and outstanding teachers. He had recruited as his Chief Resident Paul Beeson from the Rockefeller Institute (subject of a later chapter). The Brigham could not help but be rejuvenated with such an infusion of talent. Soma Weiss's personality drew people to his endeavors, and from them he had the good taste to select only the best to serve within his orbit.

I also believe that Soma Weiss influenced the Brigham permanently and significantly, because many of those who worked with him attested to his ability years later. Thirty years after his death, an appreciation of

Weiss written by James Warren appeared (*New England Journal of Medicine* 286:658, 1972). More recently, other accounts have emerged: an intern, Norman Roberg, (*JAMA* 260:3645, 1988) wrote about him and about Boston City Hospital in the 1930's, as did Eugene Stead (*Pharos*, 1987); Philip Bondy reminisced about the Brigham years (*Yale J. Biol. Med.* 53:213, 1980). And finally along comes this book on which I labor. This interest attests to the strength of the man, Soma Weiss, and perhaps also represents a reminder of our current need for strong and moral and patient-centered leadership in medicine. Soma Weiss would have been, had he lived, that sort of leader. Among his papers filed in the Countway Library, is correspondence relating to his having lunch with President Roosevelt to talk about widening access to health care (in the current jargon). One of the last entries is a letter offering him the editorship of the only textbook of medicine in the 1940's, the Cecil text, which would have become the Cecil-Weiss Textbook of Medicine.

Almost certainly, the Harvard Medical School and the Peter Bent Brigham Hospital continue to be imbued with his spirit. When Dr. Weiss died, Harvard medical students organized a student research club with Soma Weiss as their chief faculty advisor; today, the research club flourishes as the Soma Weiss Undergraduate Assembly. A large and dignified painting of Soma Weiss dominates the amphitheater of the new Brigham and Women's Hospital and, with it, he confers his blessing on the continuing medical excellence embodied by the Peter Bent Brigham medical complex.

Chapter IV

EUGENE ANSON STEAD, JR.

E ugene Stead (pronounced Sted) shared Soma Weiss's interest in heart disease and the circulation of blood and worked as research fellow under him at the Boston City and the Thorndike Memorial Laboratory for two years. When Weiss went to the Brigham, Stead went with him, returning to the hospital where he had interned in both medicine and surgery, and where he knew the faculty and the hospital staff well. When Dr. Weiss died, Gene Stead, who had already accepted the Chairmanship of Medicine at Emory University School of Medicine in Atlanta, acted as Chief of Service at the Brigham for five months before departing for Atlanta. This was a valuable experience for a 34-year-old Chairman-to-be, and Stead built a fine department at Emory in just a few years. Its reputation earned him an offer from Duke University in 1947, affording him an opportunity to head a medical service at a major health center and academic institution. During the next 20 years, Stead would be the guiding force in the academic growth and medical excellence at Duke, now recognized world-wide as one of the foremost medical centers in America. To this day, he continues to work to make Duke a stronger, more versatile institution.

Growing Up in Atlanta

Eugene Anson Stead, Sr., the father, born in Ohio, grew up from age eight in Georgia. After high school, he made a living for several years as a jack-of-many-trades while he studied pharmacy in his brother's drug store, teaching himself the trade and becoming a pharmacist licensed by state examination. Stead describes his father as a physically small man, totally fearless, and a highly opinionated fundamentalist Methodist. For example, EAS Sr., believed that most things were sinful, and that the teaching of Darwinian evolution was blasphemy. Eugene, Jr. recalls a statement that suggests that his father was also well-read and independent of mind: He blamed World War II on Henry Stimson, who, as Secretary of State, failed to condemn Japan's invasion of Manchuria. Thus, he faulted Stimson's appeasement in the Far East long before others saw Chamberlain's umbrella as the symbol of appeasement in Europe.

By the time Eugene came along in 1908 (as a second child, after Emily), father Stead had become a moderately successful pharmacist. Because he had palpitations of the heart, his doctor told him that he needed exercise. As a result, he became a traveling salesman to retail pharmacies and was away from home except on weekends and during the month of December. He was a salesman primarily for a proprietary liquid medicine called Capudine, which he sold to stores and pharmacies throughout the rural South. (As a child in the 1930's, I remember 'Try Capudine' painted on the roofs and walls of tobacco barns.) Initially, he traveled by train and rented a horse and buggy for calling on the neighboring stores. Eugene, Jr. says his father was always welcomed, both because of his strong personality and because he, as a licensed pharmacist, could and did cheerfully help the pharmacists by filling prescriptions if requested. The Capudine company must have thought well of him, because they furnished him a modest living all his life and let him work up the company-provided car hierarchy through horse and buggy, Model T Ford, Chevrolet, Cleveland, and finally a Buick.

From about ages 11-15, Gene accompanied his father on his sales journeys during the summers. He recalls the time as being rather idyllic, as he and his father drove and camped in the woods, preparing their meals and enjoying nature. Father Stead never left his religion behind, so the games they played as they drove along were such things as thinking up biblical verses for each letter of the alphabet. Gene recalls that during the times that EAS Sr. was home in Atlanta he shared pleasant times planting gardens, building a shed, and doing other home chores with his children. The father's religion meant little to the son, but Gene went to church each week with his father, explaining, "It didn't do me any harm, and it gave my father a lot of pleasure."

Of course, father was not home very much during most of Gene's growing up years. Gene remembers simply playing in the woods, flying his kite, and reading a lot. Older sister Emily had taught him to read early in life, so that he skipped kindergarten and graduated from high school at age 15. His mother, Emily Bertha White, had married Mr. Stead in 1902, and, as Gene says, they lived happily ever after. Young Emily and Eugene, Jr. were followed by Clio and Joyce, and finally by William, 10 years younger than Gene. Gene and baby Bill roomed together and have remained very close friends throughout life (Dr. William Stead is now a nationally regarded expert in the study of tuberculosis).

Gene must have been recognized as an unusual child early in his life. When he and sister Emily developed a serious pneumonia in childhood, a senior Atlanta physician, Dr. James E. Paullin, was called in to care for them. Dr. Paullin's contact with the boy led to an unusual prescription. Using the excuse that Gene was a sickly child after the pneumonia, and recognizing how inadequate were the grade schools in then rural Decatur, Georgia, outside Atlanta, Dr. Paullin simply suggested that he not be pushed to attend school too much, but be encouraged to read. By the end of high school, Gene had read most of the books in the nearby Atlanta Public Library.

In high school in Decatur, Gene easily led the boys in his class academically, but he recalls high school learning as being strongly dominated by girls while the boys were happy to be indifferent students. That sociological fact must have made Gene uncomfortable. His near-photographic memory earned him top academic standing and won him the Decatur High School's one-year scholarship to Emory University in Atlanta.

College and Medical School at Emory

The one-year scholarship got Gene into college, and he survived financially by continuing to live at home in Decatur. He usually walked the 2-1/2 miles to Emory and back each school day. Friendly persons driving between the towns frequently picked him up in the morning, but rarely at night. Gene's choices of courses in Atlanta were heavily dictated by his lack of money. He enrolled in several biology courses and eventually took all those available because his sister Emily's boyfriend had told him that the biology scholarship paid twice as much as any other campus scholarship. Stead was awarded the biology scholarship and augmented his income by tutoring his less apt fellow students.

Stead entered medical school in 1928, not through any great sense of dedication or burning interest, but because other graduate programs were full. Another reason for choosing medical school, however, related to a physician, Dr. William Bayley, with whom he played chess. No, he was not inspired by Dr. Bayley, he says, but had bet Dr. Bayley that he (Stead) could do all the busy work of anatomy, biochemistry, etc., required of medical students and still continue his relatively relaxed lifestyle, which included chess and exploring the world through books. He won his bet with Dr. Bayley. Gene Stead's photographic memory plus his study habit of intense cramming just before examinations paid off handsomely, and he rapidly became an academic leader in his class at Emory Medical School.

Stead denies being a leader in any but the academic sense at that time, but he and about a half-dozen other students found the anatomy classes too easy. They demanded a more rigorous curriculum in anatomy, and were allowed to take a more intense course. By the time that little group of students reached the third and fourth years that provided patient contact, they were clearly the leaders of the group. When Gene found that the Emory textbooks were out of date, he obtained for the group copies of Henry Christian's *Oxford System of Medicine*, and Paul Dudley White's *Textbook of Cardiology*. Although fascinated by clinical medicine, and clearly an excellent student, Stead describes himself as a loner who did not smoke or drink, go dancing, or go out with women at that time. His father's fundamentalist Protestantism was sticking to him better than he recognized!

Medical Housestaff Training in Boston

This very tall (6'2"), socially awkward young Southerner managed to get one of the most coveted medical internships in the country, the Peter Bent Brigham's internship under the illustrious Henry Christian. Gene knew about the PBBH and Henry Christian because of the medical textbook he had read. By pure luck, his first attending physician on the medical floors at Grady Memorial Hospital at Emory as a student was a Dr. Hugh Wood, later Dean at Emory. Stead presented a patient, an older man with very active hyperthyroidism, to Dr. Wood and Wood apparently did a spectacular showman-like teaching job.

Hyperthyroidism (Grave's disease) is a dramatic illness, Dr. Wood was an exciting teacher, and young Gene Stead, a very bright but untrained observer, was an appreciative and receptive student, eager to apply what he was learning to the care of his patients. The stars were certainly in constellation for young Stead, because the Dr. Hugh Wood whom he so admired had interned at the Brigham under Henry Christian. So, too, had Carter Smith, an attractive, bright young practitioner in Atlanta interested in cardiology and in electrocardiography, who found Gene Stead a fascinating younger colleague. These two fine Brigham-trained internists had no difficulty getting one of their junior progeny invited to the Brigham for an internship interview.

In those days, interns in Boston were selected from a small group of young people (almost 100% male) who were invited to be interviewed. Dr. Samuel Levine, who would become a legendary Brigham cardiologist at work there for 40 years, found himself interviewing the tall, slow-talking but fast-thinking young man from Atlanta. On the way to Boston on the train, Stead had been reading Dr. White's textbook about cardiology; he was fortunate to have Dr. Levine as his interviewer, and even more fortunate when the patient they discussed had co-arctation of the aorta. The aorta, the large artery leading from the heart, was narrowed due to a congenital constriction. This anomaly leads to the sort of dynamic vascular changes that fascinated the young doctor Stead. To overcome the constriction, the heart works hard, and high blood pressure occurs in the upper but not lower extremities. The blood pressure is low in the legs and the pulses in the lower body are absent or severely decreased secondary to the narrowed aorta. About a dozen years ago Dr. Stead was visiting me at the Veteran's Administration Medical Center in San Diego, and by sheer chance a patient with coarctation of the aorta was presented. His give-and-take discussion with the students was brilliant, and excitement became palpable in the conference room. I can imagine 50 years earlier in 1932, Dr. Levine being similarly stimulated and fascinated by the topic of aorta coarctation as reviewed by that young man from Atlanta.

Internships at the Brigham, for some reason, ran for 16 months, and Gene Stead lived in the hospital, day and night, immersed in the phenomenology of medicine and in the personalities and lives of his patients. He says he loved every minute of it.

After the internship, Dr. Christian offered Stead an 8-month fellowship in his own laboratory. After the intense internship, this training opportunity offered him some time to think, to read, and to begin to mature into his own strong, highly motivated personality. He was given room and board in the hospital and the magnificent sum of $75 per month, which provided enough money for him to begin to date a nurse, his first girlfriend. In the laboratory, he began to work on the mechanism of edema (the soft watery swelling of the legs that occurs in heart failure and other conditions). In his experiments, he took whole blood repeatedly from test dogs, spun it in a centrifuge, and discarded the protein-rich plasma and later reinjected the red blood cells to avoid anemia in the animals. On this regimen, the animals became very depleted of blood proteins, but edema occurred only when salt water was administered through a stomach tube. This important clinical observation and the publication resulting from it was directly related to an understanding of the first diuretic drug, a mercurial compound, and how it worked on the kidney to promote excretion of water and salt. Stead was struck with the fact that low protein alone did not result in edema in the dogs, and that low protein plus extra water did not cause edema; extra salt was in some way the key.

After the stint in Dr. Christian's laboratory, young Dr. Stead was anxious to return to clinical medicine and the care of patients on the wards. He decided to take a second internship at the Brigham, this time in Surgery. He says he took the surgical internship because the intern had the best job in the hospital, because he liked the Chief of Surgery, Dr. Elliott Cutler, and because he had good friends in the Surgery program. By this time, Gene Stead must have known everyone at the Peter Bent Brigham Hospital, having lived and worked there constantly for nearly two years. Bert Dunphy and Hartwell Harrison, later to be internationally acclaimed leaders in surgery and fine academic doctors, were his good friends, and they remained friends throughout life. Stead enjoyed the year in Surgery, and learned to appreciate the surgeons and how long and hard they work. He also realized that surgeons could spend six to ten hours daily working on patients who were asleep, and Stead preferred to spend that sort of time talking with his patients, understanding their illnesses, learning how they lived and how they thought. Stead terminated his surgical career, but he has always valued what he learned from that surgical internship.

He next worked for nine months with Dr. Jack

Gibson to investigate the use of Evans Blue Dye in determining blood volume (see Appendix, list of publications). When the blue dye was injected, it immediately bound itself firmly to albumin in blood plasma. The quantitative dilution of the blue color defined the volume of the plasma. Many aspects of this research reinforced his earlier experiments in Dr. Christian's laboratory, giving him a solid base of physiologic experiments on which to build his career.

To Cincinnati and Back to Boston City Hospital

Nearing the end of his nine months with Dr. Gibson, Gene Stead was showering one morning as usual at the Brigham in a shower room characteristic of those in gymnasiums and of housestaff quarters in those days. An unknown gentleman was in the stall adjacent to Stead's and they began to chat as they showered. (Both were about 6'2" tall, so their heads were well above the walls of the showers.) A Dr. Tom Spies introduced himself, and they had breakfast together. As they chatted on, Dr. Spies (a nutritionist and internist) admitted that he was in Boston on a mission for Dr. Marion Blankenhorn, Chief of Medicine at Cincinnati General Hospital and Chairman of Medicine at the University of Cincinnati. Dr. Blankenhorn was not satisfied with the abilities of his senior residents, and Dr. Spies had been empowered to find a Chief Resident in Boston. By the time they had finished breakfast, Stead was offered the job, and accepted. His usual lack of money presented an immediate barrier, however, as he could not have paid for the trip to Ohio. His friend Hartwell Harrison obtained money from his "rich uncle" to loan to Gene Stead (rumor has it that HH was, himself, the rich uncle).

Stead spent his first six months in Cincinnati as a senior resident, learning about the hospital and the staff before becoming Chief Resident. He and Dr. Blankenhorn got along well, and Dr. Blankenhorn allowed his Chief Resident to take over much of the day-to-day operation of patient care and teaching. According to Dr. Stead, it was in Cincinnati that he learned to lead others, to set his own standards, and to instill rigorous expectations in others. Cincinnati General was the quintessential big-city hospital where many very sick poor people were being cared for in an environment in which public funding to support that care was always scarce. Stead, as Chief Resident, was the leader of the medical team, and began to be referred to as "the professor," sometimes derisively, but oft-times with respect for and awe of his knowledge and talents.

Stead had not known Soma Weiss in Boston, but Dr. Weiss came to visit for a week with Eugene Ferris, a cardiologist at Cincinnati who had been a fellow with Weiss. Drs. Weiss and Stead saw patients together on the wards every day, and with their teaching skills and interest in cardiovascular problems must have put on quite a show for students and houseofficers. At the end of the visit, Dr. Weiss asked Gene to return to Boston as his fellow, at a salary of $900 per year. Dr. Stead's reply was that he needed $1800 yearly because he was helping to pay for his brother's education at Emory. The exchange continued, with Dr. Weiss saying that they never paid more than $900 at the Boston City-Thorndike. Gene's reply was classical, "You're the only man I want to work for, and I will be here until July lst, before I start my practice in Atlanta, so if you find another $900, let me know." A few weeks later, a wire arrived in Cincinnati: "Found $900." So, in 1937, the tall Atlantan returned north to Boston as Dr. Weiss's fellow and Dr. Minot's Chief Resident at the Thorndike; Soma Weiss had coopted the $900 salary from Dr. Minot for the largely titular Chief Resident, and added it to his fellowship stipend. Stead did both jobs easily.

When Eugene Stead returned to Boston, he found that Dr. Weiss had departed on an extended European trip, leaving behind a technician in the laboratory and a medical resident, Paul Kunkel. They set to work and by the time Soma Weiss returned, Stead and Kunkel had already completed their first research project, and, with help from the secretary and Dr. William Castle, a manuscript had been completed and was ready to be sent to the prestigious *Journal of Clinical Investigation.*

Within five years of returning to Boston, Gene Stead had become a major clinical investigator and had published more than two dozen papers on the dynamics of the circulation. His collaborators were his research fellows: Paul Kunkel, Richard Ebert, and, later, James Warren. Dr. Weiss's name appeared on a manuscript only when he had actively collaborated with one of his fellows, a firm rule set by Dr. Weiss. In early 1942, Stead accepted the Chair of Medicine at Emory, but following Dr. Weiss's death, served as Acting Chief of Service at the Brigham.

Chairman at Emory

Stead's decision to be considered as Chairman at Emory was a difficult one. He had become an exciting figure on the Harvard-Brigham scene, a charismatic teacher and a highly productive clinical investigator. Emory at that time was not a distinguished school and, indeed, was probably an inferior one. Emory had no full-time clinical faculty and it was obvious that the days of the all-volunteer faculty were drawing to a close. Stead's biggest concern was whether he could develop a first-class faculty in the very Southern city of Atlanta; he felt that the venture was so risky that he would hesitate to invite his Harvard friends and junior colleagues to Atlanta. Soma Weiss probably made the decision for him by saying "So far you have proved to be a man of promise; if you succeed at Emory, you will also be a man of achievement." His friends in Atlanta, particularly Arthur Merrill, whom he had known in Cincinnati, pushed his candidacy. Stead negotiated a salary of $8,000/year so that he could "live as a professor."

As soon as he announced his decision in January, 1942, his hesitancy about luring young people to Emory and jeopardizing their future careers in medicine was resolved for him. Four fine young house officers at the Brigham came to him and simply announced that they would be in Atlanta ready to work on July 1st (the usual housestaff starting date). They were John Hickam, Eddie Miller, Abner Golden, and Jim Warren. A resident already at Emory, Emmett Brannon, became his research fellow, and within a year or two Stead would recruit Paul Beeson and Jack Myers from the Brigham as faculty. The

Rockefeller Institute later provided two fellowship stipends, which went to Max Michaels and Philip Bondy. Arthur Merrill, interested in kidney disease, left full-time practice to join Gene Stead's department on a half-time basis. In addition to bringing a group of bright and dedicated young doctors to Atlanta, Stead also arrived with his wife of two years, Evelyn (formerly Evelyn Selby), who had been Soma Weiss's secretary in Boston. When Dr. Weiss moved from Boston City to the Brigham, he needed a secretary, and because he sometimes still had a little trouble with the English language, the little *lapsus linguae* defined by his colleague Dr. Romano, he sought a secretary with particular knowledge of our language, and Miss Evelyn Selby seemed ideal. She had been graduated in 1935 with a B.A. in English Literature, and after graduation had worked for four years for Miss Marks, Chair of the English Literature Department at Mount Holyoke, an all-girls college, as such institutions were known in those days. Miss Marks was writing a book about Elizabeth Barrett Browning and the Barrett family. As secretary, Evelyn was heavily involved in that literary effort, improving her skills in editing and writing during her four years with Miss Marks. Miss Wooley, President of Mount Holyoke, shared the President's House with Miss Marks and two other senior women in the academic community. Miss Marks retired to the family home in Westport, New York each summer, accompanied by her secretary and often joined by one of the other women from the Mount Holyoke group. Evelyn became an excellent writer and editor, a talent useful to Dr.

Weiss, but also useful to her new husband, who was prone to *lapsus linguae*, Deep South variety. Although Gene Stead rather glories in those lapsi, Evelyn has diverted quite a few of them over the years, and they have become a powerful editing team.

Anyway, Miss Evelyn (as Gene still frequently calls her) left Mount Holyoke to join Dr. Weiss and his team of young doctors at the Brigham as they assembled on September 1, 1939. Apparently, several of the young bachelors who joined the Weiss housestaff and faculty also noticed Miss Selby favorably, but Gene Stead won out. Their courtship was unusual, since it illustrates Gene's clever use of resources while living in a state of chronic penury. Stead, Max Finland (Chief of Infectious Diseases at Boston City Hospital), Mike Meiklejohn, a Scotsman working with William Castle, and Paul Kunkel lived in Mrs. Redmond's boarding and rooming facility on Upland Road in Brookline, an area called "Pill Hill" in honor of the many doctors who lived there. Mrs. Redmond was an eccentric lady, much given to pro-Nazi literature, and a stickler for etiquette. She dressed formally for dinner each evening, and expected her guests to assemble on time. Since the meals were prepaid, Mrs. Redmond permitted the boarders to substitute a personal guest when one of the regular boarders was not at dinner. Gene noticed that the Scotsman, Mike Meiklejohn, was prone to have other activities. He quickly made a habit of inviting Evelyn to dinner whenever he learned that Mike was to be absent. Thus, he wooed and won her on Mike's nights out at Mrs. Redmond's boarding house.

The Steads were married in Cambridge at the

Bryant Street home of Soma and Elizabeth Weiss on June 15, 1940. Because Evelyn's father had died, Dr. Weiss gave away the bride. Just as Gene had described the marriage of his own father and mother, he and Evelyn were still living "happily ever after" in 1994. Their daughters, Nancy and Lucy, were born in Atlanta in January, 1944 and August, 1945, respectively, and their son Bill would come along in August, 1948, shortly after their move to Duke. Evelyn never resumed an independent career, but helping Gene Stead and raising three children was career enough. Of the three children, Nancy and Bill are doctors working in medical schools, and Lucy combines the job of mother and housewife with a full-time job at IBM. Evelyn did find time to write, with her close friend Gloria Warren (Jim's wife and a dietician), the first low-fat cookbook, which went through three editions and sold 180,000 copies. (The royalties from *Low-Fat Cookery* paid Nancy's tuition for four years at Duke Medical School.) By practicing her low-fat cookery, Evelyn has managed to keep both Gene Stead and herself healthy and trim, and many people can attest to the excellent cuisine at the Stead home.

Not everybody in Atlanta was overjoyed to have their bright young graduate of only a few years earlier return as Chairman. Among the local doctors there was the usual "old guard" who did not want to see the medical school adopt a system of employing full-time teachers/academicians, and they were uncooperative. Stead was disconcerted to find when he arrived in Atlanta that he was Chairman of Medicine at the Medical School but was not Chief of Medicine at the School's only hospital, Grady Hospital. Indeed, Grady had two Chiefs of Medicine, one for "white Grady" and one for "black Grady." Both were busy practitioners who spent little time in the hospital. Gene let them keep their titles, but built his own reputation as a doctor and teacher whose abilities exceeded theirs — an early lesson for him and perhaps for them in how little titles mean.

Philip Bondy (later to be Chairman at Yale, following Paul Beeson) was a victim of the practitioners' malice. Bondy had interned at the Brigham, but was not kept on as assistant resident. He wrote to Stead, who offered him an assistant residency in Atlanta. As soon as he got there, he was drafted into the Army on the instigation, he learned later, of the old guard and assigned to a military unit in the Atlanta area. Not all the practitioners were opposed to him, however. The doctor who had attended Gene in childhood, James E. Paullin, had been Gene's predecessor as Chairman. Dr. Paullin continued to attend conferences at Grady after Gene became chairman and worked hard for the new regime.

Stead and his group of young physiological investigators were interested in heart failure, blood loss, and other major perturbations of the circulation. The Grady Hospital was and is a big-city hospital with predominately black patients. Each Saturday night found the emergency room-filled with patients with knife and ice-pick wounds, bullet wounds, and other ills resulting from assorted mayhem. The Stead group began to deploy themselves to the emergency room to study such patients. About that time, Drs. Andre Cournand and Dickinson Richards, at Bellevue Hospital in New York, had developed a technique to be known as cardiac catheterization, for which they would receive the Nobel Prize. Long hollow rubber tubes were fed into an arm vein, into the right (venous) side of the heart, and out the right side of the heart into the large vessels of the lung, or the large veins draining the liver. The tube allowed sampling of the blood for chemical determinations, for oxygen and carbon dioxide content, and permitted measurements of pressures in various crannies of the circulation. This was the ideal tool for investigators like Stead and his group, and it was an ideal tool to help military doctors study the kind of trauma expected in the large numbers of casualties likely to result from the looming World War II.

Dr. Alfred Blalock, Professor of Surgery at Johns Hopkins, visited Atlanta and was impressed by the work of the Stead group. He recommended that they apply to the Office of Scientific Research and Development (OSRD) of the Army for a contract to develop a cardiac catheterization laboratory to expand their research capability on the hemodynamic effects of trauma and blood loss. OSRD responded favorably, and James Warren was sent to Drs. Cournand and Richardson in New York for six weeks to learn the technique. Dr. Stead tells a story about the contract that illustrates the innocence of the times and the amateurish behavior of the young group. There were no National Institutes of Health giving out grants and contracts in those days, and the group had had no experience in estimating how much experimental materials cost and how much their request for funding should be. After the laboratory was built, equipped, and functioning, they found that the budget they had requested for future years would be totally inadequate for operational costs. Fortunately, the secretary who typed and sent the final grant was not very good at numbers, and she was off by a decimal point in all the dollar amounts. The Army did not blink and the ten-fold increased windfall was about what they really needed to operate the laboratory! Thus Emory University, of all the unlikely places, had one of the world's three cardiac catheterization laboratories — New York, London, and Atlanta.

The Emory investigators were incredibly productive. Warren (later Chair at Ohio State) and Stead were the heart disease experts and circulatory physiologists. Jack Myers (later Chair at Pittsburgh) diverted his interests to liver and visceral blood flow, pressures, and chemistry; and the versatile John Hickam (later Chair at Indiana) combined studies in lung function with work on vascular pressures and blood flow in chest diseases. Paul Beeson, too, who was later to succeed Stead at Emory and to go on to Chairmanships at Yale and Oxford, made imaginative use of the new technology. He discovered that the number of organisms in arterial blood in patients with infected aortic heart valves were much higher than those in veins; the splanchnic circulation (liver, spleen, and gut area) was an efficient extractor of bacteria. All of these creative and later to become powerful men worked and planned together in a happy and productive way under Stead's general leadership.

The cardiac catheterization laboratory was very busy during the weekends as the investigators pursued studies of blood loss and traumatic shock, the purpose of the grant. Stead's team, however, was not going to let their splendid facility lie idle during the week when trauma cases were less frequent. All sorts of fascinating patients entered Grady Hospital, and provided unusual opportunities to the young investigators, and they wrote and published many papers on the findings by cardiac catheterization in many disease states. The landmark paper, however (#38 in Stead's publications, see Appendix), was related to the cause of heart failure, and this paper created enormous interest in the 1940's. Before its publication, it was thought that when the heart could not beat effectively, blood simply began to pile up on the venous side, pooled, and caused the veins to distend and the capillaries to leak fluid into the tissues, causing edema. Not so, said Warren and Stead. They pointed out that, in any form of circulatory stress, the human body had evolved to protect its two really vital organs, the brain and the heart. If the heart could not pump enough blood for all functions, blood was preferentially shunted to brain and heart by mechanisms involving increased tone (constriction) in non-essential circulatory beds, permitting adequate flow to brain and heart. The survival principle is clear: we can postpone liver metabolism, prevent the gut from absorbing food, the legs and skin from functioning, and the kidneys from making urine, but the work of the heart and brain must go on. Warren and Stead put forth the view that this reflex that shunted blood away from the kidneys played a large role in heart failure, because failure to excrete salt and water (remember Stead's experiments on salt and water in Dr. Christian's dogs) added to the swelling and to the salty water that accumulated in the lungs. This was an extremely important concept, because up until then all treatment of heart failure focused only on the heart. Under the new concept, doctors could control salt intake, thus improving kidney function; this added a new and important approach to therapeutics. Today, most of our treatment of heart failure involves prescribing diuretic drugs, which enhance kidney function and, in turn, diminish the swelling and the accumulation of fluid in the lungs. Although the Stead and Warren paper clearly defined the issues, it would be more than a decade before effective diuretic drugs would become available.

The Opportunity at Duke:
The Private Diagnostic Clinic

Within less than five years, Eugene Stead had built a remarkably creative service at Emory, turning a glimmering opportunity into an educational program of national prominence. Research was thriving, and a group of talented and convivial colleagues had been convened who shared Stead's ideals and visions. Yet when the Dean at Duke University's School of Medicine, Wilburt Davison, came calling in Atlanta and asked Stead to come to Duke, he accepted without much indecision. What was wrong with Emory, or what was unusually attractive at Duke? At Emory, the problem was that Gene Stead had been forced to assume the Deanship, plus his Chair in Medicine, simply because there was no one else. He did not like being the Dean, and, in general, administrative things were taking too much of his time without returning much personal satisfaction. Throughout his career, he would be an educator who was also a creative and effective administrator, and not an administrator who taught and did research as sidelines.

Duke had some very positive attractions for Dr. Stead. The University and its medical school were not very old, having been established by the Duke endowment in the late 1920's and thus had no dissatisfied practitioners objecting to new methods. The medical school had been planned and built under Dean Davison, who had been an energetic 33-year-old pediatrician from Johns Hopkins when he undertook the job. By 1946, when Stead was approached by Duke, the school had an established reputation and good basic science departments. Teaching in the clinical years, however, was still largely didactic. Nevertheless, the school attracted good students from a national base, not simply from a local Southern grouping.

The greatest attraction for Stead at Duke was a private diagnostic clinic (PDC) which had been established by Dr. Deryl Hart, first Professor of Surgery at Duke, and later President of the University. Dr. Hart's interests in private patients were soon augmented when Dr. Frederick Hanes was appointed Chair of Medicine, preceding Gene Stead. Dr. Hanes was a white-maned elegant Southern aristocrat of the Hanes Knitting Company family, who had been trained impeccably in Medicine at Hopkins. Before becoming Chairman at Duke he had been in private practice in Winston-Salem for a few years. Both Hart and Hanes thought that the private patients in North Carolina should have available a fine facility at Duke, and they also thought that private practice should help fund academic growth. The plan they concocted was and is unique among medical schools. The inner workings of the plan were, deliberately I think, kept a bit murky until Dr. Hart in 1971 told the story in, *The First Forty Years at Duke in Surgery and the PDC* (Duke University Press, Durham, NC).

Dr. Stead explains that Dean Davison, when he started the Duke Medical School, knew that most of the clinicians would be required to earn their salary. The Duke endowment was simply not ample enough to provide a staff made up entirely of full-time salaried clinical physicians. As Davison surveyed current practices in medical schools, he noted that the separation of famous surgeons such as Frank Lahey in Boston and George Crile in Cleveland from their University base represented a real loss to their institutions (Tufts and Western Reserve Universities, respectively). The Brigham hospital in Boston allowed faculty to care for their private patients in the hospital, and Dean Davison felt that the reputation of surgeons like Harvey Cushing and Eliot Cutler and internists such as Samuel Levine and Henry Christian added to the luster of the Brigham. Thus, he approved and encouraged Dr. Hart's plan for Duke, in which the faculty practiced as Duke faculty members in Duke Hospital.

The Private Diagnostic Clinic (PDC) was started in 1933 at the depth of the Great Depression. Basically, the arrangement was that the clinical faculty would be what is called "geographical full-time." That term means that the faculty works for an institution on its premises on a full-time basis, but is not paid a full salary. In Duke's case, pay from the University was the token salary of $2500/year, the base salary in 1933, and additional supplements were earned. The basic agreement with the University was never written down, but in essence the PDC physicians would be expected to fulfill their teaching duties as well as provide care for indigent patients. In return, the University agreed not to know the details of earnings of the PDC members, nor to become beguiled by the earnings generated. In other words, hands off if the teaching went well.

The University provided the initial clinic space, but agreed, in lieu of rent, to accept a fixed donation to the Development Fund. The money in the Development Fund was used by the Dean, with the advice and consent of the chairs of the departments which generated the money, to further advance the overall needs of the School of Medicine. In practice, most additions to the clinical facilities, including new PDC space, were built with Development Fund money, often in cooperation with the departments, the Duke endowment, outside agencies, and private donors.

In addition to the Development Fund, each department taxed its clinicians a certain percentage of earnings to develop a Department Fund. Within a given department, salaries might be negotiated but tended to relate directly to earnings of the individual faculty person. Later, as procedures such as kidney dialysis brought in large professional fees to a subspecialty group, the salaries were negotiated within the group and with the department chairman.

In pragmatic fiscal terms, my estimate (from Dr. Hart's book) is that the basic overhead of the practice was 10-20% of gross income, usually close to 10% in the early years. The Development Fund received, in different years, 4-8% of gross, and each Department Fund's portion might vary but was generally about 10% (by my estimate). This arrangement meant that the individual practitioner had an incentive to see many patients because he always kept well over half of his earnings. The medical school benefitted directly by the Development Fund, but also indirectly because the dean could divert certain University monies (i.e., salary increment, secretarial support) to basic science departments from the wealthier clinical departments.

Dr. Hart (pages 66-68 in his book) gives a good example of the use of these funds to build various segments of the Bell Research Building. Initially, in about 1945, money from the Surgical Department Fund ($10,000), Medical Department Fund ($10,000), Dorothy Beard Surgical Research Fund ($50,000), Duke Endowment ($100,000), and Rockefeller Foundation ($10,000), built the building to provide research space for several departments, including Anatomy, Biochemistry, and Pathology. A small (1400 sq. ft.) addition in 1948 was to provide specific research space to Physiology, and again a consortium of the Dorothy Beard Foundation and the departments of Medicine and Surgery built the addition. Only $18,000 total was needed in those days for 1400 sq. ft. of space. Even in 1952, when grants from the Cancer and Heart Institutes of the NIH were available for construction, $125,000 from the Development Fund was needed to provide one-third of the cost of the third addition. Construction of the final addition was a 50-50% arrangement between the federal government and the various departmental funds.

The PDC monies, in summary, provided just the sort of flexibility that Duke needed, but it would operate well only in an amicable environment in which the overall benefit to the School of Medicine was a high priority. With its help, Duke was growing, building, and improving its quality.

Gene Stead, coming to Duke from an impoverished Grady Hospital in Atlanta, saw the opportunity immediately, seized on it, nurtured the system, and managed his departmental finances carefully and well. He and Deryl Hart were both cautious financiers who struck careful bargains, but both used their departmental funds in the strong pursuit of excellence. Both never forgot the financial as well as the educational value of private patients cared for skillfully in the Duke PDC.

Stead's Educational Revolution at Duke:
One Student's Account

I had arrived at Duke as an undergraduate in September of 1942, at age 16, and left Duke as a medical doctor in September, 1947. This rapid trajectory was not because I was some sort of genius, but because that was the way the system worked in those days. North Carolina had only 11 grades of schooling, so 16 was a common age at high school graduation. World War II accelerated education, so that I was accepted to medical school when I was 18. By going to school without major breaks, we completed three years of undergraduate credits in two calendar years. When Dr. Stead's group arrived in early 1947, I was a near-pubescent 20-year-old junior

medical student. I had coasted through the first half of
the medical curriculum, the basic science part, without
stress or stimulation, reading extensively in the human-
ities and in literature in an attempt to find out how the
world worked. Things were a little more challenging in
the third year of medical school, with the beginning of
work with patients, but the faculty left from Dr. Hanes's
era, although competent, were not stimulating to me. I
had, however, discovered the library and had stumbled
on the great benefit of using the library properly to learn
about diseases. If I had a patient with leukemia, for example, I found an article on leukemia among the current
periodicals in the library. From that article I followed the
references to key papers on the subject, read those and
found new references, and finally read the textbooks.
Textbooks in those days were often grossly out of date
because four years of war had disrupted the usual
cycle of rewriting of standard textbooks. My system of
relying on current journals was effective, exciting, and
fun for me.

My first encounter was not with Dr. Stead, but
with Assistant Professor Jack Myers, who had helped
move the laboratory from Emory to Durham. Jack came
to my ward to see patients and teach — "ward rounds"
in the medical terminology. By chance, my patient was
selected to be presented to Dr. Myers. The patient was a
man with advanced cirrhosis of the liver, very yellow
because his diseased liver was unable to metabolize bi-
lirubin, and with a huge distended belly because of
accumulated fluid from interference with blood flow
through the scarred liver. Dr. Myers started questioning

me about the man's history, and about all the physical findings and the abnormal physiology and biochemistry caused by the damaged liver. We talked for 2-1/2 hours with the patient's large belly protruding between us. The other students joined in occasionally, but mostly Myers and I discussed every aspect of liver disease. At the end of the session, Myers harumped! and walked away. I learned later that lack of adverse comment by Myers indicated great approval. What Jack Myers did not know was that cirrhosis had been the subject of perhaps my most extensive literature search just the day before, and that I have never known as much about cirrhosis as I did that particular morning when a stranger named Dr. Myers arrived for ward rounds. I was exhilarated by my own performance, but I was even more excited by the breadth and quality of our discussion. No other member of the Duke faculty could have talked for 2-1/2 hours on cirrhosis, and on that day I became totally and completely enthralled by the people from Emory.

During my last nine months as a medical student (Stead's first nine months at Duke), I was involved in the senior clerkships. In those days, the senior year curriculum was the same as the junior year, with students rotating as senior clerks through the major services of medicine, surgery, and pediatrics. In the senior clerkship, if you were an able and reliable student, you were allowed to function almost as an intern. Because of the Stead influence, plus my own use of the library, my gears became completely enmeshed in medicine and I was outstanding in those last nine months. I liked everything in medicine, and both the Departments of Medicine and

Surgery wanted me to enter their discipline. My mind was made up: Medicine under Stead and his team.

However, with the end of the War, I suddenly found myself adrift in September of 1947. The war-time student schedule was to cease, and the July-July traditional academic year was to start up again in July of 1948. I was lucky to have found an unexpected intern vacancy at the University of Maryland, and I left for Baltimore in late September of 1947 to take up my new post. In those days, interns were selected by the Chairman whenever he wanted to make the appointment. I knew that fact, and went to Dr. Stead to tell him that I wanted to return to Duke to intern again in 1948-1949. He tried hard to get me to apply elsewhere - Boston, Hopkins - and it was obvious that he could and would get me an internship in those other places. I kept pointing out that I wanted to work for him, and we left the conversation with the understanding that I would apply only to Duke, unless he absolutely said he would not have me. He never said that, and after nine months in Baltimore I returned to Duke.

By the time I returned to Duke as an intern, I was a highly experienced doctor with good surgical skills because half of the Maryland experience had been in surgery. The Duke schedule required the intern to be "on-call" in the hospital five nights a week. To me, this was really wonderful after my less than one night per month at Maryland! So I read a lot of medicine and became increasingly aware that we were developing drugs which really worked — penicillin for syphilis, pneumonia and streptococcal diseases, and streptomycin for tuberculosis and tularemia. Cortisone had come along as an experimental therapy and its risk:benefit ratio in diseases such as rheumatoid arthritis was a pertinent topic. Others of the interns were in awe of and in many cases afraid of Dr. Stead, a not uncommon attitude toward one's professor at that time, but he and I have always been friends on a near egalitarian basis. Perhaps this was because our Southern backgrounds had been similar or because I had been raised by an uncle very much like Stead whom I had always thought of as a friend. In any case, to this day, he has never spoken a cross or unkind word to me, although he did occasionally lose patience with one or another of his house officers. I, like many of his interns and residents, totally worshipped the man. The group of us talked like him, walked like him, used his figures of speech, and adopted his mannerisms. Even now, forty years after our paths diverged, a little clone of Gene Stead exists in me and may emerge with only slight provocation (e.g., two glasses of wine). When we meet somewhere, we inevitably and immediately fall into conversation as if we had just parted a few minutes ago. Gene Stead is a charismatic leader of a unique sort.

After the internship year, most of us stayed on the Duke housestaff as assistant resident physicians. Early in that year, Dr. Stead called each of us, perhaps seven or eight in all, into his office to tell us that we must leave Duke and go elsewhere for one year of subspecialty fellowship. His reasoning in this was clear: we had become good doctors and he wanted to send us out as advertisements of the Duke medical product. He was prepared to help each of us get the sort of position we wanted. I did not argue with him, because I felt I did need to work in a different program, and I also needed to decide on the type of subspecialist I wanted to become.

Stead managed to get me offers in hematology from Richard Vilter in Cincinnati and Carl Moore and Edward Reinhard at Barnes Hospital in St. Louis. I finally decided on St. Louis because I could see private patients essentially all day, every day, with Dr. Reinhard, who had built up a huge referral practice from throughout the Midwest. Professionally, it was good for me. I did get an unbelievably diverse and intense exposure to hematologic diseases during the year with Reinhard, and got a significant exposure to private medical practice while still being an integral part of the research effort.

Chief Resident Under Dr. Stead

In June, 1951, I was slated to return to Duke, and Dr. Stead had decided that I would be his Chief Resident, a job I associated with someone older and more mature than myself. The year as Stead's Chief Resident led me to think I could become a professor. The Chief Resident position at Duke mimicked that of the Chairman of Medicine. I had all the responsibilities that Stead carried, but at a lower level. My direct charge was to help all the interns and residents to advance their knowledge and to become successful doctors. All the patients were mine, in a sense, even private patients of the faculty, because all patients were cared for by housestaff, and responsibility for their care devolved eventually on the Chief Resident. The Chief Resident was constantly educating his housestaff, planning and running formal conferences, being certain that housestaff and students performed well on their wards and related well to their faculty attending (supervising) physicians. The Chief Resident and the residents assigned to each floor met each morning with Dr. Stead for Morning Report, during which patients admitted to the Medical Service the day before were discussed. One of my informal jobs as Chief Resident was to spot-check, with the resident involved, any patient whose history or physical examination suggested that the ward team was not handling the patient properly.

Stead and I naturally spent hours together each week. He was constantly probing ways to make patient care better, to improve teaching, to streamline some hospital function, or to make people more responsive and more effective in their jobs. We discussed issues and policies, and his interests shaped my understanding of medical administration as a creative and enjoyable activity. As illustrated by his sayings in *Just Say For Me* (abstracted at the end of this chapter), he sought always to define social or psychological verities out of the mass of his experience as teacher, educator, and administrator.

Stead's Personal Educational Philosophy and Style
During the years that I knew Dr. Stead, his educational philosophy did not change, nor did his personal style of teaching. Philosophically, he believed that the patient was the focus of all educational efforts. Among his housestaff and students, his definition of cardinal sins included poor patient care or lack of sensitivity to pa-

tients, particularly if the deficit in any way smacked of laziness. This led to a mild constant tension which most of us found stimulating, but some found to be intimidating. Those who were intimidated generally left his program. His demands on others were no greater than those he placed on himself. He was always around the hospital, at all hours of the day or night. This was possible because he lived in a university home, just a five-minute walk from the hospital, and whenever he was in the hospital for a meeting or working late in'his office he wandered about the wards for a few minutes, simply observing and commenting. Stead's seeming omnipresence was felt by his students and housestaff. Also, he was most reluctant to join national groups or travel away from home very much. Dr. Stead told me he learned about the dangers of the traveling professor at Emory, where his counterpart, the Professor of Surgery, was always gone when decisions were made or booty of some sort was distributed. Stead was a poor traveler, and I remember once being in his office with his secretary when he was out of town. The phone rang, and it was Dr. Stead: "I seem to be in Dallas. What am I doing here?"

Dr. Stead taught on one particular ward, the Osler Ward, which was the public ward for white women. By teaching on one ward all year, all houseofficers and most students would have personal contact with him. Also, the Osler Ward had fewer "interesting" patients, and one of Stead's talents (like that of his mentor Soma Weiss) was to find any patient interesting in some way. Because most of the women on the Osler stated their main problem to be that they were "weak and nervous," it took a master teacher to make rounds interesting to the students. His rounds started promptly at 10:00 a.m. and ended whenever he wanted to stop, usually after 1:00 p.m. He held the student responsible for knowing specific medical and personal information about the patient, as well as general medical information about the patient's disease. Only when the student's fund of information was exhausted did he shift his questioning to the intern, and eventually to the resident — e.g., going up the ladder of responsibility.

He remained staunchly convinced that teaching could, and should, be totally egalitarian. Anyone in the group who had knowledge to contribute was listened to, and his or her input, not its hierarchical source, was valued for its content. Dr. Stead reinforced his egalitarian concepts with his famous "I bet a nickel" strategy. He never bet his nickel on any piece of information that he knew concretely, but bet by deductive reasoning. When he bet a nickel, the student or houseofficer who accepted the bet would be busy in the library searching for the facts that established who won the nickel. About half the bets were voided: the answer was not found. Dr. Stead won most of the nickels, but any student or intern who won a nickel was likely to frame it, along with the question whose correct answer won the nickel. Since Dr. Stead usually carried no money in his pocket, it was usually a nickel supplied by his secretary and friend, Bess Cebe, that the student or houseofficer carried away after delivering his or her proof to the professor.

The Duke housestaff program reflected some of Dr. Stead's specific educational techniques. He believed that houseofficers, interns in particular, should stay in the hospital most of the time in order to have informal contacts with patients and to interact informally with one another. Thus, we were on-call constantly, except for two nights a week. The majority of houseofficers in the early years were unmarried, and this policy did not bother us very much. Later, as more of us were married, and had children, the on-call schedule drew our wives and children to dinner in the doctors' dining room on nights when the work was slack. This social custom helped make the housestaff an extended family. Wives visited together in the dining room, getting to know one another.

Morning Report is an educational activity which was, and is, common in medical centers. In essence, a group of residents meets with their Chief to present and discuss patients admitted the day before. There are a number of variations on the format, but Stead had a unique one. He met each morning at 8:00 a.m. with his Chief Resident and about four or five residents in charge of different wards. The variation peculiar to Dr. Stead was that no one was forced to present patients, or was even required to discuss anything medical. Any topic could come up — yesterday's Duke football game, a movie, a book, a social issue. In practice, we usually presented patients and occasionally discussed some other topic. The professor made it clear to us that no one had to speak, but all had to stay from 8-8:30 a.m. Periodically, a group would decide to say nothing, but such was the power of Stead's personality that I, at least, cannot remember a "silent" report lasting longer than 10 minutes.

Dr. Stead had started a "Sunday School" at Emory and transferred it intact to Duke. This was a Sunday morning, 9:30-10:30 a.m., formal conference in which one of the houseofficers (or perhaps a fellow or junior faculty member) gave a formal presentation on some topic of his own choosing. Many of the senior faculty sat in the front row while other houseofficers and students made up the audience. By ending the conference at 10:30 a.m., we did not interfere with 11:00 church services in the religious South. Most of us remember our Sunday School lessons vividly.

Most of the unique features of the Duke teaching program in internal medicine were in the day-to-day operation and the intense personal input by Gene Stead. His comments were thoughtful, creative, useful, whether on organizational matters or related to diagnosis or care of patients. He had a remarkable ability to discuss a specific issue and relate it to a general principle. Almost from the time he arrived at Duke, his housestaff and students began to collect Steadisms. In the mid-1960's, anticipating his retirement, two Chief Residents, Fred Schoonmaker and Earl Metz, collected a sequence of Steadisms in a little pocket-sized paperback entitled *Just Say For Me*. The little volume is no longer in print, and Drs. Schoonmaker and Metz have kindly agreed to my reprinting portions in this book. Some of the Steadisms look a little dated after more than a quarter of a century, and some seem to have translated poorly from the original Steadian language, but most have pertinence and wisdom for today. Another book about Dr. Stead was published in 1978, by Galen Wagner, Bess Cebe, and Marvin Rozear. This book *E.A. Stead, Jr.*, (Carolina Academic Press, Durham, NC, 1978) was subtitled with another famous Steadism *What This Patient Needs is a Doctor.* That Steadism could devastate a houseofficer or student who had just finished presenting a patient whose course was complicated by too many consultants, too much advice, too many procedures, too many drugs, too little creative reasoning.

Selections From Just Say For Me[2]

1. One can't treat all patients as equal because not all have equal needs.

2. Long after the fever is gone changes in structure may persist. It should be obvious that people don't get well all at once. In a sick person many changes take place that require some time to return to normal. It has always intrigued me that so many doctors hold on to the naive notion that once an underlying defect is controlled, the patient is well.

3. The staff is made up of doctors who exist to care for patients. A physician must believe that patients can legitimately make demands on doctors and that because the ill are not rational these demands do not have to be rational. It's not bad for people who are sick not to feel well.

4. I never threaten the patient who refuses to follow my instructions. The opportunity for learning is the same.

5. Take care of people, not illness.

---

[2] Fifty selections from 342 quotations in the complete manuscript.

6.   All too often we are too eager to talk about rather than talk with our patients.

7.   I never feel sorry for the doctor. The sick never inconvenience the well.

8.   Some people have to be right and feel that they are right. I don't worry too much about who is right or wrong, but about what is best for the patient.

9.   Many patients go from doctor to doctor thinking that they are sick and are never told that they are really well in a way they can understand. If a hundred people listen to a Beethoven symphony, some will be in ecstasy and some will be bored. These are not good and bad people, but people with different central nervous systems. Some people interpret almost all sequels from their central nervous systems as signs of sickness. They are not sick, but just have different receivers.

10. The art of medicine is not confined to organic disease; it deals with the mind of the patient and with the behavior as a thinking, feeling human being. The essential skills depend not simply on instruction but on emotional maturity, manifested by sensitive self cultivation of the ability to see deeply and accurately the problems of another human being. The challenge is further magnified by the fact that the examining physician is himself a human instrument, subject to error due to the events in his own biography.

11.   The restoration of the patient's comfort and con-
       fidence should begin with his initial contact with
       the physician. Gentle, thorough and interested
       interrogation and examination prepare the way
       for more painful procedures that may be essential.

12.   There is clearly a difference between the physician
       who has doubts about his interest in clinical med-
       icine and the physician who has doubts about his
       ability. I have always had much more patience
       with the latter.

13.   I'm sure it is natural to feel hostility toward the
       "alcoholic." An amateur can feel any way he
       wants, but a doctor is a professional.

14.   A doctor doesn't really need much knowledge, as
       he can look most things up. But he must have
       much emotional stability and ability to perform in
       an air of uncertainty.

15.   Tact, sympathy and understanding are expected
       of the physician for the patient is no mere collec-
       tion of symptoms, signs, disordered functions,
       damaged organs and disturbed emotions. He is
       human, fearful and hopeful, seeking relief, help
       and reassurance. To the physician, as to the an-
       thropologist, nothing human is strange or
       repulsive. He cares for people because he cares
       for them.

16.   No greater opportunity, responsibility or obliga-
       tion can fall to the lot of a human being than to
       become a physician. In the care of the suffering,

he needs technical skill, scientific knowledge and human understanding. He who uses these with courage, with humility and with wisdom will provide a unique service for his fellow man and will build an enduring edifice of character within himself. The physician should ask of his destiny no more than this; he should be content with no less.

17.   A good clinician ceases to make a distinction between work and play. A child equates play with good and work with bad. When a physician does this, clinical medicine becomes intolerable for him.

18.   In maturing, a physician finds that he can deal with life and death more comfortably.

19.   Many physicians too calmly bury their mistakes.

20.   A doctor ought to be able to tell when a dying patient has stopped suffering so that he can direct his attention to the suffering family.

21.   A physician must have great tolerance for he sees people at their worst.

22.   The word physician equals a willingness to serve.

23.   A doctor should be an expert in the problems of dying so that he can be helpful to the layman who has had no experience with death.

24.   The secret of success is to devise a social system which allows for change. The only thing you know for certain about a new faculty member is that he will change. You do not know the direction or rate of change, but you know that change will occur. The social system of the university should accept

the challenge of this uncertainty and allow its faculty to live many different lives.

25.   The role of the faculty is to set the atmosphere and example so that those in clinical medicine may try out their wings.

26.   The most common error is for the doctor to keep on doing at the age of 50 what he clearly enjoyed at the age of 30. For the majority of teachers, their real excitement wanes after fifteen years. They should pass the torch to the youngsters and move on to other areas of responsibilities in the school or community. We should enjoy the young, not compete with them. The young should gain responsibility while they have the drive and enthusiasm to enjoy it. In this way the profession will more effectively mold the lives of men.

27.   Students are not emotionally involved in adult problems, but try to change their curriculum and see what happens.

28.   You build stronger medical centers not by getting better teachers but by getting better students.

29.   Education does not make a man more tolerant. Some of the best educated people I have known have been the most intolerant.

30.   I'd like to see all medical school examinations open book. Books are so useful.

31.   Internship and residency are the golden years in the life of a physician who practices medicine. They are the years when he first becomes a pro-

fessional worker, the years when patients first are willing to entrust their bodies and minds to his care, and the years of close association with bright young colleagues and mature doctors. These are important formative years, and they shape the conduct of future young physicians more than any other experience.

32.   Two years in a hospital, night and day, is necessary to see how illness looks - to see what the people behind the patient look like in all circumstances.

33.   If you can't get your work done in 24 hours, you'd better work nights.

34.   I'm not so immune to the simple pleasures of life that I don't enjoy hearing a young man say that he has learned a lot from me, but realistically I know it's not so. Bright men teach themselves.

35.   Learning is an active process and each of us learns more when we teach than when we are taught.

36.   To give or to teach, much time must be given. Both the student and the teacher must learn by investing time.

37.   Research should be carried out with residents and fellows to stimulate their thinking. With older staff research is a means for keeping minds alert and teaching interesting.

38.   Can a physician choose to practice and teach excellent clinical medicine in a University center and

devote no time to research? Well, there are two ways of getting money to support a doctor. One is from patient fees. One is from research grants. And as sub-specialities grow there will develop differentiations within each of them. Some will do basic research. Others will be more clinically oriented. Those with grants depending on patients will be helping to support the clinicians in some cases. The criterion for staying in a University center should be excellence of performance. It should be presumptuous to state which area that excellence should be.

39. There is a marked difference between the appearance of a disease and what it means to the patient.

40. That man is not a far sighted biological creature is evidenced by the way he kills off all the able in war.

41. I learned early that many people like to fish and play golf. I like to work with my head.

42. Modern medicine deals with curable disease. This is where the glory lies.

43. I would rather be called to see someone who is frightened than to see someone who is dying. The results of treating the first are obviously so much better.

44. What's culture in North Carolina is insanity in New York.

45. The young and the old have different functions. The young are able to give new and more useful

information, while the older more wisdom. They can generalize in problem areas from a broader outlook.

46. None can give authority, it must be taken.

47. I've had no difficulty dealing with life's great problems, just in finding the right classroom.

48. There are many different patterns of dying. In a hospital it is a social affair. People are continually doing what good people are expected to do in this setting.

49. When I was young, I never imagined then anyone would ever pay me such a good salary for doing exactly what I wanted to do.

50. There is no advantage in being young unless you believe in yourself.

Eugene Stead and the Evolution of Duke as a Renowned Medical Center

To paraphrase Soma Weiss's comments to Gene Stead, Duke was an institution of promise when Stead went there in 1947 as Chairman of Medicine, and had become an institution of great achievement by the time he resigned as Chairman 20 years later. People give Stead most of the credit for Duke's evolution to greatness, but he acknowledges the critical importance of other major figures at Duke. When Mr. James B. Duke started his foundation, Duke's President, William Few, was fortunate to hire a young pediatrician from Johns Hopkins, Wilburt

C. Davison, as Dean. The new Dean had boundless energy, supervised the physical building of the school, hired
the first faculty, recruiting heavily from Johns Hopkins;
most were still there in the 1940's when I was a medical
student. Duke was, in many ways, "Dave's medical
school," as Gene Stead describes it.

Dean Davison would serve for 33 years as Dean,
providing leadership and being in overall charge until
1960. He was not a micromanager, but achieved balance
and helped bring consensus and set goals and standards.
He was an honest and reliable man, a fascinating conver-
sationalist who worked for Duke and not for Dean
Davison. He was respected nationwide, but his own emphasis was to serve Duke first, then the State of North
Carolina, the South in general, and the cause of children.
He wrote a little handbook of pediatrics which provided
a unique system to allow the reader to follow a symptom
through the maze of the book to arrive at a diagnosis and
treatment. My copy of *The Compleat Pediatrician* has long
since been lost, but I would like to see one today to sat-
isfy myself that it was, as I remember it, a work of genius,
unique and eccentric.

Davison's personal little black appointment book
was a fondly remembered fixture. When he agreed to a
commitment with one of the staff, he wrote it in his little
black book, which he kept in his wallet. Once something
was in the little black book, it was a guarantee to his
colleagues for he always kept his end of the bargain.

Dean Davison's excellent taste in people was reflected, I believe, first in his selection of Fred Hanes as
Professor of Medicine to begin to build a department,

and, later, his selection of the young and somewhat controversial Eugene Stead to improve it and to strive for greatness. Deryl Hart, Professor of Surgery and later President of the University, was a strength in building a strong surgery department and, as discussed earlier, in conceiving the Private Diagnostic Clinic (PDC) and setting its policies. In the basic sciences, Philip Handler in Biochemistry, later President of the National Academy of Sciences, and in the 1960's Daniel Tosteson, now Medical Dean at Harvard, helped forge excellent and creative departments.

Gene Stead gives Dr. Walter Kempner a great deal of credit for Duke's achieving a national and international reputation as a medical center for patient care. Kempner, a German who was invited to this country in the early 1930's by Dr. Hanes to do research on kidney disease, became enamored of the idea of treating hypertension with a rice and fruit diet. Hanes insisted that Kempner be allowed to join the PDC so that he could obtain his own private patients for these studies. The rice diet was questioned by other doctors then, but looked at with current knowledge, the diet probably did no harm. Its extremely low-sodium low-protein content would be expected to treat hypertension, heart failure, and kidney failure fairly effectively.

The diet contains no cholesterol and no one can eat enough rice and fruit to gain weight. Thus, the diet was excellent for high-cholesterol problems such as heart attack and stroke and for weight loss in the morbidly obese. The rice diet was touted as a panacea. The diet was consistent with life because Orientals had subsisted on it for centuries, but it was acceptable to American patients only as a last resort and when presented by Dr. Kempner, a man of forceful character who was totally rigid about the rice diet. It became, to the patients, a religion as well as a treatment.

People flocked to Durham for the rice diet, were evaluated in the hospital, treated for weeks or months in his "rice houses" in town, and cared for by the hospital if acute complications arose. Meticulous clinical records were kept and urine and blood studies were recorded. But, except for one descriptive paper in the *American Journal of Medicine* about 40 years ago, the advantages and disadvantages of the rice diet were never evaluated by Kempner's peers, but achieved a cult-like status. The dilemma for Duke in allowing a program of unproven worth to continue, was obvious to those of us working as students and houseofficers. The diet did succeed to some extent in alleviating cardiovascular disease, and at that time there was absolutely *no* alternative treatment. The lack of peer review kept the rice diet from being adopted in other medical centers, as did the sheer problem of getting people to eat it. Only Kempner's dominating personality could get patients to accept the regimen, and to pay to endure it. Hollywood moguls, powerful men of business and politics, scions of wealthy and prominent families flocked to Durham and to Dr. Kempner. I remember one powerful Hollywood producer, with tears of gratitude in his eyes, as Dr. Kempner in full regalia of starchy white coat and full retinue of about six assistants, came by and allowed him to add half a tomato to his diet!

In 1947 when Stead arrived, this sort of behavior,

considered semi-charlatan in nature, was being questioned by many members of the Duke faculty. David T. Smith, the gentle man who was Acting Chair after Dr. Hanes's death, was told by the Executive Committee and Dean Davison to fire Kempner. Dr. Smith refused, saying that Stead was a cardiovascular expert and could decide whether Kempner should be kept. Stead came, reviewed the records of Kempner's patients, and decided to keep him. The two men, both zealots in certain ways, remained firm friends. With the help of the excellent care that the PDC group gave to his patients, Kempner did, indeed, spread the image of Duke as a great center of clinical care to a national and international clientele.

The Kempner enterprises provided handsome operating funds for his research, and I presume he also allowed wealthy patients to donate to his own work and to Duke. I feel sure that Kempner was a major support to the Department of Medicine and to Dr. Stead's general academic program. Cynical people have, over the years, criticized the Stead-Kempner relationship as being heavily influenced by finances. I believe that both men have always been individuals of strong beliefs and principles, and remain by nature mutually respectful colleagues. Duke was the beneficiary of their enduring and continuing friendship.

During the 1950-1951 year when I was at Barnes Hospital in St. Louis during my hematology fellowship, I was essentially out of touch with Duke. When I returned as Chief Resident in June of 1951, casual chatter among the housestaff indicated that "Dr. Stead had mellowed," which many people attributed to son Bill's arrival in the family. But I also heard a hint, on my return, that Stead had had some sort of administrative trouble and had threatened to resign. As we continued our year of close association, I thought he seemed more careful of how his actions affected others, and more prone to seek true consultation on decisions. I learned that he had instituted monthly departmental faculty meetings, an interaction that had not been common practice before this year.

The administrative problem that had caused him to alter his leadership style, it turned out, was one of his own making. The story, as told by Dr. Stead himself in the Wagner-Cebe-Rozear book, was that he had decided to take away the University's stipend, only $2500 yearly, which went to each member of the private group (the PDC), and replace it with equivalent money from the tax that the PDC paid to the Department. The PDC group rebelled, feeling that the small stipend was a recognition of their role as genuine members of the Duke faculty, rather than adjunct clinical helpers.

In the fight, Stead tendered his resignation and it was promptly accepted by the Dean and the Executive Committee. Dr. Wiley Forbus, senior Chairman of Pathology, came to Gene and reviewed the opportunities he was tossing away at Duke and asked him to withdraw the resignation. His anger abated and mollified by Forbus, Stead did so, but was astonished to hear Dean Davison say that he could not be reinstated without a vote of the Executive Committee. Somehow, Davison then found it hard to get a proper quorum in the Committee, and the vote was postponed. Finally, after what must have been an anxious time, Gene Stead was reinstated by a one-vote margin. I view this as an example of Davison's genius as Dean. The episode forced Stead to review his situation and his options, forced his senior colleagues to think about Stead's institutional assets and liabilities, and the engineered delays gave time for things to simmer down and for Dr. Stead to mend some tatters. The more mellow Gene Stead who chaired those newly instituted interactive faculty meetings each month had become more modest, partly as a result of introspection but largely as a result of being forced to sign a written agreement to hold regular department meetings and to make major decisions by majority vote. This episode made Stead a better leader, and solidified his attachment to Duke, at the same time helping him to develop the broad support he needed to continue as an effective leader. Thereafter, he never looked at other jobs.

Eugene Stead's overall vision for Duke was that it would become a renowned producer of doctors of high quality through its medical school and its residency programs and specialty fellowships. To produce good doctors, particularly the highly specialized doctors whom he considered to be at the cutting edge of clinical medicine, he recognized the need to teach them how best to care for patients and at the same time to make clinical advances through patient-centered research. Duke, because of the reputation of the PDC, attracted large numbers of patients with interesting diseases, referred from all over the South. The achievement of overall scientific excellence, from the research bench to the bedside, was absolutely essential to his vision of the medical center. The PDC departmental tax helped him build research buildings and support bright young faculty, while the revenues from the PDC also brought modern improvements to the hospital. This was the era — 1950's and 1960's — when the federal government through the National Institutes of Health (NIH) was priming the pump of biomedical research. Duke, with strong clinical programs, good scientific research, and stable, enlightened and receptive leadership, received a deserved share of federal funds.

The Growth of Medical Subspecialties at Duke

Like his mentor, Soma Weiss, Stead could not accept the concept of narrow medical subspecialization for himself, although he saw its value for others. He wanted to maintain an overview of human disease to enhance his own intellectual growth, as well as to aid his teaching of housestaff and medical students. As a leader of his department and of Duke, however, he realized that subspecialization, which was already operative at Duke in 1947, would be a necessary outcome of the increasing complexity of medical care.

When Dr. Stead arrived at Duke in 1947, most of the subspecialties we identify today were already developed and accepted, but they were often divisions represented by only one faculty member. Hematology, oncology (cancer), cardiology, pulmonary diseases, infectious diseases, allergy, dermatology, rheumatology (arthritis), endocrinology, metabolism, and clinical pharmacology existed in some form. Only nephrology (kidney disease) was not identified, because as a specialty it was nascent throughout the medical community in 1947.

The twenty years of Stead's chairmanship (1947-1968) coincided with the growth of medical subspecialization in the U.S. and the emergence of specialized scientific disciplines enhanced by awards from the categorical divisions of the National Institutes of Health (NIH). As the NIH grew after World War II, its training grants became the base support for subspecialty training at universities, and Stead tried to insure that Duke got its share by strengthening the divisions so that they would compete well for grants. His methods were simple, in that he left the subspecialty group under its old leader, but added key faculty members to enhance the scientific strength of the discipline. The Durham Veterans Administration Hospital opened in the early 1950's, allied with Duke Medical School and providing additional training potential for young physicians in a setting paid for by the federal government. Stead often appointed his young potential stars to a VA-based position.

The Division of Gastroenterology provides a good example of subspecialty growth. When Gene Stead arrived at Duke, a remarkable man, Julian (Judy) Ruffin was in charge of Gastroenterology. Ruffin had achieved a national reputation through studies on the absorption and metabolism of vitamin A, and with other colleagues had described aspects of pellagra. An excellent clinician, Ruffin had trained most of the gastroenterologists in practice in North Carolina. He was their beloved father-figure to whom they referred patients with difficult problems. His research consisted entirely of clinical observations, but he made important contributions. A colleague, a clinical pharmacologist at Duke named

James Hendrix, had sought out and studied patients with a rare form of diarrhea called Whipple's Disease. He and Dr. Ruffin would show that long-term antibiotic treatment benefitted patients afflicted with this miserable disease. A popular treatment at the time to cure ulcers was the freezing of the stomach by inserting into it liquid nitrogen enclosed in a balloon. When Dr. Ruffin reported poor results and dangerous complications from the procedure, no more stomachs were frozen in the United States.

Meanwhile, Dr. Stead had recruited a young man, Malcolm Tyor, to head the radioisotopes unit of the Veterans Hospital. Tyor brought the new technology of isotopes to the field of gastroenterology, and also introduced modern methods of direct visualization of the stomach and colon (endoscopy). When Dr. Ruffin retired, Dr. Tyor moved from the VA to Duke as his replacement, while Dr. Ruffin continued his clinical practice and teaching for a few additional years. The specialty of gastroenterology prospered well at Duke, developed good NIH research and training grant support, and is now solidly established in the modern era of molecular biology.

Cardiology became the supreme subspecialty at Duke, in part because of the number of patients with heart and vascular disease, and in part because Dr. Stead merged his group so nicely into the existing cardiology program at Duke.

When Stead and his group of young and talented investigators arrived from Atlanta with their cardiac catheterization laboratory, they found a fine clinical cardiologist, Edward Orgain, already at Duke with a large, PDC-based practice. Orgain was a handsome, elegant, nattily dressed Virginian who was one of the great teachers and doctors at Duke. Since Stead's interests were in cardiovascular physiology, his group augmented Dr. Orgain's talents in what turned out to be a frictionless collaborative effort. Orgain trained first-rate clinical cardiologists and Stead was mentor to scientific cardiovascular physiologists. Perhaps because they were equal in ability, there was no conflict between them, and each enjoyed respect and admiration from students and housestaff.

Stead's group of clinical investigators used their catheterization laboratory as a research tool. The cath lab often generated interesting data pertinent to patients, and I remember erudite notes on the chart, written by Jack Myers or John Hickam, about the findings of cardiac catheterization and their interpretation of these findings. But the cardiac cath labs we know today were more than a decade away,

In the early 1960's, Henry McIntosh joined the faculty at the VA Hospital and began to write systematically defined notes on all cardiac catheterizations. When Myers, Hickam and Warren left Duke for positions elsewhere, Stead brought McIntosh from the VA Hospital to Duke Hospital first as Chief of the Cardiovascular Laboratory and later as Chief of Cardiology. McIntosh had broad interests and competence, starting programs in hyperbaric oxygen and in kidney dialysis, while functioning primarily as a cardiologist. Dr. McIntosh build a reputation at Duke, and in 1971 went to Baylor as Chairman of Medicine. McIntosh was succeeded by Andrew Wallace, and the Duke cardiovascular program became even larger, more varied, and internationally known.

Gene Stead played a supportive and encouraging role in guiding the cardiology division, but was not heavily involved personally during his years as Chairman. He always considered the Chairmanship his full-time job. After retirement in 1968, he began to resume activities in cardiovascular disease, bringing statistical expertise and the Cardiovascular Data Bank to clinical studies in the Duke Cardiac Intensive Care Unit (CCU). Stead tried unsuccessfully to get the NIH interested in computerizing the monitored events in the CCU. He found piecemeal funding, and started the Duke Cardiovascular Data Bank aimed at helping to guide doctors in their treatments and interventions. It was an effective teaching device because the doctor could see an electronically recorded phenomenon in his or her patient and call on the data bank for similar experiences with other patients. It was popular with housestaff, and, as the years went on, the Data Bank became the focus of many grants and research publications about heart attacks and coronary heart disease. Duke is now an important center for cardiovascular disease, and is particularly effective in the application of computer technology to clinical medicine.

The examples of gastroenterology and cardiology reflect the changes that occurred in all the medical subspecialties at Duke. Oncology, fueled by Stead's prescient appointment of Wayne Rundles as Chief, might also be singled out for special comment. The oncologists combined surgical abilities with the pharmacologic expertise that was Rundles's specialty. All the Duke medical subspecialties did well under Stead. By controlling both the salaries and the academic appointments, Stead had direct input into recruitment of faculty and the configuration of academic programs.

Research Training Programs

Duke's most innovative program, perhaps, was the Research Training Program, a concept that evolved in the late 1950's as a result of a conversation between Eugene Stead and Philip Handler, the stimulating Chairman of Biochemistry, as they sat together on a return flight to Durham. Stead and Handler discussed the problem of how one could train young clinical doctors or medical students to do modern science, and how one could retrain older clinical faculty in ever-changing scientific methods. The talks that began on that airplane continued later and the concept of a Research Training Program (RTP) evolved into a program plan that they submitted to the NIH for funding. Their idea was to form a multidisciplinary faculty group to be primarily responsible for the RTP; this group would have few assignments in traditional courses or to specific departments. This group of scientists would provide a one-year intensive research experience for medical students, housestaff, junior faculty, and occasional senior faculty members. These students would work primarily with one investigator, but would receive special formal training by the RTP faculty in research technologies and biostatistics so that they could explore the functions of broad areas of science.

James Wyngaarden at that time was a major investigator at the NIH in urate metabolism and gout. Stead and Jack Myers wanted to recruit Wyngaarden to Duke, and thought they had a strong enough rheumatology group to attract him as Chief of Rheumatology. My predecessor as Chief Resident, Grace Kerby, provided teaching and clinical care in rheumatic diseases. A senior clinician of the PDC group, Elbert Persons, had teamed up with Duke's dynamic Professor of Orthopaedic Surgery, Leonard Baker, to obtain an NIH training grant in rheumatic diseases. Wyngaarden accepted the Duke position, and was the logical person to direct the Research Training Program.

The NIH bought the concept wholeheartedly because the program basically was designed to upgrade the scientific skills of young people. Wyngaarden recruited an exceptionally fine faculty group that included Daniel Tosteson, Chair of Physiology and Pharmacology at Duke. This was an exciting educational venture, and other schools adopted the program. (Paul Beeson promptly established a similar program at Yale.)

The success of the Research Training Program, its creativity and the excitement it aroused, is attested to by the subsequent careers of some of the major participants. Philip Handler became Director of the National Academy of Science. Wyngaarden went to Pennsylvania as Chairman of Medicine, before returning to Duke in 1968 as Stead's successor, and later became Director of the National Institutes of Health. Daniel Tosteson left Duke to become Dean of the University of Chicago School of Medicine before moving on as Dean at Harvard.

Stead and the New Curriculum at Duke
Gene Stead was first and foremost a medical educator. He made innovative changes in medical education for doctors, primarily through his shrewd assessment of the learning process. The Research Training Program, in which some medical students relinquished clinical medicine for a year to learn research methods, was a great success under Wyngaarden and Tosteson. Building on this achievement, Gene Stead began to talk about a new medical school curriculum which would embody his ideas about letting students be free to explore science in a stimulating environment. He wanted to offer a first year basic science curriculum that would rely less on traditional courses and more on the exploration of new findings in research. The second year offered the standard clinical clerkships of Medicine, Surgery, Obstetrics, and Pediatrics; students elsewhere had to wait until the third year to have contact with patients. Students would return to science courses as electives in the third year, a time to reinforce the basic sciences after students had been actively involved in taking care of sick people. The fourth year would remain largely unchanged, with elective opportunities for clinical or research subjects, ventures overseas, and the like.

Stead began to talk about these ideas around the school, and also began to speak at national meetings about Duke's exciting new curriculum. Deans, other chairpersons, and senior faculty at Duke began to hear about Duke's new curriculum from people in other schools, and came home to find out what it was all about. Stead gradually won people over, a key recruit being

Clarence Gardner, then Chair of Surgery, who gave up a three-month surgical rotation (Medicine did likewise) so the new plan could work. One casualty was the Research Training Program, which was superseded by a whole third year in research. As is the nature of people, various faculty approved the plan in principle, but needed space and new faculty members to execute it. Handler and Stead convinced the Commonwealth Foundation to underwrite the new curriculum with a generous grant.

Years later I told Stead that I thought his experiment had failed because no other school had tried to duplicate the curriculum. He replied, with characteristic lack of modesty, "I have never been able to explain the lack of creativity among most medical faculty in this country." He then provided his own serious critique of the new curriculum at Duke. The relaxed convivial and collegial relationships that he envisioned between faculty and students in the first year basic sciences did not transpire. The basic science teachers feared that they were teaching too little, and loaded the first year with lectures. Faculty members always have trouble with the concept that the amount of teaching in formal lectures may be inversely related to the amount of learning by students.

The introduction of clinical medicine in the second year was a resounding success with students who were impatient to learn how to interact with their patients. Moreover, they were less jaded than students in a traditional curriculum and had not lost their enthusiasm when they began their research in the third year. Stead estimates that more than 25 percent have experienced a meaningful research exposure upon which they were able to build after their clinical residency training. More importantly, perhaps, Duke is now the only medical school in the country that can boast a distinct curriculum. The early exposure to patients and the year of meaningful research are attractive features to many young people contemplating a career in medicine, and Duke undoubtedly recruits some of the country's best young scholars to its classes. This result, alone, would seem to justify a revised curriculum, and it is surprising that some other schools have not adopted a similar educational concept. It should be noted that this is an intensive study program — two years of basic science are covered in the first year, followed by the National Board Examination that students in other schools take following the second year. If students are not well-prepared before entry to Duke Medical School, this can be a stressful experience.

Stead's Crowning Educational Initiative:
The Physician's Assistant Program
Gene Stead was constantly toying with educational experiments, and he often commented that the innate abilities of nursing and medical students were similar, but that nursing students preselected away from hard science, making it difficult to teach beginning nursing and medical students in the same class. In clinical areas, however, it was quite clear that both groups could be taught together.

At Duke, he encountered an unusual nursing instructor, Thelma Ingles, who taught in a style not unlike his own and was even able to admit it when she did not know something. Ms. Ingles was about to take a sabbatical to get a Master's Degree, when Gene suggested she enter medical school for one year and learn to solve patient-centered problems under his personal tutelage, three hours a week. She did so, and matured remarkably. Later, she put together what would become a highly successful two-year Master's Degree curriculum in Nursing Care for graduate nurses. Stead's department provided her with teachers, and the venture seemed to be a great success until the students graduated. Certification bodies in the nursing profession refused to accredit the Duke medical experience for nurses because there had been no standard curriculum with hours, goals, objectives, and examinations.

Later, Stead and Ms. Ingles sponsored a nurse-run ward (no private duty nurses) which functioned well for a time but disbanded eventually because of major insensitivity and minor but persistent harassment by hospital administrators. The program had been appreciated by patients and fiscally enriching for the hospital, but these attributes had been insufficient to maintain the program. With these rebuffs, Gene Stead abandoned nursing education.

The teaching of medical topics to non-physicians, however, confirmed his educational premise that bright people could learn much of medicine without a formal medical school background. He was intrigued with the idea of physician assistants, and their value to rural practitioners. Stead had been asked to undertake the educational updating at Duke of rural family practitioners in North Carolina, but found it was impossible because when the rural doctors were away, there was no one to take over their practices. Stead knew that one well-known practitioner in Garland, North Carolina, Dr. Amos Johnson, was a fine doctor with a large practice but had time to attend meetings and to be prominent in state and national medical organizations. The secret of Dr. Johnson's success, Stead found, was that he had trained a helper, a black man who had started as a servant, but gradually learned to take over the practice informally.

Having an assistant meant that Dr. Johnson had the freedom to develop his talents in medical politics.

Stead also knew that Army and Navy corpsmen functioned effectively in medical care. Also, he had seen Mr. Smith, a hematology technician at Duke, doing bone marrow aspirations, a procedure in which a large needle is inserted into the sternal breast bone, just above the heart, and marrow quickly sucked out; it is a frightening procedure, but Mr. Smith did it better than anyone else. The cardiologist, Henry McIntosh, had trained off-duty firemen to "moonlight" as effective helpers in his cardiac intensive care unit where nurses were in short supply.

Based on such casual observations, and after much discussion, the formal Physician Assistant Program was initiated and the first class enrolled on October 6, 1965. Despite much resistance by physicians both at Duke and in the medical profession in general, the program began. Andrew Wallace, the cardiologist, did most of the work in defining the curriculum, with help from a number of colleagues. An experienced nurse educator, Kay Andriole, took over the first students (4 full-time and 4 part-time). The program was successful in that graduates were immediately snapped up into useful and well-paying jobs. In the 1990's, the Duke program was a stable component of Harvey Estes's Department of Community Health Services. It graduates 40 physician assistants each year. Nationwide we now have 20,000 certified physician assistants. Gene Stead achieved, indirectly, what he failed to achieve directly. The success of the physician assistant training programs was threatening to the nursing profession, and their rigid opposition to non-traditional roles for nurses began to soften. Today both physician assistants and nurse practitioners fill many roles in general and specialty care, and both are highly regarded health practitioners.

Without Gene Stead's stature, his persistence, and his leadership, these changes might not have occurred, or would have evolved more slowly and in a different configuration. The physician assistant-nurse practitioner movement may be his most widely recognized achievement in a fruitful and productive career as educator.

Buddy Treadwell, The First Physician Assistant

When Dr. Stead told me about Dr. Amos Johnson and his black physician assistant in the 1980's, I decided to learn more about the man and his work. I placed a telephone call to Dr. Amos Johnson in Garland, North Carolina, and a friendly, chatty Southern operator said she did not know a Dr. Amos Johnson. Since my last contact with Amos Johnson had been 40 years ago, it seemed quite likely that he had died or moved from Garland since I had been a resident physician at Duke in 1953. Hoping to locate a relative, the chatty operator said there were Johnsons in Garland, and connected me with a Mrs. Al

Johnson: She, too, was friendly, and no, she was not a relative of Dr. Amos Johnson, but had been his patient before he died about 15 years ago. Yes, everybody in Garland had known Buddy Treadwell until his death just last year in 1990, but his wife Lucille was still there. Lucille Treadwell was pleased to have a telephone call from California about her husband, of whom she was obviously proud. Buddy graduated from the local segregated high school and while still a teenager he became sort of a handyman around Dr. Johnson's office. He was bright and likeable, and his relationship with Dr. Johnson evolved into a lasting friendship. They went hunting together (quail, pheasant, and a few wild turkeys, I suspect), and one of the few times that Dr. Johnson's office was closed was during bird hunting season in the Autumn,

Buddy started doing what Lucille calls "little nurse-like things" taking temperatures and blood pressures. Gradually he, under Dr. Johnson's constant tutelage, began to do more and more things. People trusted and respected Buddy, says Mrs. Treadwell, and they all loved him, she says. Thus, he grew as an extension of Dr. Johnson to become a respected practitioner as he and Dr. Johnson worked together for 36 years.

Dr. Johnson died in 1974 when he was 65 years old. He (and Buddy) thought he was having a sudden recurrence of the asthma he had had as a child, but he died enroute to Duke by ambulance. An autopsy showed pulmonary emboli — blood clots that formed in the veins of the legs and broke off to land in the lungs. Asthma-like symptoms often are a major complication of pulmonary emboli. Even good doctors like Amos Johnson and his experienced assistant Buddy Treadwell will mistake the gasping wheezes brought on by blood clots landing in the lungs with the true wheezing of asthma.

After Dr. Johnson died, Buddy Treadwell continued to work at the clinic for a time, under different doctors. But it was not the same, and finally Buddy went his own way, and the clinic passed out of existence. With four children and ten grandchildren, he and Lucille had a busy family life. In 1985, Buddy developed angina and required a surgical by-pass operation at Duke, and did well until angina returned in 1990. He went back to Duke, seemed to be doing well, when he died suddenly of a heart attack.

Toward the end of his life, Buddy could count many accomplishments and had received recognition — as a Mason, as deacon in his Baptist church, and by a special certificate from the Duke School of Physician Assistants, acknowledging him as the "first" P.A. When he died, his home and his grave overflowed with flowers. Buddy had always liked flowers, and said he wanted them when he died, even though he conceded that the money used to buy flowers might better go to some worthy cause. Lucille says she thinks Buddy deserved his flowers, and the folks in Garland seem to have agreed.

Eugene Stead, Blacks and Desegreaation

Eugene Stead spends a lot of time justifying his acts of altruism as simply a reflection of his pragmatism. Because he is such a convincing person, he makes a strong case for his reasoned approach, but I am certain that his actions on occasion belie this cerebral and pragmatic way of looking at problems. Gene does say that very early on, growing up in Atlanta, he realized that this very poor part of our country was spending far too much money operating dual or even multiple systems of everything — transportation, schools, recreation facilities, hospitals. It was clear to Stead that the costs of running multiple separate medical systems for blacks, whites, men, women, and children generated an unnecessary fiscal burden, a burden that constrained growth of more worthwhile aspects of medical care.

His actions about segregation began in Cincinnati in 1936, when he was Chief Resident, and when Dr. Blankenhorn was out of town. He simple desegregated the ward services because there were insufficient beds and resources to operate separate sections in this busy, crowded public hospital. Cincinnati is a very Southern city, with a high proportion of black residents, and one might have expected an outcry. I suspect that patients and staff alike had recognized the expense of the dual system, but in any case, desegregation was readily accepted. Also, Cincinnati lies slightly north of that magic Mason-Dixon line that, before the Civil War, separated slave from free, and after the war, marked the segregated South.

At Duke, Stead started by desegregating the clinics, and in that undertaking, under the guise of economy, he had the full support of the Clinic Director, Dr. Julian Ruffin, a Virginia gentleman. Early on, a Dr. Robert P. Randolph, a black physician in town, came to ask for permission to work and take care of patients (black patients primarily) in the clinics at Duke. Stead agreed readily, but pointed out that he had no real control over the actions of staff, housestaff, nurses, other personnel, or patients. Dr. Randolph replied "Dr. Stead, I have lived and worked in Durham for 58 years, and I know how to handle things." And handle things he did, volunteering his services in the clinic a half-day weekly.

Slowly, Stead began to desegregate the ward services. As his Chief Resident in 1951, I participated when he and the hospital hired the first black graduate nurse to work on the wards and assigned her initially to the white male ward. I had had no experience with working with blacks in a professional capacity, but strongly supported the action. During all of her first day, I hovered about to help dampen trouble, but nothing really happened. Only one patient, a man from South Carolina, objected to her presence and left the hospital to return home. The rest of the patients did not mention the black nurse, I suspect because whites were accustomed to black people caring from them and simply accepted the nurse in her service role. Slowly, Dr. Stead desegregated the patients on the wards, beginning with the female wards. The hospital system in 1951 was racially separate and not in any way equal. As Chief Resident, I was an attending physician on the black wards, located on the top floor under the flat roof. It was summer, and the temperature on the floor was often over 90 degrees fahrenheit at 7:00 in the morning. Several sick patients added mild heat stroke to their litany of problems. Air conditioning was a new technology in the 1950's and not yet available in southern hospitals.

Durham had an all-black hospital, the Lincoln Hospital, that was undergoing a regeneration in the 1950's. A remarkably dynamic and effective young black surgeon, Dr. Charles Watts, arrived in Durham in 1950 as Chief of Surgery at Lincoln and as Director of the Hospital. He moved rapidly to obtain a commitment from Dr. J.B. Johnson, then Chair of Medicine at the premier all-black medical school in the country, Howard University, to allow two interns from his program in Washington to rotate through the fledgling Lincoln Hospital program in Durham. But Dr. Johnson had a proviso: that Dr. Stead would personally take an interest in the program. Stead agreed to do so, and in addition provided regular teachers to the Howard interns from his senior house-staff-junior faculty group. Among those who volunteered and provided real leadership were two senior residents, Charles Mengel and Patrick Henry. They found the experience a rewarding one, and by the late 1950's were boasting about the good doctors being trained in the program.

Dr. Watts received funding from grants and formed the Lincoln Health Service, with a private clinic for blacks modeled after the Duke system. As the Lincoln program flowered, some training rotations at Duke were substituted for those at Lincoln and some Duke housestaff reciprocated by rotating to Lincoln. But in the early 1960's, Dr. Johnson retired at Howard and the flow of interns ceased. Lincoln began to recruit its own interns to the program, mostly graduates of Howard and Meharry University in Nashville.

Several good practitioners were emerging at Lincoln. Dr. Charles Johnson had been trained in endocrinology at Duke; Dr. Charles Curry had been a Fellow in cardiology at Duke; and Dr. Donald Moore joined the staff in obstetrics. In the late 1960's, Gene Stead appointed Charles Johnson to his previously all-white faculty with a statement reputed to be, "Anyone who does not like it can leave." No one left, and in 1970 as segregation was ending, Charles Johnson was appointed to the Duke PDC, bringing with him his large practice of mostly black patients. Charles Johnson is now (1991) an Associate Professor at Duke and President of the National Medical Association, a mostly black physician group with about 16,000 members. He constituted a strong force for integration of Duke, and has been a guiding figure to younger minority students and physicians. Said Johnson, in an article in the Duke Medical Center publication *Perspectives* in 1990: "Stead was avant garde — for a white man to do what he did. He certainly incurred wrath and hostility..." Commented Stead laconically: "Not everyone thanked me."

That story refutes any notion of Gene Stead as a pragmatist, although he would probably claim pragmatically that his efforts in the 1960's were simply designed to put Duke, in the 1990's, in a favorable position for recruiting minority students and faculty. We can interpret his actions as emblematic of the sort of long-range leadership Stead provided, but I prefer to see a quixotic Gene Stead, doing what was right because it was right, and Duke later reaping its just rewards for his actions.

Update and Assessment of Eugene Stead

Eugene Stead resigned his Chairmanship at Duke, to be effective in 1968, when he had completed a 20-year term. He was at the height of his reputation locally at Duke and nationally, only 59 years old, and no one could really believe he was going to retire from the Chairmanship. A search committee was appointed; they decided to reoffer him the job, and he had to reiterate that he was *really* retiring. He told me then and now that his primary reason for retiring was age: he had never encountered a chairman who did as good a job after age 60 as he had done before age 60. I believe this is generally true, because the really successful chairman derives his success and his pleasure from working with students, housestaff, and junior faculty, helping them grow. The senior faculty require very little except an occasional pat on the back, or a hand up or a push down as they manipulate for space and personnel. The Chair, then, ages but his real constituents remain with a median age of about 30. Somehow, that age gap seems to increase logarithmically after about age 55. But Gene Stead was almost uniquely suited by constitution and personality to remain biologically young, and he could have continued longer if he had wanted to do so. He admits that he had become disinterested in the little details of running a department. The satisfactions derived from being a great father figure and role model do not replace altogether the effort of keeping up with the administrative details. He clearly did not want to continue and James Wyngaarden, his successor, brought different strengths and talents to the job, and Duke prospered.

As with other tenured professors, Gene's salary would continue until age 70, and the Dean had given him the freedom to work as he liked. Needless to say, Duke did not lose money on Gene Stead, and, indeed, he could be considered a fortunate growth stock like Xerox or IBM. Stead understood that it would be helpful to the new chairman to be free of his presence for a while; he and Evelyn spent the 1968 calendar year at Cornell Medical School in New York City, teaching and helping the Commonwealth Foundation with some of its projects. On their return, Gene resumed a generous teaching schedule at Duke, back at his old stand on Osler Ward. He helped the cardiologists in computerizing their cardiac care unit, and, as mentioned earlier, was a significant catalyst for the use of computers elsewhere in the medical school. He tried to give visibility to geriatrics, and at one time was medical director for a 350-bed Methodist home for the aged. He enlisted the family (Bill and Nancy, his two doctors) in some of his ventures. He and Nancy, as one example, wrote a charming description of medical problems in the nursing home (reference 187 in the bibliography reproduced in the Appendix).

Gene and Evelyn Stead became an editing team when, in 1966, he undertook the editorship of *Medical Times,* a medical publication sent free to huge numbers of doctors. This venture was fun because it provided Gene a weekly forum to write about anything that struck his wide-ranging fancy. He edited *Circulation*, the leading journal specializing in cardiology research, for a number of years. In 1991, and for several years past, he has taken on editorship of the *North Carolina Medical Journal*, and made it one of the best of the state medical journals. From ages 70 to 77, he accepted an appointment as a Distinguished Physician of the Veterans Administration, and the Durham VA Hospital became his base of operations for teaching and writing. At age 82 in 1992, he still worked in Durham one day a week, teaching students on Fridays.

Before he retired as Chair, he had bought acreage on a lake near Bullock, North Carolina, about 50 miles from Durham, and decided with characteristic self-confidence to build a home for himself and Evelyn, confident that he was as smart as most carpenters. He was and is, and he did build his house, and later built another house for guests. From the children's song, "Puff, the Magic Dragon," came the whimsical name of Honah Lee for this whimsical family project. And so it remains - Honah Lee, now a lovely family home.

Gene and Evelyn have made a strong bid for extremely long lives. During the 1950's, Gene had decided that he should eat a low-fat diet, because he liked to eat a lot but did not like to get fat; a low-fat diet was the practical solution. Evelyn's expertise at low-fat cookery has not only rewarded her with a best-selling book, but may well have lengthened their lives.

Gene Stead had enormous impact on Duke and considerable influence generally in American medicine. He is an activist-philosopher whose personal growth was continuous and has never ceased. Continued growth over more than 60 years is a rare phenomenon. Dr. John Horton is quoted in the Foreword of the Wagner-Cebe-Rozear book, "People respect, admire and love Dr. Stead because within the turmoil of his life he seems to have a simplicity, directness, and detachment which makes him able to be calm and helpful. Furthermore, his character is virtuous. In times when most men are so selfish, his qualities of selflessness and dedication loom large."

Chapter V

PAUL BRUCE BEESON

P aul Beeson was a medical resident at Rockefeller Institute in New York City when, unexpectedly, he was invited by Soma Weiss to become his first Chief Resident at the Brigham. Later, he was to join Eugene Stead in Atlanta as his second full-time faculty member, and to succeed Stead as Chairman at Emory five years later. He was Chairman at Yale for 13 years, and from there went to Oxford for almost a decade.

Paul Beeson has an entirely different personality and leadership style from those of Soma Weiss and Gene Stead, far more subtle and complex. Mrs. Louise Castle described Soma Weiss as exuding energy when he entered a room. When Gene Stead entered a room, his self-confidence, which was not quite arrogance, dominated his environment. When Paul Beeson entered a room, slowly a feeling of warmth suffused the area, elevating the mood and the conversation. I have a lithograph by the Mexican artist, Francisco Zuniga, showing an Indian woman holding a candle in her lap, her head and face encircled by a glow; it reminds me of the subtle Beeson

aura. I wonder if Mrs. Castle would concur that Paul
Beeson exudes kindness and universal warmth.

Birth and Childhood in Alaska

Few boys ever entered the world with such debt
and bonding to their fathers as did Paul Beeson. Dr. John
Beeson, being the most reliable medical practitioner of
Livingston, Montana on October 18, 1908, delivered his
wife Martha of their second son, Paul, some eight years
after the first son, Harold, had been born. From birth,
Paul was closely bonded to his somewhat reticent but
powerful father and to his equally strong mother. They
lived for 60 years after Paul's birth, and he was a duti-
ful and devoted son during all those years.

Martha Ash and John Beeson had met and married in Livingston, Montana. Both were school teachers
who had followed Greely's dictum, "Go west, young man"
(and young woman) and ended up in Montana. The teachers married, and in 1889 moved to Chicago so that John
could attend Rush Medical School. While in medical
school, their son Harold was born. After completing medical school, John and Martha returned to Montana,
although John did manage a year of surgical training in
New York. So, Dr. John Beeson became, in Livingston, a
true general practitioner of medicine and surgery.

John and Martha Beeson were almost a prototype
of the young Westerners of the turn of the century. Martha had grown up in Missouri, where Grandfather Ash
had fought for the Confederacy, and John's Iowan Grandfather Beeson had fought for the Union forces in that
divisive and devastating Civil War. John and Martha each

went to college, he to Valparaiso, Indiana and she to Northwestern in Chicago, before being hired for their first teaching jobs in Livingston. My wife Dorothy and I were planning to drive to California from Kentucky in 1976 and noted that our route would take us through Livingston, Montana. We asked Paul for the old Beeson street address, and in Livingston we found the little white house that had been the Beeson home. Its plain, unadorned simplicity reminded me of similar houses in the Grant Wood paintings that were featured on the covers of *Collier's* magazine in the 1930's.

Harold was thirteen and Paul five when the family moved from Livingston to Seattle, where Dr. Beeson hoped to establish a practice in a town larger than Livingston. He was not very successful, perhaps because his quiet manner and his surgical interests were more suited to the towns of the frontier than to the niceties of city practice. At that time, the United States was busy opening up Alaska and was building a railway from Fairbanks to Anchorage and Seward. Dr. Beeson applied for the position as Assistant Surgeon for the railway, was accepted, and shortly thereafter became Chief Surgeon. He stayed in Alaska from 1916 to 1935, first as Chief Surgeon on the railway and then as a practitioner in Ketchikan. At age 63, in 1935, he bought a practice in Wooster, Ohio, joined with son Harold, then a physician and urologist, and established a practice that grew into the Wooster Clinic of today. Dr. Beeson worked in Wooster until he reached 84 years of age, and then retired to La Jolla, California. His wife said that he had retired too young, and always warned Paul not to do the same thing.

Dr. John Beeson must have been quite a person. While in Alaska, he became famous for a trip by dog sled from Fairbanks to the little settlement of Ididerod in an attempt to save the life of a banker and gold miner who was thought to have empyema, a chest infection that needed surgical drainage. Dr. Beeson completed the heroic trip, but found the patient dying of tuberculosis. Every year one reads in the newspapers about the famous dog sled race in Alaska from Fairbanks to Ididerod, an adventure that still captures our imagination. I only saw Dr. John Beeson once, while he was a patient at Yale-New Haven Hospital having a needed cholecystectomy when he was more than 90 years old. Paul Beeson was shaving him when I walked into the hospital room, and the old gentleman (now quite senile) was rambling on in a confused way. That scene of Paul shaving the prattling old man solidified my feelings that there existed an unusually strong and silent bond between father and son.

Paul Beeson's school years, and his growing up, took place in Anchorage, a town he enjoyed as a youngster. Anchorage was the gateway to the vast territory of Alaska, and its climate was considerably milder than that which we usually associate with Alaska. He enjoyed the countryside, as well as the town, was the outstanding student in Anchorage schools, and age 16 had completed high school and was ready for college.

Dr. John Beeson worked in his medical practice while Mrs. Beeson tended to all things related to house and children. When Harold had reached college age, she literally took him to Seattle for the better part of a year as he enrolled in college, and when Paul was ready, he and his mother similarly went off to college, to the University of Washington in Seattle. Mrs. Beeson took an apartment for the year and saw Paul off to a proper start in life. Paul loves to tell the story of how he entered premedical courses, rather than the business course which had been the plan in Anchorage. Mrs. Beeson took her son to a clothiers to buy a suit and new shoes before starting classes. The sales clerk, a nice and personable young man, mentioned that he had just graduated in business from the University last year. After completing her purchases, Mrs. Beeson promptly marched out, with Paul in tow, and presented him to the college dean, saying, "This is my son Paul. He will study medicine." Her son Paul was not destined to fit shoes! Mrs. Beeson was not one to suffer from self-doubt.

Thus it came about that Paul followed his father and his older brother Harold into medicine as a career. After her year in Seattle, Mrs. Beeson betook herself back to her husband in Alaska, who by this time had moved his practice to the town of Ketchikan. Paul lived in his fraternity in Seattle and completed the pre-medical curriculum in three years, before enrolling for medical school at McGill University in Montreal, again following Harold's footsteps. He enrolled in McGill's five-year medical course in 1928 and lived with Harold, also a student at McGill, for part of his medical school time.

Paul describes college and medical school, during which he often lived in fraternities *in lieu* of dormitories, as a monastic life. Obviously he studied hard and effectively. I saw Beeson's early edition of *Cecil's Textbook of*

Medicine (the textbook he was'to edit in later years) that he had owned as student and resident; he had carefully edited his copy by underlining pertinent passages in ink, using a straight-edge ruler to guide the pen. However, the monastic life did not preclude Paul's learning to drink whiskey with appreciation, but with moderation. That same monastic life also provided him with great experience in the game of poker. Both literally and figuratively he has played poker with skill and daring for all of his life.

Internship, Residency, and Two Years of General Practice

He was accepted as an intern by the University of Pennsylvania, which was a highly coveted spot in 1933. It was a two-year program, with the first year spent rotating through specialty programs and the second year split equally between medicine and surgery. This training was excellent for general practice, and a two-year mixed intern program was mandatory for licensure in the State of Pennsylvania until almost 20 years ago. Dr. Beeson has always felt Penn was the pre-eminent medical school in the 1930's. The faculty included O.H. Perry Pepper, a respected internist who ran the Department of Medicine. T. Grier Miller and William Abbott (well known for their tube for deflating the bowel) were Penn's gastroenterologists. Francis Wood (later Chairman) headed cardiology, and Isaac Starr and Eugene Landis were cardiovascular physiologists and scientists. Detlev Bronk, later President of Rockefeller University, was at the medical school [in Philadelphia] in 1933. Donald Pillsbury was among the world's premier dermatologists, editor of the comprehensive textbook of dermatology. Beeson's Chief Medical Resident was Ludwig Eichna, later a distinguished physician and professor in New York. After completion of the two-year internship, Paul had received excellent medical training and was prepared to pursue his life's work.

In 1935, he joined the family practice in Wooster for two years, but it became clear to him that general practice was not his calling. As an example of his discomfort with surgery, he tells of receiving a call from the hospital while he was on duty. A young woman friend of the family was recovering from a cesarian section when suddenly the stitches broke loose and her hospital bed was literally filled with her intestines. Paul took one look at this situation, recalled the life-long tremor of his hands, and called his father for help. Dr. Beeson came, immediately replaced her intestines into the abdominal cavity, and sewed up the incision right there in her hospital bed. There were no antibiotics in those days, but she recovered totally and uneventfully. Paul Beeson, however, had been made acutely aware of his own sense of futility during her unnerving episode.

Through a McGill classmate, Frank Horsfall, Beeson learned that the medical service at Cornell in New York had a vacancy for a medical resident, and he decided to apply, with the active support of his mother, who realized that life as a general practitioner in Wooster was not Paul's calling. He was accepted at Cornell and left for New York in the summer of 1937.

Chance again played a major role in his career, changing his focus from medical practice alone to one combining teaching, research, and patient care. He was

enjoying his medical residency at Cornell, but was unexpectedly offered a medical residency next door at the
Rockefeller Institute Hospital. Paul's friend and classmate, Frank Horsfall, later to be a distinguished virologist
at the Rockefeller, was getting married, and a group of
friends gathered for a prenuptial party that became a bit
of a brawl. Thomas Rivers, head of the Rockefeller Institute Hospital, was at the party, took a liking to Paul, and
in the midst of the revelry offered him a job as a resident.
When heads cleared the next day, Paul found that he still
had his offer from Dr. Rivers. The residency involved
working on the pneumonia service headed by Dr. Colin
MacLeod; the main activity was to develop pneumococcal-
typing vaccines and to treat patients with antisera
specific for the type of pneumococcus that had caused the
patient's pneumonia. The type of pneumococcus is determined by a complex carbohydrate capsule on the microbe
that determines certain aspects of its virulence. Although
Beeson viewed himself primarily as a clinical resident at
the Rockefeller, he was influenced by the research orientation at the Institute; many of his later research activities
stemmed from work he did during his two years at the
Rockefeller. He shared a laboratory with MacLeod and
with a close friend and colleague, Charles Hoagland.

In the lab, Beeson probably was more successful
than he now admits. He was first author, with Hoagland,
on a paper about the carbohydrate that determines the
blood group A of human red cells. He also, with Hoagland, found that infused calcium carbonate could block
the muscular shaking of chills brought on by fever — a
finding of possible use in treating patients with rheuma-

toid arthritis. Much of Paul's later work and interest in the mechanisms of fever began at the Rockefeller from these clinical observations. He, with Hoagland and Walter Goebel, wrote three papers which called attention to the similarities of the carbohydrate on the capsule of type 14 pneumococcus to the carbohydrate on human blood group A. Type 14 has the largest capsule of any pneumococcus, and is the most virulent and lethal for humans of the pneumococcal strains.

More important to Beeson than the specific residency experience itself was the excitement he felt at the Rockefeller - a place ablaze with stimulating research. Rene Dubois, a renowned bacteriologist and general biologist, worked across the hall, and he and Selman Waksman were discovering bacteria from soil samples that produced substances that killed other microorganisms. These early experiments laid the conceptual groundwork for the discovery, soon to follow, of penicillin by Alexander Fleming in England and of streptomycin by Waksman. Oswald Avery was discovering the basis of life in nucleic acids; his brilliant experiments established the foundation for much of modern biochemical genetics.

At the Rockefeller at that time, a large volume of clinical research concerned the induction of fever in patients in an attempt to treat diseases, syphilis and rheumatoid arthritis in particular. The rationale for its use in syphilis was clear enough: The spirochete which causes the disease might be killed at temperatures which the body could produce without fatal damage. The rationale in rheumatoid arthritis was less clear. Beeson and the other Rockefeller residents injected killed typhoid bacilli intravenously to the patients to produce the fever and chills. It was well known that each patient required larger and larger daily doses of the killed typhoid organisms to produce fever. The patients became tolerant of the organisms to produce fever and the tolerant patient could accept doses many thousand-fold higher than the initial dose which induced fever and chills. Much of Beeson's later work concerning the mechanisms of fever and the tolerance to fever induction by portions of the typhoid organism would reflect those early clinical experiments at the Rockefeller.

The Brigham Under Soma Weiss and the Harvard Field Hospital Unit in England, 1939-1942

Soma Weiss, in Boston, had just moved from Boston City Hospital to the Peter Bent Brigham Hospital, and needed a chief Resident. Someone mentioned Beeson to Weiss, who then went to New York to interview him. Beeson was immediately enthralled by Weiss, and presumably Weiss was impressed with Beeson because he offered him his Chief Residency. By 1939, Paul Beeson was an experienced 31-year-old physician; he had had two years of internship at Pennsylvania, a year of residency at Cornell, two years at Rockefeller, plus two years as a general practitioner. When he arrived at the Brigham, he found, among his assistant residents, such people as Jack Myers, later to be Chairman at Pittsburgh, Gustave Dammin, later Chair of Pathology at the Brigham, and Richard Ebert, later Chair of Medicine at Arkansas and at Minnesota. These alert young physicians kept their chief resident on his mettle. Among Soma

Weiss's research fellows and junior faculty were Gene Stead, Charles Janeway, later to be Professor of Pediatrics at Harvard for many years, and John Romano, who became Chairman of Psychiatry at Cincinnati and at Rochester. Paul learned a great deal under Soma. He watched Weiss delegate responsibility to his young colleagues at a time when wisdom tended to be equated with age in most other medical institutions. Beeson also noted that Weiss influenced everyone he encountered, perhaps because he was interested in his housestaff as people and thought of them as future colleagues, not as lackeys. It was an exciting period for a young man from Anchorage, associating with highly talented young people under a leader both caring and charismatic.

President James B. Conant of Harvard University wanted to demonstrate Harvard's support for the embattled British nation already caught up in World War II; he established in Salisbury, England the Harvard Field Hospital Unit, associated with the American Red Cross and made up of medical volunteers, to care for military personnel and civilians disrupted by the war. The Salisbury Fever Hospital was a referral hospital for about 200,000 people from the surrounding areas. The emphasis was on infectious diseases, and Paul Beeson was appointed Chief Physician and served in England with that Unit from 1940-1942; the unit disbanded when the bombing by the Japanese at Pearl Harbor thrust the United States into World War II.

While in England, Beeson had charge of the hospital staffed by four or five doctors and a group of Red

Cross nurses, among whom was a petite, dynamic young woman from Buffalo, Barbara Neal. Their courtship and marriage in Salisbury were to instill in them a love of England that would later permit them to live and work happily in the England of the 1960s and 1970s.

Beeson had a busy time professionally as well as socially in Salisbury. His unit became involved in an extensive epidemic of trichinosis in Wolverhampton, which Dr. John Shelton described in *Lancet* in 1941. Trichinosis is a disease caused by a worm usually found in pigs and can erupt in man when raw pork is eaten. After being ingested, the worms invade the intestine and pass into the circulation where they lodge in many organs, but are found particularly in muscles. As these worms filter out of the bloodstream, the capillaries at the end of the finger nails seem a favorite filter site, leading to splinter hemorrhages in a line at the end of the nails. Beeson has a slide of a young Wolverhampton bride whose wedding photo shows the typical hemorrhagic fingernails of trichinosis.

England in 1941 was unaware of trichinosis because English hogs were free of the disease. During the war, however, sausage was imported and was often eaten raw, particularly by young women. Sheldon explains this as an outcome of the chauvinistic attitudes prevalent at the time. Young women tended to rush off to work with raw sausage spread on bread, or they nibbled raw sausage as they cooked, while the male of the English species expected, and got, his properly boiled dinner. Anyway, Paul Beeson was the expert from America and his review of trichinosis in *Lancet* (see Publications in Appendix,

Reference 11) is a splendid example of his terse, informative, no-nonsense style of writing, and of thinking. As part of the reaction to trichina worms, as well as to other parasites, the human body mounts a response characterized by eosinophils in the blood, and eosinophils in tissues surround invading worms. These beautiful blood cells had no known specific purpose in 1940, and they and their function continued to fascinate Beeson. On his return to England in 1965, more than 25 years after the Wolverhampton epidemic, he would do important research on trichinosis in rats, and on the function and control mechanisms of eosinophils.

Beeson also became an expert on meningitis during that brief two years in England when he was given the records of over 3,000 cases. His report was a classic and definitive one, emphasizing that death was a less likely outcome if diagnosis was made quickly and treatment with sulfadiazide initiated promptly. This was important for the care of an army of young men living together in barracks, a situation that rendered them prone to contract infections like meningococcal meningitis.

Perhaps his most important observations in England related to the description and understanding of serum hepatitis, now known as hepatitis B. The military were concerned that so many young inductees living in the closed and crowded society of a military barracks had not had mumps. Beeson and his group collected serum from patients who were convalescing from the mumps, pooled the serum samples, and gave the serum containing mumps antibodies to newly exposed recruits.

Although the new recruits developed fewer cases of mumps than would have been expected, many of the soldiers developed hepatitis instead. The English experience with hepatitis following the injections of pooled serum suggested that the serum had contained an agent that caused hepatitis. At that time, however, the only recognized hepatitis (now known as hepatitis A) occurred in epidemics related to food contamination. Such infections were common among troops concentrated in barracks and eating from a common food source. Thus, the association of the serum infections and hepatitis could have been coincidental.

When Beeson returned to the United States he encountered six patients at Grady Hospital who had developed hepatitis following blood transfusions, and reported these patients in the *Journal of the American Medical Association*. This was an important clinical observation, since blood transfusions would be used with increasing frequency as elaborate surgical operations were developed. The discovery of serum hepatitis (now known as hepatitis B) was to be the single most important observation attributed to Dr. Beeson. Almost half a century later, the same clinical detective work that Beeson pursued in 1942 would define AIDS, like serum hepatitis, as a highly infectious agent carried in the bloodstream of asymptomatic people.

By the time he left the Harvard Unit in England, Dr. Beeson was eminently qualified for a faculty position. As noted here, his clinical experience had been gained at several prestigious institutions, and the Rockefeller had given him exposure to good laboratory research. The breadth of his interests was reflected in his work, but it was evident that infectious disease problems were his primary interest. His accomplishments in 1942 at age 34 included many attributes that one looks for today in young faculty: diversity of clinical experience, publications reflecting interest in both basic research and clinical observations, ability to take the lead in directing projects as well as to collaborate, and good taste in colleagues and in areas of emphasis. He was certainly ready to join a faculty, and only Soma Weiss's death kept that first faculty appointment from being at Harvard and the Brigham.

Emory University in Atlanta, 1942-1952

Two assistant professorships in infectious diseases were open in 1942 when Dr. Beeson was considering positions, one at Cornell and the other with Eugene Stead at Emory. Cornell was Beeson's first choice, because he had been there as a resident and would thus work closely with his old colleagues and mentors at the Rockefeller, just adjacent to Cornell-New York Hospital. He had a firm offer from Stead, however, and had not yet received one from Cornell when Stead, with characteristic forcefulness, insisted that Paul respond to his offer by a specific date. Just before midnight of the deadline, Beeson sent Stead a telegram accepting the position in Atlanta. The next morning, he received an offer from Cornell, but Beeson did not consider breaking the agreement. He said later, "I accepted a position at Emory at midnight, and I could not go back on my word."

With characteristic modesty, Beeson says now

that the Emory job was sheer good luck in that he would "never have amounted to anything" in academic medicine had he gone to Cornell which was adjacent to the Rockefeller and full of outstanding young academic physicians. He cites his basic shyness and lack of aggressiveness as reasons he would not have bloomed in New York, but others might fantasize a wholly different history for Cornell had that quiet and unassuming yet tenacious and high-principled young man joined Cornell's faculty at the beginning of World War II. In any event, the game was played out in Atlanta, and within four years Paul Beeson had risen from Assistant Professor to Professor and Chairman.

Beeson claims that the Emory experience really brought out his abilities because he was the only specialist in infectious diseases within 1,000 miles of Atlanta, and, therefore, was forced to develop his skills. He also points out that when he arrived in Atlanta, Gene Stead assigned a laboratory and technician (Liz Roberts) to him. Somehow, until then, Beeson seems to have viewed himself as basically a physician making clinical observations. With Gene Stead supplying a laboratory and expecting results, no one would have dared not to become a scientific investigator! Also, as the director of Grady Hospital's microbiology laboratory, Beeson expanded his knowledge of microbiology and acquired a window into the wide spectrum of infections in that crowded Atlanta city hospital known to its devotees as "the Gradys."

Paul Beeson quickly evolved into a classical clinical investigator, using his Grady experience and his research laboratory. His major contribution was to the understanding of how bacteria caused fever, and later how white blood cells from pus cause and sustain fever. He also had an uncanny ability to draw on clinical experience to solve problems. Stead and Warren were beginning to study the heart and circulation, using catheters passed into the heart and needles into the large arteries. Beeson wondered about the differences in the number of bacteria in blood of patients with infected heart valves — was the amount of bacteria higher in the arteries (blood that had passed through the lungs) or in the veins? It turned out that microbes from the heart valve came off evenly into the flowing blood, and the numbers were about equal in artery and vein — in other words, the lung does not sequester bacteria. The surprise came in a purely fortuitous event. In one patient the heart catheter slipped through the heart and lodged in the large hepatic vein draining the liver; upon investigation, Beeson found that the blood in the liver contained almost no bacteria. Jim Warren became skillful at deliberately catheterizing the hepatic vein, and the same observations were confirmed in six patients. The liver, then, had an enormous capacity to scavenge bacteria from the bloodstream. These classic observations were an exciting by-product of Beeson's questioning mind and the Warren-Stead technology. A few months later, those experiments would never have been performed because penicillin was discovered and was found to cure bacterial endocarditis, a disease until then always fatal. A potentially dangerous heart catheterization would not be condoned after penicillin proved so effective in treatment.

In addition to his classic work on removal of bacteria from the bloodstream and on the mechanism of fever, Beeson was making major clinical observations on many of the diseases common in the clientele of The Gradys — such diseases as rat bite fever, the venereal infections chancroid and lymphogranuloma venereum, and the leptospiroses, an unusual group of infections contracted from rat urine contaminating the human food chain.

In 1947, Gene Stead left for Duke, taking with him his bright young academic team of Jack Myers, John Hickam, and Frank Engel. Beeson was by now quite well-known nationally and well-regarded locally, and Emory promptly made him Chairman of the Department. James Warren stayed on at Emory for several years as Professor of Physiology, before joining Stead at Duke as Chief of Medicine at the new Durham Veterans Administration Hospital.

During his six years as Chairman at Emory, Beeson rebuilt the department mostly through the growth and support of local people. Philip Bondy had come to Emory from Boston as resident in medicine as part of the Stead exodus of 1942, was promptly drafted into the Army, but returned to Emory under Beeson and developed into a first-rate endocrinologist. Bondy would later leave Emory with Beeson, and at Yale University Medical School would take over the renowned endocrinology/metabolism group headed by the aging and ailing John P. Peters. When Beeson left Yale in 1965, Bondy succeeded him as Chairman. Ivan Bennett was a local Grady resident who worked with Beeson in infectious diseases and rapidly became a highly regarded investigator. He, also, would leave Emory with Beeson in 1952, emerge as a strong teacher and clinical investigator at Yale, and then leave Yale to head the infectious disease group at Hopkins. Later he became Chairman of Pathology at Hopkins and Dean and subsequently Vice Chancellor at New York University. Paul and Barbara Beeson, despite being Northerners, had adjusted quite well to the Deep South of Atlanta, and liked it. Sons John and Peter had come along and the Beesons were planning a definitive house in Atlanta, lovingly designed by Barbara. Meantime, Beeson was on one of those annual pilgrimages to the clinical research meetings in Atlantic City, quietly sitting in a stall in the men's room of The Haddon Hall Hotel, when he heard two gentlemen walk in, chatting together as they emptied their bladders in a nearby urinal. One, forever unidentified by Dr. Beeson, said to the other "Oh, we (at Yale) will go down to Emory and get Paul Beeson to replace Francis Blake." Beeson waited for news from Yale, heard nothing, and decided to go ahead and build the house. The house was barely completed when Yale did, indeed, come to Beeson, and it was not until 1985 that Barbara finally designed another house just to suit her, their current home in Redmond, Washington.

Building a Department at Yale, 1952-1959
(The Early Years)
    Yale, as a major bastion of the Ivy League, had a medical school and a department of medicine, both probably with reputations better than their recent accomplishments. The Department of Medicine had been

chaired for many years by a charming and elegant man, Francis Blake. Blake, like Beeson, was an expert in infectious diseases, had a small group of colleagues, but the department was essentially run as two units, a general group under Blake and a highly sophisticated (for its day) scientific metabolism unit that included endocrine and renal disorders, under the direction of John P. Peters. Peters was a revered man who had trained a number of young people who later became important figures in academic medicine, and who had provided invaluable leadership in bringing biochemistry into the mainstream of clinical medicine. Francis Blake found this strong Division of Metabolism an asset to his Department and the source of much of the reputation of the Department of Medicine at Yale.

Paul Beeson arrived at Yale and resented the independent style of Peters and his group, and was, in turn, clearly ignored and belittled by Peters. After two department meetings in which he was openly opposed by Peters, he scheduled no further meetings until Dr. Peters died in 1955. Meantime, Beeson continued to recruit very young people as heads of divisions. Those early appointments included Stuart Finch (hematology), Howard Spiro (gastroenterology), Gilbert Glaser (neurology), and Aaron Lerner (dermatology).

Along with his external recruitees, Beeson also liked to promote his own young people from Yale's housestaff and fellowship group, fitting jobs to their particular talents. One example was Seymour (Sandy) Lipsky, now dead, who loved gadgets and biochemistry, and became a leader in liquid chromatography; he later moved from the medical school to the Department of Chemistry at Yale College. Alvin Feinstein ran a superb second year course for medical students in physical diagnosis, aided by his strong tendency to quantitate and evaluate the effectiveness of important aspects of clinical medicine. This interest led him to a highly distinguished career as a clinical epidemiologist.

Ivan Bennett was a powerful teacher and investigator in the new infectious diseases group. Elisha Atkins was recruited from Barry Wood's group at Washington University in St. Louis. Lawrence Freedman and Vincent Andriole, Yale houseofficers, grew into semi-autonomous status within Yale's infectious disease group. Fred Kantor and I had our own visible sections (allergy and rheumatology), but worked amicably together and with the infectious disease people, forming a loose consortium that we called the I-3 Group — Infection, Immunity, Inflammation. Paul Beeson was our leader scientifically and clinically.

Of the pre-Beeson department, Gerald Klatskin had developed a highly regarded section on liver diseases. Cardiology and pulmonary diseases followed their traditional pattern of growth. In oncology, Paul Calabresi and Joseph Bertino built on their knowledge of pharmacology, Bertino with a primary appointment in the Department of Pharmacology. Within Jack Peters's old metabolism group, Franklin Epstein developed a truly distinguished section of renal diseases without feeling the necessity for an independent group. Indeed, most of the individuals felt their loyalty and effort going into the department first, a division second. Philip Bondy, in time, replaced Dr. Peters and built a diverse endocrinology group with a strong base in biochemistry.

Meanwhile, the housestaff was improving progressively and appointments to Yale Medicine became highly competitive and valued. Students at other schools became keenly aware of the quality of leadership provided by Dr. Beeson, and his dedication to the personal growth and clinical abilities of young doctors. Beeson, himself, was the principal ingredient because he stayed at home and worked with the housestaff and personally heard about each new patient in Morning Report rounds. Hearing about clever diagnostic or therapeutic maneuvers clearly pleased the Professor, while a dampened facial expression was all that he needed to let the housestaff know that they had handled a patient poorly. Often, with his Chief Resident, he would drift off to see some patient with an unusual disease who perhaps needed encouragement. Beeson accepted occasional personal private patients whom he and his Chief Resident managed, together with the housestaff. He saw those patients at least daily, including weekends, and sat down and explained carefully the medical problems to them and their families. Although his private patients were not numerous and his care of them was low-keyed and personal, it was evident that he took care of patients because he liked caring for them. The example for housestaff and students was more valuable than a dozen brilliant lectures.

As a result of his forthright leadership, Yale became one of the most desired internships in the country, competing perhaps only with Massachusetts General Hospital and Johns Hopkins. An invitation to become his

Chief Resident was, in essence, the highest honor a houseofficer could achieve and usually became the stepping stone to an academic career.

Beeson also understood the importance and distinction between the two titles, Professor and Chairman and Physician-inChief of the teaching hospital, which usually by rote tradition fell to the Chairman. Both as Professor and as physician, he made rounds everywhere that came within the Yale orbit: Yale-New Haven Hospital, the Memorial Unit (private) and the West Haven Veterans Administration Hospital. The symbolism of those rounds was not lost on housestaff and students, and his expectation of excellence was apparent at all three institutions. Beeson's Professorial/Chief of Service rounds were not noted for their sparkle or their flashy diagnostic coups. I doubt if any of us will recall many episodes of sudden brilliance, nor remember bon mots or aphorisms. What came across from Beeson's rounds was the image of an intelligent, prudent physician and a caring, sensitive, polite, and thoughtful man. Former Yale students all remember those teaching rounds.

Unusual Leadership: The Challenge of Sputnik

By the end of his first six years at Yale, and as he was preparing for his sabbatical year in 1959, he had built an unusual environment in which all strove to reach their highest capabilities because they were excited by the atmosphere of learning and not because they were coerced. All were loyal to Beeson and to Yale, loyal to one another, and self-confident and proud. Beeson tends to say, and I believe to really feel, that he was not a leader.

One wonders how he defines leadership because he was a leader in the eyes of others and of his own faculty for his ability to bring out the strong points of each individual and to motivate people to work well together. An example of this was his performance at the time of Sputnik.

In late 1957, the USSR, whom the United States then considered our sworn enemy, was thought to be retarded in scientific and technical skills. Suddenly, while the United States was proudly discussing plans to put a basketball-sized object into orbit in outer space, these "primitive" Russians launched Sputnik, the size of a refrigerator. Sputnik successfully orbited the earth for more than a year, during which the United States underwent great soul searching to discover how to regain our competitive advantage over the Russians. Paul Beeson met with our department weekly to delineate avenues in which we could advance the science of the United States. He invited Keith Cannan, formerly a Professor of Biochemistry at New York University and then head of the Division of Biological Sciences of the National Academy of Sciences, to visit our department and to describe the problems the Academy had in operating the atomic Bomb Casualty Commission (ABCC). Data on the long-range medical effects in the survivors of the bombings constituted vital information for a world in the atomic age at a time when we feared the USSR might use its technology against us. Dr. Cannan's proposal was that Yale take responsibility for the Medical Service of the Atomic Bomb Casualty Commission (ABCC) by rotating one member of the department to Japan every two years. The department would provide the continuity necessary for successful scientific operation of ABCC's medical studies.

Junior staff at ABCC would come from our own draft-eligible young house officers who could be selected to enroll in the Public Health Service to go to Hiroshima rather than to other military service. The department liked the project and felt that the proposal was good one for us because it provided a concrete way for our department to help our nation.

Cannan's visit occurred in about February or March, 1958. After we had agreed on the project in principle, the problem remained as to who would or could go in July. Finally, I went to Dr. Beeson and pointed out that I had had experience in radiation biology, was a hematologist, and that I would go if he wished. At this time I was Chief of Medicine at the West Haven VA Hospital and replacing me at short notice was an inconvenience to him, but he did not hesitate to honor his verbal agreement with the Academy. My interest in things foreign was piqued by Japan, itself, and by the unusual medical and political problems resulting from the bombing of Hiroshima and Nagasaki.

In retrospect, a measure of Beeson's unusual leadership qualities is reflected in some of these appointments. In 1956, the West Haven Veterans Administration Hospital, which had previously been an independent facility, became closely associated with Yale. I have never known the politics of that change in affiliation, but suddenly all the housestaff and most of the faculty level people at West Haven were gone, and Dr. Beeson's small department at Yale found itself responsible for the care of a large population of veterans, just four miles away in West Haven. The operational transition time was only about four months from the time the affiliation was announced.

Because my wife Dorothy was working as a resident at West Haven, and because we lived only two blocks from that hospital, I knew the situation better than most of the young people at Yale, and knew its pitfalls and problems. Dr. Beeson called me to his office, told me that Yale was taking over the West Haven Hospital in July of 1956 but could not recruit a larger Yale housestaff to staff it until July of 1957. He accepted that I understood the problems of the job, but emphasized the stipulation of the affiliation with Yale.

This was the strong leader, as well as the skilled poker player at work. He knew that I needed a permanent faculty job, at Yale or elsewhere. He knew that the West Haven affiliation would be difficult, and was basically too risky for a senior academician to undertake, and he knew that time was very short, indeed. Also, he recognized that his own position would be damaged if the Veterans Administration affiliation did not go well. Both Beeson and I understood all of these factors as he quietly offered me the job as Chief of Medicine. The experienced poker player added a little inducement in the form of a bit of healthy competition as he mentioned that if I was not interested in the job, he would discuss it with Frank Epstein. Epstein and I were good friends, and I admired him enormously and felt he was the most talented of all the young faculty at Yale. By approaching me first, Beeson gave me the ultimate vote of confidence.

Thus at age 29 I became the youngest Chief of Medicine ever appointed in the VA system. The gamble paid off. By the time the housestaff arrived a year after I began, I had rearranged the Medical Service and by hard work and energy had managed to care for the patients during that year without housestaff. By July, 1957, I had arranged for the housestaff program to include a third year of residency, paid for by the Veterans Administration. Until then, the third year of Yale's internal medicine program was mandated by the American Board of Internal Medicine, but executed by selecting third year residents who were willing to work for nothing — Yale had no stipend. Teaching at West Haven went well, as both Beeson and I chose faculty with strong interest in teaching, as well as competent investigators.

Looking back at it, Beeson's gamble on me was in the mode of Soma Weiss, putting trust in young people he respected and giving them responsibility. The young people, in return, trusted Dr. Beeson to continue to be interested in them and be concerned about their academic growth. That trust helped me decide to go to West Haven, and then to Hiroshima. I was succeeded in Japan by Stuart Finch, Lawrence Freedman, and Kenneth Johnson. All of us had a wonderful experience in Japan, helping the Atomic Bomb Casualty Commission bring the first statistical and computerized clinical research program to fruition. Trust in Paul Beeson and in his integrity allowed each of us to disrupt our careers at critical periods in our development; each of us felt that we gained from the Japanese experience, both personally and professionally.

Beeson's Personal Illnesses and his Research

During those first six years at Yale, Beeson's accomplishments were interspersed with long periods of hospitalization, at least during 1953 and 1954, as he underwent repeated major surgery to correct a congenital communication between his rectum and his bladder. This condition required colostomy to divert the fecal stream from the rectum and the urine from the bladder to an artificial opening in the abdominal wall, followed weeks later by tedious surgical dissection to correct the malformation between the bladder and the rectum, and many months later a reconnecting of the colon to the rectum. Each surgical procedure was fraught with complications, and he was seriously ill on several occasions.

I believe that Paul Beeson, the patient, directly influenced Paul Beeson the astute clinical observer who, in turn, asked key questions of Paul Beeson the clinical investigator. Since childhood, undoubtedly as a sequel of the rectal-bladder communication, Beeson had had episodes of fever and chills, not always accompanied by symptoms of urinary infection. At Emory, his technician Liz Roberts had, on several occasions when he was having fever and chills, cultured colon-type bacteria from his bloodstream. Dr. Beeson says he decided to undergo surgery because of fear of developing bacterial endocarditis. He had already learned from his clinical research that his liver would remove most of the bacteria efficiently, but those experiments with James Warren had taught him the serious dangers of a bacterial infection on a heart valve. By the early 1950's, we had a satisfactory array of antibiotics to treat infection, but surgery on the heart and replacement of damaged heart valves was still years away.

If one reviews Beeson's publications (see Appendix), some of his finest research at Yale involved those themes familiar from his own personal medical experience. With Ivan Bennett, he continued basic studies on how fever is produced. With Bennett, myself, and others, he continued to expand his knowledge about bacteremia and how the body handles microbes suddenly released into the bloodstream. He began to ponder the reasons for infections in the bladder and in the kidney, and the relationship between the two that involves a communicating urinary tract. Working with Lucien Guze, Lawrence Freedman, and Heonir Rocha, he pioneered studies of the mechanism of kidney infection as a sequel to bladder infection. Almost certainly influenced by his own personal experience, buttressed by his research, he wrote an editorial in the *American Journal of Medicine* in 1958, "The Case Against the Catheter," which radically reduced the use of a catheter, common at the time, in diagnosis of urinary infection and in routine post-operative care. This influential editorial undoubtedly helped patients enormously because it changed the way physicians treated infections in the bladder and kidneys, infections which are common and potentially dangerous.

Years later, in England, working with David Durack, he would revert to his interest in bacterial endocarditis and ask what factors favor bacteria lodging on a heart valve during the course of bacteremia.

Yale, 1959-1965 (The Later Years)

Before describing Paul Beeson's London sabbatical and his final years at Yale, let me discuss how our personal friendship evolved over the years. My first memory of Paul Beeson was in 1949 when he was an official Visiting Professor with us at Duke. John Muller, a classmate and friend, had returned to Duke after internship at Grady, full of admiration and respect for his Grady Chief, Dr. Beeson. Beeson was not charismatic in the mode of Stead and Myers, but in his own environment Beeson has a natural grace that distinguishes him in a very special way — special, but very much an essential part of his institution or his department. His innate shyness always made him nervous when performing outside his own territory, or outside his particular field of personal knowledge. In watching him over the years, I learned from him to always "run scared," to be better prepared than my casual Southern nature might dictate. By continuing to strive and to challenge himself in those aspects of his professional activities in which he felt some insecurity, he improved and polished his natural skills. When I read Russell Baker's remark that I have used as the frontispiece of this book, "It's important to strive but absurd to strut," I thought of Paul, and hope that the quotation fits all those in the Soma Weiss lineage.

It was pure chance that took me to Yale in 1954 at the end of my two years in the Army at Walter Reed Army Medical Center in Washington, D.C. I felt that I needed more university-based training and experience, and decided to look for a place that was doing research in white blood cells rather than research on anemia and red blood cells, which had been my interest at Walter Reed. I encountered Dr. Jack Myers at the Spring meeting of the medical research societies in Atlantic City, told him I was looking for more training and research on white blood cells. He countered that he did not know about specific research fields, but that Paul Beeson was going to Yale from Emory and that if he (Jack) were a young man, he would consider working at Yale under Beeson because he would surely run a good department.

I did inquire, and found that Beeson had just hired a young hematologist, Stuart Finch, to head his section at Yale and that Finch was working on granulocytes, one of the white cell family. I wrote to Stu Finch, who said he would be delighted to have me, but had no salary support. About that time, I was at a small meeting of Washington hematologists and told George Brecher, head of clinical laboratories at the newly created Clinical Center at the National Institutes of Health, about my conversations with Finch. Brecher, whom I knew only casually, informed me that the NIH was thinking about supporting careers in medical research and that he would try to fix it up for me. He did, and I went to Yale with two years of support at $6,000 yearly in what must have been the earliest precursor to the NIH Clinical Investigator Award.

I liked Yale from the outset. Finch had some research projects ready to go, and I started work on them immediately. Our office and laboratory were across the hall from Dr. Beeson's office, and I got to know Beeson early in the Yale stay. His laboratory was just down the hall, staffed by Liz Roberts, the experienced technician whom Beeson had brought from Atlanta.

As I settled in during the fall of 1954, Beeson was just recovering from the last of his series of operations that would lead to the permanent correction of his rectal-bladder fistula. I was working on white blood cells and their function in preventing bacteremia, a topic of interest to Dr. Beeson and we talked about experiments. Our actual collaboration evolved so naturally and easily, that I cannot remember how it transpired, and it ended only when I went from Yale to the VA Hospital as Chief of Medicine in 1956. In retrospect, I suspect some of our early contact was not so casual and accidental, because the old Grady group (Stead or Myers) had probably told Beeson about me. Also, Ivan Bennett had just left him after four years of close association, and Beeson probably missed having a young man to talk to about his experiments. Finally, I tend to be outgoing, cheerful, and self-sufficient, and I think Dr. Beeson found it easy to relax with me without feeling the weight of his position as Chairman.

Barbara Beeson was several years younger than Paul and my wife Dorothy a little older than I, and the two spouses got along well. Paul and Barbara's youngest child, Judy, was the same age as our middle daughter, and that gave our wives something in common. I cannot recall the occasion, but we had the Beesons to dinner in about 1955 at our little rented house in West Haven, along with my friend and collaborator Harry Merryman who was interested in freezing blood for permanent storage. We drank whiskey, told a lot of funny stories, and enjoyed the evening, but we did not see much of the Beesons socially until after our return from Japan in 1960. I sense, in retrospect, that I was so busy running that VA Medical Service from 1956-1958 that our social life was quite minimal. Our friendship actually grew around the Sputnik-inspired venture in Hiroshima where I was to organize a sustained medical follow-up of the survivors of our World War II attack at the Atomic Bomb Casualty Commission. The Hollingsworths were off to Japan in the summer of 1958, and Paul and Barbara Beeson, by chance, were to leave for a one-year sabbatical in England at the same time. Beeson and I were spending some time together professionally, planning the Hiroshima-Nagasaki program; we did not want the Yale effort to fail. Because we were both leaving in July, mutual friends tended to entertain both couples at farewell parties, and we spent a lot of time together in those few weeks before July 1.

Correspondence between England and Japan matured our friendship. While Beeson was in England, I sent him many of the plans and working documents of the project in Japan, including protocols and comments about many of our sub-projects related to physiological measurements of aging in the irradiated Japanese, compared to their controls. We measured such things as graying of hair, skin elasticity, muscle strength, blood pressure, rapidity of response to a stimulus, acuity of hearing, and incidence of bacteria in the urine. All these tests were performed in the Hiroshima-Nagasaki clinics that we operated, our "patients" being a random sample of irradiated and non-irradiated individuals. We did not expect to find accelerated aging in the radiation-exposed, although that was the hypothesis we were testing. We applied the rigor of clinical research to the overall project of detecting illness in what was, basically, a random population of adults in Hiroshima and Nagasaki.

Dr. Beeson, I suspect, derived a vicarious pleasure from hearing of our exploits, and I am sure he was pleased with our success in generating an upbeat atmosphere for the study and in designing a stimulating operation for the Academy. He knew most of our young people, who were our own Yale housestaff drafted into the Public Health Service and designated to work with us. I began to get regular, perhaps weekly at times, handwritten blue aerograms commenting on various projects. As time went on, the exchanges of blue aerogram notes became more general in nature. Beeson wrote about his research with Derrick Rowley, which was going well. Barbara Beeson sometimes took to the typewriter to describe the home and children in London.

The Beesons returned from sabbatical in the summer of 1959, much refreshed and enthusiastic about the value of a sabbatical year. He had been studying the unusual susceptibility of the kidney to bacterial infections, and found that portions of the kidney inhibited the action of complement in blood serum. Since complement is needed to kill most bacteria, this observation helped explain why kidney infection, pyelonephritis, was common. Beeson did this work with his own hands since he had no technicians, and published it promptly in the prestigious *Journal of Experimental Medicine* (reference 66 in C.V., see Appendix).

The Hollingsworths remained in Japan for another year. We continued to correspond regularly and Beeson arranged for Stuart Finch to replace me at the end of that year as Chief of Medicine at the Atomic Bomb Casualty Commission and to bring with him a fresh cadre of young housestaff-level people. I returned to my job at the VA Hospital in West Haven in July, 1960, but in early 1962 joined the Department at Yale as Chief of Rheumatology and Director of the Clinical Research Center.

Dr. Beeson felt rejuvenated after the sabbatical, but he did not again work in his laboratory. The chores of running a department were too great. When he went to Yale in 1952, the Department of Medicine had fewer than 20 faculty members. When he left in 1965, he was overseeing a faculty that had increased to more than 100. Housestaff numbers had increased only moderately, but the number of fellowship slots had forged ahead as the various faculty subspecialty groups obtained federal funding from the NIH to support the training of doctors as scientists and to bring basic scientists into clinical medicine. At this time, too, Dr. Beeson realized that Yale needed a place where private patients could be seen in a modern and comfortable clinic setting. He generated the money to build the Dana Clinical Center. Many, perhaps the majority, of the patients who allowed me to do studies on fluid from their rheumatic joints were recruited from private patients seen by me in the Dana Clinic. Good care and good research are absolutely compatible. Largely through Beeson's efforts, Yale also built a magnificent laboratory building adjoining the Dana Clinic.

Beeson's years at Yale, 1952-1965, coincided al-

most perfectly with the period of pump-priming by the
NIH to expand the medical research establishment. The
nation struck out on a determined course that was expected to lead to the cure of all human diseases. Each
year the government set a target budget for the NIH, and
a generous and enthusiastic Congress gave more than the
amount requested. Paul Beeson commented recently that,
during those years, he was never sure whether he was
asking too little or too much. The department budget in
money allocated by Yale University was only $250,000.
Like most faculty members, I never saw a copper cent of
Yale money for myself or for my programs during 13
years at Yale. Almost everything we did was paid for
from the grants we solicited competitively from the NIH.
My grants even paid for the phone bill! I believe those
pump-priming years were not wasteful; they laid the
groundwork for a biomedical research endeavor that has
sustained sensible growth and excellence to the present
time. The NIH budget, although now counted in many
billions of dollars, is still a small percentage of our national expenditures and even of the amount spent on health
care. If, as I believe, we are beginning to see the final
spurt towards the conquest of disease, history will record
this country's vision in funding biomedical research in the
20th Century as one of the crowning achievements of
mankind.

Paul Beeson was an unusual person to preside
over the growth of Yale's Department of Medicine during
those expanding years. One part of his nature, the part
that most of us saw most readily, is conservative, retiring,
and, indeed, almost minimalistic. He thrived on doing

simple things like mowing the lawn, wanted to keep his Department small and intimate, and did research that is classic because of its simple and pure approach to the questions posed. The other part of Beeson, however, is the poker player who liked to win the way most people like to win. That part of him also wanted to see his Yale colleagues growing and expanding in mastering their disciplines. He took pride in their achievements particularly as those achievements led to better care of our patients, but he was also proud of the standing the Department had achieved in American academic medicine. This truly unassuming and conservative man whose honesty and integrity were evident to all was, in many ways, the ideal person to attract funds to Yale, contrasting as he did with the more flamboyant entrepreneurial department heads that reigned during that period. Few granting agencies would have sensed in Paul Beeson the satisfaction he derived from those fortnightly poker sessions with three or four of his closest colleagues, nor the skills he demonstrated at the game.

During those latter years at Yale, Beeson was steadily writing and editing larger and larger portions of one of the great world-wide textbooks of medicine, *Cecil's Textbook of Medicine*. For many years, the Chairman of Medicine at Columbia University, Robert Loeb, was the Chief Editor of this multiauthored and highly authoritative textbook, and it became known as the Cecil-Loeb text. Beginning in 1963 and continuing for more than 15 years, Beeson and his close personal friend and colleague, Walsh McDermott, at Cornell, were co-editors of the book. Beeson was an excellent editor because of his innate simplicity, directness, and understated style. He could spot irrelevancies, transpose a loose phrase or two, strike out a few extraneous words, or split the long sentence into two and behold!, a tersely elegant statement emerged. Beeson enjoyed the editing, and the income was most welcome to his growing family and to a man who never had a salary above $35,000 a year until he was 66 years old and had retired from Oxford. Those of us working with Dr. Beeson were almost unaware of the enormous amount of work he put into the Cecil Textbook, which was completely reviewed and revised every three years.

When Dr. Loeb retired at Columbia (in 1960), Beeson's eminence and close association with the then *Cecil-Loeb Textbook of Medicine* made him a natural choice to succeed Dr. Loeb as Chairman at Columbia. I remember that he visited New York on perhaps two or three occasions, and I was concerned that he might leave Yale for the larger and perhaps more prestigious Columbia University Chair of Medicine. He turned it down. Recently I told Beeson that I had feared he would take the job at Columbia and then wondered why he had not. He countered quite succinctly that the Columbia Chairmanship paid even less than he was getting at Yale and he could not afford it!

During the Yale years and extending throughout the Oxford years that would follow, Beeson got a great deal of pleasure out of an informal group of academic researchers who met to discuss progress in infectious diseases. The group was particularly interested in learning about host defense mechanisms — why, for example, white blood cells migrate to infected tissues and cause pus to form. The group in the early years consisted of several of Beeson's colleagues at Yale, along with the nucleus of people associated with Walsh McDermott at Cornell, and W. Barry Wood at Johns Hopkins. They met yearly, alternating among the three cities, with the host city providing a program during the day and a pay-as-you-go cocktail party and dinner in the evening. The three leaders, all good friends and mutual admirers, set a wonderful tone of fun, excitement, and quest for excellence in research. McDermott headed the Department of Public Health and Preventive Medicine at Cornell, and was wise and effective as a national leader in medicine. His fame came from his key role in the discovery of effective chemotherapeutic agents to combat tuberculosis and for leading the effort to eradicate tuberculosis in the United States. Barry Wood had been an outstanding Harvard athlete and scholar in the 1930's, and had followed this promising start by going to Washington University (Barnes Hospital) at age 32 as Chairman of Medicine. Sometime in the mid-1950's he became Vice-President of the Johns Hopkins Medical School, a move he soon regretted and relinquished to become Professor of Microbiology at Hopkins. Wood, like Beeson, was interested in the mechanisms of fever.

Those three men were leaders in the study of infectious diseases, but also in academic medicine generally; their informal scientific meeting provided an important forum in which they could interact with young people and share some of their research ideas. All three were elegant men, perhaps even fastidious, and were somewhat miffed by the sobriquet, "Pus Club," which some wag had used to define the group. Thus, when Beeson moved to Oxford, the slightly inebriated membership selected the name Interplanetary Society to indicate that they could meet anywhere, anytime. The Pus Club/Interplanetary Society became a powerful force in academic medicine as the junior members grew older, assumed chairmanships, and returned to the meetings with their own junior associates in tow. Robert Petersdorf, a Beeson Chief Resident at Yale and later a faculty member at Hopkins, went to Seattle as Chairman at the University of Washington, Ivan Bennett to New York University, Leighton Cluff from Hopkins to Florida, David Rogers from Cornell to Vanderbilt, Donald Kaye to Women's Medical College in Philadelphia, Edward Hook from Cornell to the University of Virginia, and I went to the University of Kentucky. Many others benefitted from the Weiss/Beeson heritage at those meetings and progressed to major academic jobs.

I learned a lot from the Interplanetary Society, although I was a somewhat peripheral member of a club that had no official membership. Academic professors must have meetings that serve a purpose, but leaders with heavy responsibility also benefit from relaxing with a congenial peer group. I had the Interplanetary Society in mind when I invited a group of West Coast Veterans Hospital Chiefs of Medicine and their spouses to join me in an informal yearly meeting at Borrego Springs near San Diego; these meetings have served to meld this group over the last decade.

The Yale Years, 1959-1965 (continued)

As the pleasures of the 1959 sabbatical receded in memory, and as Dr. Beeson progressed further into his second 6-year term as Chairman of Medicine at Yale, he seemed a little tired and a little reserved. That flirtation with Columbia may have heightened the restiveness. He had been a chairman since 1946, and the job requirements had changed enormously during those years. He was quite nostalgic about his lapsed research and talked periodically about eosinophils and potential experiments on the mechanisms of eosinophilia. At home, I suspect times were ripe for a change. John and Peter were grown young men, at Yale as students, and heavily involved as members of the generation of the early 1960's who were trying to make sense out of the Vietnam War. Yale was a center of anti-war agitation, but I do not recall thinking very clearly about that War until 1968, and I do not recall discussing it with the Beesons. However, being parents of draft-aged sons during that period must have been a dreadful strain.

Beeson's restiveness was clearly evident when, one night in 1964, he called to his home a group of close friends and colleagues to discuss the burdens of the chairmanship. The group consisted, as I recall, of Thomas Amatruda who had succeeded me as Chief of Medicine at the West Haven VA Hospital, senior professor Gerald Klatskin who had been acting chairman during Paul's sabbatical, Philip Bondy who had been with Beeson for more than a decade at Emory and Yale and was an obvious heir-apparent to the chairmanship, and myself. I believe either Elisha Atkins, Fred Kantor, or Lawrence

Freedman were also present. Dr. Beeson later indicated that he had found that meeting unsatisfactory. He discussed with us the enlarging and increasingly onerous chores of a chairman, but the group did not feel that he could or should relieve himself of any one of his readily identifiable responsibilities — taking Morning Report with housestaff, recruiting interns, teaching medical students. I believe we were correct, since the successful chairman must keep a hand in all those activities. Although it is possible to delegate or reject some of these tasks, they are generally considered to be very important aspects of the job.

As events transpired, shortly thereafter Beeson was to receive an offer to become Nuffield Professor of Medicine at Oxford University in England, an offer he accepted with joy and without compunction. Sir George Pickering, the senior medical person in the Oxford constellation in the dean-like position of Regius Professor, had approached him about the job. Once licensure requirements had been overcome, Beeson was free to return to England.

The Beesons, full of excitement and pleasure over the new appointment, told us about it as the two couples were just sitting down in our seats at a Woolsey Hall concert. Dorothy and I listened to their excited account, and both of us simply burst into tears and had to leave the concert and walk home. I could not conceive that people like Paul and Barbara Beeson, as American as that proverbial apple pie, would voluntarily and happily leave this country at the peak of his career and accept a position in England. To me, it was as if the master poker player was suddenly playing for matchsticks rather than real money.

I tried to keep my true feelings from Paul and Barbara, and from the other members of the department, because I realized that my negative attitude would be non-productive or even damaging. We arranged a big departmental party as a send-off, with much talk about an Oslerian type move from America to England. I went to Dean Vernon Lippard and suggested that Yale, too, adopt a positive view of an unfortunate loss. Lippard was clearly miffed at me for the suggestion and Dr. Beeson for taking the Oxford position.

It was not until I spent a sabbatical year at Oxford in 1967-1968 that I saw for myself that Paul Beeson was content with life there. He describes those nine years as the happiest of his life and career, and I now understand his decision. It was a purely personal choice by Beeson, undertaken for personal and not professional reasons. As it turned out, some aspects of Dr. Beeson's career were enhanced by the Oxford move and, altogether, he enjoyed a second and different career in England from the one he had had in the United States.

The Oxford Years, 1965-1974

When, at age 57, Beeson accepted the Nuffield Professorship at Oxford, I do not think he had any clearly defined goals in mind. But Paul Beeson could not simply fade away, and by the time he left New Haven he had become well informed about the job and about the Department of Medicine at Oxford, and was already beginning to think about changes he might make. By the

time we took him, wife Barbara, and daughter Judy down
to the boat dock in New York from which they would sail
to England, I was quite convinced that the master build-
er of Emory and Yale would quietly begin to build in
Oxford.

Oxford is very different from an American university, and medicine at Oxford more different still. Oxford
University is a coalition of semi-independent colleges. The
colleges admit undergraduate students and are responsible for all their basic education. Students live in the
colleges, have their meals and classes there, and venture
out only in the later stages of their education when they
need special facilities such as laboratories. Various scientific disciplines were assigned special University buildings
for their research and for certain student teaching. Science teachers were affiliated with their discipline and
also with one of the colleges as an academic base, should
they choose to use such a base.

The very bright Oxford students who studied medicine began their medical studies in their colleges and
proceeded to learn advanced science disciplines in
specialized buildings for anatomy, pathology, and biochemistry. The clinical disciplines were concentrated at
the Radcliffe Infirmary, a quaint and quite inadequate
rabbit warren of buildings and add-ons, bearing little
resemblance to an American hospital like the Yale-New
Haven Hospital Beeson had left. Because the Radcliffe did
not have enough patients or sufficient technical facilities
for the well rounded education of all the undergraduate
medical students, Oxford maintained clinical affiliations
with several London hospitals where students could elect

to receive their clinical instruction. This arrangement suited the powerful London hospitals, since they received excellent Oxford medical students. Oxford clinicians were left with half the students for clinical teaching, but most of their time was spent taking care of patients and educating and training postgraduate students or "registrars," who were roughly equivalent to interns and residents in the United States.

Oxford has no single Department of Medicine or of Surgery as we know it, but separate units called firms, which consist of a senior physician, perhaps two or three junior staff, and registrars. Most firms were not headed by people with academic or professorial appointments. Each firm is in charge of 20 to 40 patient beds and is presided over by an authoritative Head Sister (nurse) and the physician head of the firm. Admissions were shared among the firms. Each firm ran its own follow-up clinics, and depending on the interests of the head physician, a firm might be partially subspecialized. George Pickering, as Regius Professor, undoubtedly also provided some overall guidance and coordination of the firms. Sir George, hobbling about on two walking sticks because of his degenerated hips, attired in the magnificent garb of the Regius, was certainly an active part of the Oxford scene in the 1960's, and he had great influence and power.

Beeson, as the Nuffield Professor, inherited a 40-bed firm at the Radcliffe, and Sir George (who was also an internist and an expert in hypertension) had a 20-bed firm. There were three or four other firms headed by physicians without academic appointments. In Beeson's farewell address to our Department at Yale, he stressed particularly his pride in the expert care that our Department could render to a patient with any disease. I also measured our Department at Yale, and later departments elsewhere, by my personal yardstick of how confident I would feel there as a patient with any known disease. I thought Dr. Beeson would miss modern subspecialization in England and its benefits to patients, but he seemed quite content to function, as one of his registrars later described it, as a general practitioner among a group of subspecialists.

Actually, I think Beeson was quietly strengthening the subspecialty aspects of the other firms. Cardiology, gastroenterology, and oncology were already represented among the firms, and, in the mid 1960's, those three groups controlled most of the special procedures that might prove actually life-saving. Professor Beeson began a series of social evenings every fortnight among the heads of firms, and that group began to plan informally how to share one another's skills and procedures by cross-consultation, and to discuss additional needs of the entire hospital. Under Beeson's leadership, teaching sessions of the individual firms were amalgamated into a single Grand Rounds format.

Paul Beeson's willingness to accept the Nuffield beds as a generalist firm reflects, I suspect, two different realities. Being the generalist and letting the other specialists expand was good internal politics. Had Beeson seemed self-aggrandizing or threatening, the natural resentment of the British in having one of their coveted named Professorships go to an American would have heightened, and Paul Beeson does not thrive in a contentious environment. The second reason for accepting the generalist role is perhaps more personal. We have noted Beeson's pleasure in simplicity. He was, by this time, a superbly competent physician who was comfortable that he could decide when a patient on his firm needed highly specialized intervention, and he was respected enough among his colleagues to get that specialized attention when his patients needed it. One example of his simple approach to patient care occurred shortly after he arrived in Oxford. The registrars took him to the ward to see a semi-stuporous old woman just admitted with a markedly subnormal temperature (35°C), expecting the expert on fever to want a lot of laboratory tests and diagnostic procedures. The Professor looked at her briefly, turned to the sister and said, "Sister, close the window, bring her another blanket, get those two electric fires (heaters) over here and she will be all right." Simple hypothermia during the cold and damp winter claims as many as 5,000 lives among the poor and elderly of Britain; it would never have occurred to Beeson to do tests on an old woman who just needed to come in out of the cold.

Professor Beeson generated some local support (and perhaps some grumbling animosity) by instituting something he termed a "bridge" course that tied clinical medicine at the Radcliffe to the specialized and scientifically sophisticated departments on South Parks Road where the separate buildings that housed pathology and biochemistry were located. The idea was to let students see the relevance of sophisticated science taught by world famous researchers to good clinical practice. We Americans might call such a course Pathobiology. To establish the course, Beeson obtained generous grants from the Commonwealth Fund. The funding included a new building at the Radcliffe for research and teaching. He was also able to establish clinical research units in both Clinical Immunology and Diabetes, activities not previously represented at the Radcliffe. The "bridge" course was popular with students and young faculty, but did not really excite some of the senior, entrenched people at the hospital. Dr. Beeson says that the course is hardly discernable in the current Oxford medical curriculum, but at the time the concept was fresh and the new resources that came with the bridge course were most welcome.

Early on in his Oxford career he did something that exemplifies both his courage and his willingness to do something that was right, if not politic. Sir Hans Krebs, Nobelist and one of the foremost biochemists of the mid-twentieth century, had fled Germany when Hitler came into power and then pursued his career in England. At age 65 he was retired from the Chair of Biochemistry at Oxford, as mandated by the University, but his colleagues in biochemistry were unwilling to allow him to continue working in his standard laboratory (although some small space probably would have been offered). Beeson offered Krebs a large laboratory in his Nuffield department, where he could bring his research group. Sir Hans ran a productive research program during Beeson's entire nine years at Oxford and hosted sabbaticals for several eminent professors of medicine from the United States, including Harvardians Alexander Leaf and Franklin Epstein (formerly at Yale). That appointment by Professor

Beeson probably annoyed some of the Oxford establishment, but I suspect a larger group was pleased that Oxford's seeming ungraciousness to Krebs had been quietly corrected, without rancor.

Beeson's professional life in England was moving along well by the time the Hollingsworths decided to spend a sabbatical year in Oxford (1967-1968). We selected Oxford primarily because of the Beesons, but I had been a great admirer of James Gowans and his work at the Sir William Dunn School of Pathology. Primarily because Paul Beeson recommended me, Gowans invited me (primarily a clinician) to his highly sophisticated research group.

Gowans in the early 1950's had made one of those rare seminal observations in science by documenting that small lymphocytes do not just sit in tissues, but migrate from tissues to blood and back again. They live for many years and carry immunological memory back and forth. This extraordinarily basic observation set the groundwork for modern immunology, and brought Gowans eventually to his position as Director of the National Research Council and a knighthood from the Queen. He and his group were very kind to me, and later Beeson and Tony Basten would work closely with the Gowans group. James Gowans and Paul Beeson were good friends and respectful colleagues throughout Beeson's Oxford years.

By the time we arrived in 1967, Beeson clearly was enjoying the patient care and teaching on his 40-bed ward, was having fun experimenting with new ideas such as his bridge course, and his research was reviving as Rhodes Scholars and others with a Commonwealth award flocked to Oxford. After several months in a small flat in downtown Oxford, Barbara was enjoying refurbishing a splendid country house in the Oxford suburb of Boar's Hill.

Tony Basten, with whom I later spent my 1988-1989 sabbatical year at the University of Sydney in Australia, became Beeson's first research fellow at Oxford because he had been assigned to Professor Witts, the predecessor in the Nuffield Chair. Basten had had no research training and, from Beeson's menu, selected the subject of experimental trichinosis and eosinophilia. Beeson had developed a rat model of the parasitic disease. Basten started by simply defining the clinical aspects of the illness in rats and the elaboration of the eosinophilia, described in three papers in 1970. With Gowans, he and Beeson showed that lymphocytes controlled the eosinophilic response. Later, a tall and sophisticated young Englishman, Christopher Spry, and Mark Boyer from the United States, would continue the eosinophil story. They continued collaboration with the Gowans group, finding that lymphocytes secreted substances that caused and subsequently modulated the eosinophil response. Beeson had always been fascinated by the odd fact that eosinophils completely disappear from the blood during any acute bacterial infection; he worked with a young visiting American doctor, Elizabeth Morgan, on the disappearance of eosinophils during acute infection and their reappearance during recovery.

The eosinophil work continued throughout Beeson's tenure in Oxford with Australians Ron Walls and David Durak, and culminated in a monograph in 1977 in collaboration with an American junior colleague, David Bass. Ever since that epidemic of trichinosis in Wolverhampton during World War II, Beeson had been fascinated with the subject of eosinophils, and his work at Oxford provided the first original scientific approaches to the problem, marking the field as his own.

In addition to work on eosinophilia, he undertook another important area of research while at Oxford. This research reflected his early fascination with bacterial endocarditis and, more specifically, with what causes bacteria, during the course of bacteremia from any initial source, to occasionally but not usually infect a heart valve. David Durak made the major contribution to these studies, although the design of the work clearly mirrored Beeson's earlier work on localization of bacteria in the kidney in pyelonephritis. These elegant experiments were highly successful and again provided major understanding of an important clinical problem by using simple methods along with impeccable logic.

My concern that the Oxford move would remove Paul Beeson from the American academic mainstream turned out to be totally unfounded. If anything, he became even more influential in the United States. Some of it was luck, and all of it depended on the trans-Atlantic airlines. The luck part was that his time in England coincided with the Vietnam War, a time when children rejected parents, young people generally were alienated from their elders and from the government those elders supported, and medical students and housestaff tended to view their professors as natural antagonists. I doubt that Beeson's mild-mannered although firm authority at

Yale would have survived those years, and he certainly would have been miserable as a leader during a period when challenge-the-leader was the order of the day, particularly in volatile private universities such as Yale.

The trans-Atlantic plane was a necessity dictated by both professional and personal reasons, and Paul broke his habit of staying at home. In England, it seemed to be the expected norm that senior professors undertook long pilgrimages to the former colonies, from Khartoum to Karachi, from Cape Town to Casablanca. Beeson's brief forays to the United States were hardly noted by his Oxford staff, particularly since be was almost never on vacation. (We had a 4-day holiday with the Beesons in the Channel Islands in 1968, and that was their first vacation since a camping trip across the United States in the early 1960's.)

His trips back to the States were usually a mixture of business and responsibility to family or friends. His aging parents were still alive in La Jolla when he went to England, and the boys were still in New Haven. After completing Yale, and with a great deal of soul-searching, Peter enlisted in the Army. John, always interested in music, decided to proceed on a major musical career.

Shortly after leaving for Oxford, Paul Beeson was elected to the National Academy of Sciences. He was President-Elect of the Association of American Physicians, and those Council meetings brought him back to the States several times a year. He was on the Board of the Scripps Clinic, a welcome appointment because the board's two meetings in La Jolla each year gave him an opportunity to check on his parents. He received several honors, and enjoyed invitations to be the visiting professor at different medical schools. For example, he and Barbara came to Lexington to visit us in 1970, and at a party for faculty they seemed to have time for a little special chat with everyone. Altogether, Beeson was proving proficient as a commuter between the two countries while enjoying life at Oxford.

The Beeson lifestyle became very English. Their Boar's Hill home provided a welcome respite for many an American visitor who was given lunch or dinner or sherry in the Great Hall, as their huge living room was called. Barbara had her barn, her three acres of land, and a series of ponies and horses. Her mare, Cecil, joined the household later, foaled and was flown over the North Pole to Seattle when the Beesons moved there. She continues to be a part of their life in Redmond. As Judy grew up, she and her mother shared their passion for horses, and spent much time attending gymkhanas and other equine events in the countryside around Oxford. The boys occasionally visited from the United States, and the family became clearly bi-continental.

While Barbara and Judy Beeson were busy with the Boar's Hill estate and their horses, Paul was enjoying the social life of a senior Oxford professor. He became a Fellow of Magdalen College when he came to Oxford, and he often walked up the street from the Radcliffe Infirmary to Magdalen for lunch in Commons. A Fellow was expected to dine in college at High Table at least weekly, and Beeson enjoyed those evenings. Fellows appeared at about 7:00 p.m. in their proper academic robes for sherry before dinner, and then marched in through low-table students to assume their positions at High Table, seated by seniority down-table from the Master. A superb dinner was served — soup, a fish or savory dish with white wine, meat with red wine, dessert. Then the High Table retired to another elegantly tabled room for cheese and biscuits with port and madeira, and finally to yet another antique-filled room for brandy. Beeson enjoyed his Magdalen College association throughout his nine years at Oxford and was pleased to be made an Honorary Fellow when he retired in 1974.

Paul Beeson did not revolutionize British medicine during his years at Oxford, but he did widen the scope of Oxford medicine to include more basic research and did produce a bit of useful perturbation in the entire system. His most lasting contribution, however, will not be measured in educational change, but in the fine cadre of young Commonwealth scholars whom he nurtured into excellent clinical investigators.

The end of the Oxford years was dictated primarily by the mandatory retirement age in the British system. The Radcliffe Infirmary was about to be replaced, after two decades of planning and building, with the fine new John Radcliffe Hospital. Paul Beeson felt that he should not move into the new hospital and establish policies, plan space utilization, and hire staff in the last year of his tenure as the Nuffield Professor. He made the decision to retire at age 66 in 1974 so that his successor might be appointed in time to become responsible for the decisions to be made about the new hospital.

Two or three years earlier, the Regius Professor, Sir George Pickering had finally yielded to good medical advice and had the famous surgeon Mr. Charnley give him two new Charnley hips. Sir George walked well after this, and decided to accept a Mastership at one of the Oxford colleges in order to exchange the mandatory Regius Professorship retirement age of 67 for the head of college retirement age of 70. Beeson, then, expected to be appointed Regius and thus follow Sir William Osler, who had left the United States to become Regius Professor. Beeson would also, incidentally, be allowed to work a year or two longer at Oxford. The appointment was about to be announced when some clerk in the Queen's Household discovered that the incumbent Regius must be British or Commonwealth born; Osler had been Canadian, but Beeson was standard American.

The Queen made Dr. Beeson an Honorary Knight Commander of the British Empire, the foremost acknowledgement that England can bestow on a foreigner in recognition of outstanding service to the Crown. The investiture service was an elegant one, according to one report by a young colleague who was invited to attend. Americans tend either to revere or to denigrate British knights and their ladies, but I think it entirely fitting that Paul and Barbara in their last year in England were Sir Paul and Lady Beeson, even though the titles are honorary. They did, indeed, contribute significantly to England, and were a gracious proper British couple during their years in Oxford. Incidentally, Americans who may be unimpressed with the honor of the knighthood would certainly be impressed with the medallion that accompanies this honor.

The most amazing thing, in a way, about those

Oxford years was the steady and progressive change in
the Beeson's political sentiments over that decade. Beeson wrote his mother weekly all his life. As if to preserve
continuity, he and I corresponded weekly during many of
those years in Oxford, and I wish I had saved the correspondence, which reflected the Beeson's happy lives in
Oxford and their profound change in political ideology.
Paul and Barbara Beeson were both mid-western, conservative Republicans, living and working with a group of
us at Yale who were quite liberal and usually Democrats.
The Beesons kept one of those big commemorative mugs
on their mantelpiece in New Haven, a mug bearing the
likeness of President Dwight Eisenhower. In England,
they gradually moved politically to plumb center and then
clearly shifted to the left as their concern increased about
our involvement in Vietnam and our expensive but socially unequal health care system. They became more
comfortable with the more liberal democrats, but retained a warm fondness for General Eisenhower. This
was an incredible change in viewpoints for people then in
their late fifties and early sixties.

I remember writing to them about the break-in of
the Democratic Headquarters, the caper later known as
Watergate, and predicted that it could lead to President
Nixon's downfall and impeachment. By the time the Watergate scandal really broke, they were more insistent
than we that Nixon be impeached. This change in political thinking, undoubtedly fortified by the Vietnam War
and the British reaction to our (the U.S.'s) Vietnam policy, changed Beeson's thinking about medicine. He
became much more interested in all patients having ac-

cess to primary care rather than in fewer patients having the most modern and intensive sort of care. He developed an interest in the problems of older people, the costs and sometimes the indignities that often accompany serious illness or death in the aged. The Beesons had always been conservationists, but, again, their local concerns spilled over to broader concerns such as stopping nuclear warfare and promoting global ecology. They would return to the United States in 1974 as political activists and committed environmentalists.

Seattle, 1974-present

Had mandatory retirement been less rigid in England, perhaps the Beesons would have stayed on in Oxford. Although deeply American in their roots, they liked Oxford and still look on the years there as their happiest. Their property on Boar's Hill in Oxfordshire had become a showpiece of a country estate. Although they had no firm home in the United States, they debated very little about whether to return home. Rather, the debate was where, and what should Paul do. I had been urging Dr. Beeson to consider having his name proposed for the position of Distinguished Physician of the Veterans Administration. At that time, those positions were totally open-ended as to the retirement age and required no major commitments. The pay was adequate, and the award was a national honor that could be undertaken at any VA Hospital.

That advice, augmented and encouraged by Robert Petersdorf, who was then Chief of Medicine at the University of Washington, was finally accepted, and they would move to Seattle where Beeson became Distinguished Physician at the Seattle VA Hospital and Professor of Medicine at the University of Washington, positions that he held until he retired in 1980, at age 72. These have been years of quiet personal contentment and considerable accomplishment.

At the VA Hospital, Dr. Beeson decided to earn his keep by making ward rounds as attending physician-teacher for six months a year. As usual, he set high standards for himself in that any negative comments from evaluations by students would tell him he was getting too old. As far as I know, he never got anything but A's on these evaluations. It was wonderful for University of Washington students and housestaff to have him as their senior mentor, and the VA Medical Service was fortunate to have so much voluntary time of this truly Distinguished Physician. He resigned in 1980 because the VA in Washington, D.C., started to initiate time limits and reviews for their dozen Distinguished Physicians.

Update and Assessment of Paul Beeson

In resigning from the VA, Beeson was responding to VA policy, but he certainly was not responding to his mother's admonition: "Paul, don't retire too young like your father." (Remember, Dr. John Beeson was 84 years old when he left his practice in Ohio for retirement in La Jolla.) After the 1980 retirement, Paul Beeson did not teach again, but he maintained a keen interest in all aspects of medicine — clinical care, research, education, medical economics, and medical history. He regularly attends and participates in the weekly Medical Grand

Rounds at the Seattle VA Medical Center.

Much of their post-retirement effort and interest went into politics. At the local level, Barbara became a true activist in local government, particularly as it impinged on the environment, as Redmond and the other Seattle suburbs grew rapidly. In this effort, Paul was the editor and strategist for Barbara. They were effective in promoting orderly growth to Redmond, I believe, although they felt that they did not succeed in some of their more specific goals. Barbara's effectiveness in part stemmed from her and Paul's careful research of issues, aided by Barbara's first-hand knowledge of the land around Redmond, gained from her daily horseback rides on Cecil.

On the national political scene, the new political liberal, even radical, Paul Beeson emerged as a major medical spokesman against nuclear war. President Reagan and his Secretary of Defense, Cap "The Knife" Weinberger, came into office in 1980 issuing statements Paul found incredible about the use of nuclear weapons against the Soviets. Physicians for Social Responsibility (PSR) emerged as a major organization opposed to nuclear weapons and nuclear war, and Beeson became a national leader of PSR. His impeccable academic credentials, including his name-recognition as a co-editor of the Beeson-McDermott Cecil's *Textbook of Medicine*, made him remarkably effective in the antinuclear effort. He chided me, with my experience in Hiroshima as head of the Atomic Bomb Casualty Commission, into becoming active, and I headed the San Diego Chapter of Physicians for Social Responsibility from 1981-1987.

Both of us, looking back on the PSR effort, feel that respectable physicians really did help in the maturation of American political opinion about the dangers of nuclear weapons. With the collapse of communism worldwide in the early 1990's, this effort already seems somewhat antiquated and quixotic. Looking back on it, however, both he and I agree that political activism by physicians is most effective when they bring professional expertise to the problem.

In the early 1980's, Dr. Beeson became interested in the health problems of the aged, and in the problems that an aging population presented to our health care system. He headed a prominent national committee on the role of geriatrics in medical education, and the report was widely accepted and departments of geriatrics are increasingly common in our medical schools. An accepted content of a geriatric curriculum has evolved from advice by consensus groups, and by 1990 the first Geriatric Subspecialty Board certification was offered to internists and family practitioners. As part of this effort in geriatrics, Beeson also, for a few years, edited one of the journals in the field.

He has continued to write creatively about medicine, often with emphasis on historical events or on educational issues. In his curriculum vitae (see Appendix), he lists as an award being selected as the Co-Editor of the *Oxford Companion to Medicine*. It may have been an honor, but it also represented an enormous amount of work in the editing of a most unusual two-volume publication, which is essentially a medical encyclopedia. He often writes about the advances that have come about in medical practice during his lifetime, and currently is toying with the concept of a comprehensive book on medical advances in the last 50+ years.

On the personal side, Paul and Barbara Beeson have had remarkably few illnesses and enjoyed vigorous good health in 1994. Dr. Beeson had developed osteoarthritis of one hip and had a hip replacement in 1987. In his characteristic low-keyed way, he told only a few people about the operation, and had the procedure performed in the local Redmond hospital with an ex-Navy orthopedist as his surgeon. Nothing terribly bad happened, but the operation itself was uncomfortable, and the new hip made the affected leg significantly shorter than the normal one, requiring a small lift in his shoe and a lot of physical therapy before he was free of pain. I invited myself to visit for a week when, by telephone, it was clear that things were not going too well in the postoperative period. We saw the surgeon, looked at the xrays, and arranged for an independent physical therapist. It was gratifying (and amusing) on our return from Australia in the summer of 1989, as a guest of the Beesons, to look out the window and see Paul, at age 80 with an artificial hip, climbing the 5-foot fence of the horse corral to give Cecil her bran. Barbara had assigned him that chore, and made certain that he would climb the fence by deliberately not building a gate on that part of the enclosure of the field!

Barbara's health in 1992 was excellent. In the early 1980's she had had severe pain in both shoulders, was miserable, and could barely ride Cecil. I saw her at the time, socially, and urged treatment with one of the cortisone-type drugs. She responded, and slowly was able to stop that drug. Tony Basten, our mutual friend from Australia, was a house-guest during that time, and felt that she had a disease called polymyalgia rheumatica, which responds quite specifically and dramatically to cortisone. In any event, she recovered completely. When I spent that week with them after Paul's hip surgery, I took Barbara for some needed plastic surgery of her eyes, which she had planned but postponed because of Paul's problem. Her upper eyelids had become so redundant that she could scarcely see except through a small slit. The surgery was a great success, but when I brought her back to the house, Paul Beeson was shocked to see her with stitches all about the eyelids, and huge black-eyes from the bleeding — normal for the procedure but startling to see.

Eldest son John, a talented conductor with the New York City Opera, has raised two step-children. Peter, a lawyer in New Hampshire, has two small sons. Judy Beeson, like her mother, was never interested in academics, but is an avid horse person. This interest took her to Italy and eventually to the lovely resort town of Cortina. She is now a true European, married to a lawyer and ski enthusiast, and busy teaching English in a private school and raising two small children.

Assessment of Paul Beeson

Leadership ability is a personality trait usually attributed to Soma Weiss and Gene Stead, and is evident in their actions. Charismatic is another word often used to describe them. Paul Beeson's stature as a leader is much more difficult to explain. It is as enigmatic as his smile. Some important leadership traits are obvious. He is a true gentleman at all times and in all circumstances, but is not stuffy. His sense of fairness, and the honorable nature of his decisions, are a trait we all admire. Judgement is a difficult personality trait to quantitate, but all of us agree that his judgement of people and issues is remarkably fine. But these features of his personality, alone, do not truly explain why all of us who worked under him loved and respected him to the extent that we over-achieved greatly in order to meet the standards we thought would please him. I believe that the magic ingredient in Beeson's leadership was his concern and interest in all of us, personally, in his students, in his colleagues, and particularly in his interns and residents. He is still concerned about us, about our health and about our achievements.

When I began this monograph, Paul Beeson began to save and send to me letters that he received from former students or colleagues. He was interested in defining leadership because he had been asked to participate in a symposium on leadership in medicine. He and his colleagues were curious to learn more about why we felt his leadership. I wrote some of our mutual colleagues, asking them to write me about their impressions of whether Paul Beeson had succeeded as a leader. Excerpts from the letters that Dr. Beeson had received spontaneously and that I had solicited are quoted verbatim to give a flavor of his unique leadership qualities.

Excerpts from unsolicited letters to Beeson from former medical students or residents:

"I was reading *The Pharos* of A.O.A. when I saw a book review by you. I was delighted to be able to find your whereabouts. I'm sure you do not remember me as one of your still scared and wet behind the ears medical interns at Grady in 1948-49. I will always be grateful for your gentlemanly patience and kindness to me as a medical student. At one time in my junior year I seriously considered that perhaps I had no place in medicine as the result of the teaching practices of one particular member of the Dept. Of Medicine, but you caused me to think otherwise.

There are three men in my life who have made a difference for me. They are my father, Heinz Weens (a Professor of Radiology), and you. Thank you."

"I hope the address I have for you is valid and that this letter finds you in good health. You may not remember me from Yale Medical School, but I was in the class of '58. The reason I am writing is to thank you for the years in which you provided a positive example for me (and many others) and for your kind counseling when I was a sometimes angry and/or confused young man. The example you set has been of great help to me over the years."

~Sitting alone at my desk on this Sunday evening, I just took a break to eat some soda crackers and a glass of pineapple juice. That combination brought back memories of the Fitkin and Winchester wards when I would keep myself going at 3:00 in the morning as a house officer by raiding the refrigerator for that combination of pineapple juice and soda crackers.

I can't let that wonderful memory fade this afternoon without dropping you a brief note to thank you, as I perhaps may never have done entirely, for the wonderful years of training you provided at Yale for this bright fellow from Utah by way of Harvard. I think we had all the rigor that has been associated with the Spartan house officerships of a Robert Loeb and a Max Wintrobe. But without sacrificing standards, we also had the dignified gentle warmth and good humor of a Paul Beeson."

The following are excerpts from letters that I solicited from our mutual friends and colleagues:

"We have all speculated from time to time on wherein lies Beeson's greatness and I am sure that the words to follow will not add a great deal of illumination. First there is the shining integrity. One always had the impression one was dealing with a straight person; no guile, no hidden agenda, no political maneuvering. Second, Beeson could focus on you in a way that made you think you were the sole object of his preoccupation at that moment. He projected a sense of caring about the individual and that was manifested in many ways. Even today, he knows the names of wives and children of many of the people who passed through his departments throughout his career, because he made it a point to learn them. Whenever one of our children was born, a hot plate or some other small gift appeared to punctuate the happy occasion. His handwritten invitations to Christmas parties; Barbara and his decoration with shrubs gotten from the Yale golf course for those parties; all contributed to the self embodiment on our part of his ideals. He created a sense of worth in an individual by caring about that individual and making the individual feel that he or she was important to Beeson and therefore should perform at a level commensurate with that importance. In doing this, he created an atmosphere in which individuals tried to do better than they might otherwise do, just because they didn't want to fail this high opinion that Beeson projected of them to them.

"Lastly, in addition to the integrity and the focus, we all recognized in Beeson a person who practiced the ideals of medicine of which we had only remotely conceived when we became interested in medicine. By this I mean he cared about patients; he was a good example. When he had patients in the hospital he would come in to see them whether it was a weekend or a holiday, not because the patient was sick and needed his expert advice, but because he said many times that the patient in a hospital really looks forward to seeing his doctor and he thought it important that the doctor appear. He cared about his patients. He didn't lecture about it; he just showed it. That struck a cord in all of us who would like to think that doctors should care about their patients and that we should be like that. He also cared about science and getting it right. Somehow he conveyed the notion that science was not the glitter or the sparks of a new finding but rather the substance and the durability of the finding that mattered. His idealism was mature, self practiced and not the sophomoric kind projected on the rest of the world."

"I have always felt that Paul Beeson was a unique leader and an extremely effective one. Paul did not have charisma. He was not forceful in an overt way. He did not rule through fear. Instead he was the only truly effective leader with whom I have had personal contact who led successfully because almost everyone respected him, liked him, and even loved him. Paul Beeson always came through as a compassionate, fine human being who sincerely cared about people. He was in many ways a humble man who had his insecurities and never fully appreciated his own enormous talent. He had the ability to project himself into a situation and see it not only through his own eyes but with the eyes of the participants at the lowest levels. There are a number of anecdotes that stand out in my memory of him because they illustrated so well his humanity and his fairness. On one occasion, a patient with pneumococcal meningitis who was receiving 10,000 units of intrathecal penicillin daily in addition to systemic penicillin therapy, suddenly went into status epilepticus and died. It turned out that the nurse who was preparing the penicillin dose for the resident who was injecting it intrathecally made an arithmetic error and gave him 1,000,000 units of penicillin. As soon as Paul heard about this terrible tragedy, he went to the patient floor and sat down with the young nurse and resident to comfort them. In the process he told them that we are all members of a team and that we all shared the successes and the failures. He told them that since he advocated intrathecal penicillin therapy, he had played as much a part in the therapy of that individual patient as they had. His actions meant a great deal to them and helped them recover from their terrible feelings of sorrow and guilt."

"His strength of presence in combination with a gentlemanly reticence represents a unique set of attributes that I have never seen duplicated in academic medicine over the past twenty eight years. In fact, I sometimes wonder if our current milieu would recognize and reward such a person should he appear on the scene. This is brief and to the point. Dr. Beeson might approve."

"As I look back, it seems to me that in many ways Paul was a psychological father to me; his influence remains paramount within me. I know that I modelled myself after him as a physician — always learning, reaching for the highest level of creativity and commitment of which I was capable, combining teaching with patient care, and above all, pursuing the highest level of personal and professional integrity. Paul combined genuine modesty with a tenacious pursuit of learning and creativity — a very rare combination (in a profession which accommodates/invites very narcissistic personalities). Paul believed in traditions which served to unite people and make them feel at home — and he was willing to fill the role of tradition-maker and keeper."

"My first experience with Paul B. Beeson was as a third year student on Fitkin I when I was selected to present a case of viral hepatitis to him on student rounds. It was clear from the resident that this was a unique opportunity to impress the Professor so I read widely on all aspects of hepatitis and presented all the pertinent positive and negative findings. Paul Beeson complimented me on the presentation, and from that moment on - I became an intense admirer of the man and began to appreciate some of the awe in which his residents held him.

The call to be Paul Beeson's Chief Medical Resident was completely unexpected, and perhaps in many ways unwanted. However, the fact that he had selected me over my contemporaries was such an enormous vote of confidence, that I knew at that moment that an academic career was my future. I suppose few Paul Beeson Chief Residents would dispute that that year was the most rewarding of their professional life. During that year, not only was the amazing and encyclopedic clinical acumen of Paul Beeson evident, but his great humanity as well. Whenever he saw a ward patient on consultation, he would seek out a family member to explain his findings and offer some encouragement.

Clearly Paul Beeson was a giant in the academic community of his time. He influenced a generation of academicians who became successful in their own right but who were always proudest of being 'Beeson Men' (there were no 'Beeson Women' at that time — what a shame). Paul Beeson was unique in a time of unique and powerful chairs. Those who worked with him strove their professional lives to measure up to his standards. I doubt whether Professors of Medicine will ever have that unique role in molding the careers of a generation of academicians again."

Let us let Paul Beeson have the last word, in a letter to me on January 14, 1989:

"I can understand that you are having difficulty getting anyone to describe me in terms of leadership. I never felt that I was a leader. I felt I had responsibility, and realized that I had power (in such matters as promotions, space allocation and salary). But my only intent was to get good people, and create conditions that would allow them to achieve whatever they wanted, at whatever level they happened to be. The one principle I followed was that the success of the department depended on getting good house staff. They teach the students, take care of the patients, and are the best pool from which to draw future members of the department."

Chapter VI

LESSONS FROM THE LEGACY

I t may seem trite to talk about goals, but I have been amazed and discouraged by the number of people in senior academic positions who are skilled and knowledgeable about all the technical parts of their jobs, but have never really understood what academic medicine is all about. The goal is quite simple and basic: to create an environment in which people work productively, enjoy their work, and grow professionally. By definition, such an environment offers challenges and rewards, but is basically a happy and supportive place. Paul Beeson felt that Soma Weiss had evolved a sort of Camelot at the Brigham. Beeson himself had built at Yale the sort of environment in which a group of young faculty were working together to build a cohesive department. There was little jealousy among us despite our similar ages and we were productive often beyond our basic talents. The best of young people, sensing this productive and happy environment flocked to join us as students, house officers, and fellows. We were content but not complacent. I, at least, would have stayed at Yale University

indefinitely to support the joint enterprise as long as
Beeson remained the leader. Gene Stead, in one of his
broad philosophical statements, put it a little differently
when he said, "The job of a department chairman is to
create opportunity." I would add one of my own frequent
admonitions to senior faculty, which is that they must
nourish the young.

The product of such an environment is people —
good doctors, thoughtful teachers, skilled and enthusiastic students, and good citizens of an institution and of
their city and country. The success of the endeavor is
easily measured by the success and productivity of the
people it generates, and, in turn, by the people who elect
to enter its environment.

The idea that pain and fear and greed and suffering are somehow essential ingredients for a successful
human enterprise has no true counterpart in history. Yet
somehow our society and our medical micro-environment
are progressively fostering these ideas. A caring profession like medicine must care for its members if its care
of patients is to reach the perfection that we seek.

This section of the book is a discussion of some of
the problems in building a Department of Medicine, some
attributes that help, some practical advice. I will draw
liberally on the wisdom of Weiss, Stead, and Beeson in
bolstering these assertions.

Integrity

Integrity is a personal quality that means more
than honesty, although honesty is a major ingredient of
integrity. The sort of integrity that people feel in Paul

Beeson, for example, implies an externally perceptible code of behavior that influences day to day decisions, and to a major extent allows one to predict most actions in advance. Integrity involves moral principles, but not a rigid set of moral rules. Weiss, Stead, and Beeson were all perceived to be men of great integrity by their peers and their younger colleagues alike. One easy measure of integrity involves how often their actions that stemmed from their integrity are recalled by others. Many times I have heard Stead or Beeson comment: "Soma would have . . ." and others of my generation, contemplating an action, evoke the thought, "I wonder how Dr. Beeson (or Dr. Stead) would handle that."

Integrity involves follow-through of actions promised. Stead describes this sort of integrity in 'Dave' Davison, the founding Dean at Duke and Duke's leader for almost 40 years. Stead frequently mentioned Dave's little book kept in his pocket in which he recorded anything agreed upon; once recorded, it would be done. As our environment gets more complex, my memory sometimes fails while my honesty and integrity are both still intact. To guard against such failures, I try to buttress each promise with a written note of agreement, or by my signing off in agreement with detailed reports that I request of my colleagues, or simply by dictating a memorandum for record. These multiple devices are the equivalent of Dean Davison's little book.

Institutions have integrity only insofar as the leaders of the institutions possess that personal quality, whether the institution be government, business, university, or medical school. Therefore, integrity is, to me, the

most important element to search for in leaders, and I
believe that one can sense integrity in people. I am ap-
palled, sometimes, at how often we settle for the expedi-
ent in our leaders and, to the extent that we compromise,
so declines the integrity of our institutions.

On Showing the Flag: Visible Leadership

Gene Stead first taught me that people watch the
leader's actions and only then pay attention to his words.
They follow the flag of the leader. If the leader wants a
behavior pattern to evolve, he must practice that behavior himself, as well as order or urge it done. Stead made
ward rounds more often than any member of his staff.
Rather than mention his irritation with the cigarette butts
on the floors in the ward doctors's office, he arrived for
rounds a few minutes early one day and swept the floor
— he did it only once, since afterwards the floor somehow
managed to have been freshly swept before his rounds.
When he wanted the housestaff and the nursing staff to
work together more closely, he spent more time with his
Chief Nurse. He worked in the outpatient clinic for a time
to integrate its operation with the inpatient service.

All the people who remember Soma Weiss comment on his remarkable rounds at Boston City Hospital
during his years at the Thorndike Laboratory. These
were remarkable teaching sessions, apparently, and
people came from all over Boston and, indeed, sometimes
from all over the world. You can be sure that Dr. Weiss
was always there, and did not suddenly call up and ask
his Chief Resident to make these rounds for him. At Yale,
Paul Beeson had Grand Rounds on Saturday mornings

and he was always there — five minutes early in his traditional seat in the auditorium. He did not lead the rounds, nor comment very often, but everybody knew he was there, watching attentively. Case presentations by interns were a carefully drilled three-minute exercise. Orchestrating Grand Rounds was a major activity of the Chief Resident and provided an ideal way for the Yale Chief Resident to achieve academic growth. At Duke, Gene Stead met with his residents each Sunday morning. They were expected to discuss one topic in discriminate detail, and Stead and his key lieutenants were invariably present. In reminiscing about Duke, someone remarked that the presenter at those Sunday School sessions remembered those topics forever.

Saturday mornings became a regular work time at Yale because of Grand Rounds, and because Paul Beeson used this time to simply be available. Mostly, he was in his office with the door ajar, but he might drop into one of our offices or labs for a chat about something, or he might go to the wards to see a patient he was concerned about. The point was that Beeson was having a relaxed morning in the hospital, catching up on little things, visiting a bit, doing a little extra something for patients, colleagues, or simply for the institution. Others adopted his work pattern. At Kentucky, I copied his pattern on Saturday mornings and let this be the time when faculty, students, and house officers knew I was around in an unstructured time period. I must admit, however, that one of the joys of my job as Vice-Chairman at the University of California in San Diego has been getting back Saturday mornings for my own selfish personal use.

Helen Ranney, the Chair, was a prodigious worker and
showed the flag for both of us on Saturdays.

The Product is People: Young Doctors

The educational system is for educating people,
mostly young people. Therefore, the educators, the leaders, must like to spend much of their time with young
people, trying to help understand them and their needs
in order to foster the best environment for their education. In selecting a leader or a department chair, this fact
should be kept in mind and the leaders be selected in
part because they like and respect young people. People
always comment on Soma Weiss's trust and respect for
young doctors, as exemplified by the talented group of
young faculty whom he took with him to the Brigham.
Paul Beeson certainly entrusted to me, at an early age,
important jobs in the department, including the Veterans
Administration affiliation and the project in Japan with
the Atomic Bomb Casualty Commission. And he gave me
the jobs and let me do them as I saw fit, rather than giving me a title and issuing directions to me and through
me to others. Eugene Stead encouraged a group of talented young colleagues, let them go off to become department chairpersons elsewhere, and then cheerfully grew
their replacements.

Demeanor, Attitude, and Manners

False attitudes and deportment cannot be maintained over a span of time, but desirable natural attitudes
can be fostered and undesirable ones can be suppressed.
My guess is that Weiss, Stead, and Beeson were born

with mostly desirable character traits. However, I am reminded that Dr. Ferris, in his eulogy to Dr. Weiss, pointed out that much of Weiss's knowledge and productivity were derived from hard work overlaid on a fine mind and a good attitude. Weiss, Stead, and Beeson all demonstrated true integrity, and conducted their lives with decency and civility. They were polite men, basically outgoing in their personalities, friendly and respectful of others. One cannot imagine them being disrespectful, greedy, or uncivil. These generous features of their personalities were, I suspect, part of both their innate selves and part of their conscious intellectual effort towards self-improvement.

Their innate integrity served to shield them, I believe, against the crassness or vulgarity in talk and actions of others. On hearing the Nixon White House tapes, the vulgarity and the lack of respect of others which the vulgarity reflected filled me with shame and disgust. One cannot imagine Soma Weiss, Eugene Stead, or Paul Beeson closeted with staff and colleagues and talking in that way. One cannot imagine them filling their days with snide comments, crude stories, or denigrating remarks about others. Talk and demeanor are closely linked to behavior.

There was nothing posed or false in these men, and their fine attributes did not preclude anger. Weiss made no pretense of accepting slovenly work. Stead's anger was legendary and we all avoided him until it cooled. Beeson, when angry, would turn white and silent. But these occasions were infrequent and they were basically generous to and tolerant of others.

Verbal and Written Communication

By common consent, Soma Weiss was a magnificent communicator. Everyone was fascinated by his usage of words and his ability to express new thoughts in a creative way. In writing, he certainly was facile and productive, and had he lived, he would have been the editor of *Cecil's Textbook of Medicine*. To me, the best example of his skill in written communication is a long letter in the Countway Library collection of his papers analyzing the candidates and the job of Professor of Pharmacology at Harvard. I suspect this was his first major University committee assignment, and the letter was written to the renowned Professor of Physiology, Walter B. Cannon. His intellect and his skill at written communication stand out in this carefully crafted communication.

As a youngster, Eugene Stead had read extensively and became a great admirer of the apt phrase used creatively. He had no hesitancy in using unusual words in ordinary discussions, and could build elaborate verbal pictures as he talked extemporaneously. When I first knew him, he built word structures so complicated that, on occasion, I would get worried that he would overextend himself and be unable to complete the sentence. It was a little like the tension one feels in watching the high-wire performer at the top of the circus tent. His penchant, however, was to discuss a problem elaborately and then sum up the problem with one of his Steadisms. People loved to hear him talk, but he could also listen. His writing has a distinctive flavor that one knows emanates from Eugene Stead. He tells the story of the young editor who offered to teach him to write; Stead replied that he had gotten used to his own way of saying things.

In reviewing the attributes and accomplishments of these three men, their ability to write and edit journals and textbooks stands out. Textbook writing is a form of teaching that is permanent and reaches thousands of students. The ability and willingness to edit constructively is an obvious advantage to a professor hoping to help young people fashion their careers. Also, I suspect that an experienced editor has acquired skills that help prepare materials for the endless committees that are a part of academic life. Committees rarely solve problems, but they do elucidate problems and, more importantly, educate the committee members. In my own career, I viewed textbook writing and rewriting, and editing, as boring. In retrospect, I suspect the boredom would have been far less had I learned these skills well, as these men did.

Chapter VII

THREE MEN:
SIMILARITIES AND CONTRASTS

Superficially, Soma Weiss, Eugene Stead, and Paul Beeson seem quite different. Certainly their backgrounds and personalities are quite different. Weiss was a sunny, outgoing man with a remarkable energetic presence who, I suspect, had a true genius as a communicator and teacher. Paul Beeson points out that anyone who ever met Soma Weiss remembers him, and tends to recall exactly when and where they met. From age 20 when Weiss arrived in this country, natural leadership was one of his major and acknowledged character traits. Eugene Stead learned a lot from Dr. Weiss about leadership. As he points out, he was a shy young man and only when he undertook the position of Chief Resident at Cincinnati did he learn that he had leadership qualities. In Paul Beeson, humble and a bit insecure by nature, leadership came because of his personal quest for excellence and his sensitivity to his colleagues, young and old.

Each could and did lead, but leadership alone is not enough. Leadership without clear and appropriate goals can become demagoguery. They strove constantly for excellence in their educational environment, and for a happier, healthier, and more productive society.

Recently I was discussing these three men, their similarities and contrasts, with Professor James F. Gifford, Jr., archivist and historian at the Duke Medical Center. He suggested that each man, in addition to his innate personality, actually functioned in a somewhat different position in the rapidly evolving era of scientific medicine. Soma Weiss might be categorized as the great Educator-Investigator, we thought, with the remarkable ability as a listener that characterizes the great clinician. Eugene Stead was a clinical investigator, evolving into the revolutionary Philosopher-Educator with great skills in defining what Sir Peter Medawar has termed, "the art of the soluble." Durham, N.C. now advertises itself as the City of Medicine, and some perceptive person dubbed Stead as Philosopher-King of Durham. Paul Beeson might be considered a Scientist-Educator. Certainly his interest in producing important science continued throughout his career although he functioned primarily as an educator.

Professor Gifford suggested that Beeson's impeccable integrity was the integrity of the scientist, functioning in an education environment. That comment hit a receptive chord with me because I recall a conversation with Dr. Beeson about some experiments we were doing. I told him that I thought we could stop doing the experiments because the results were already statistically significant. He seemed a bit uncertain and was not quick to agree with me, so I asked him how he would decide when he had done enough experiments. His reply was, "I would just keep doing them until I was absolutely certain that the results were correct." Beeson's comment has stayed with me as a prime example of his integrity.

Giving Honor to Learning

In recent conversations with Dr. Stead, he has emphasized the importance to the individual and to society of appreciating the value of learning, and the worth of learned people. Certainly Weiss and Beeson would, I believe, subscribe to the concept that respect for learning is one important aspect of the way we define civilization. In our medical schools today, one hears too much denigration of one's colleagues's scholarship. The scientist may complain that his colleague is not sufficiently "basic" in his approach to research. The clinicians tend to denigrate their laboratory-based colleagues's efforts in science as too esoteric, while the scientists fail to appreciate that clinicians may have acquired worthwhile knowledge through experience in patient care. If we all honored the learning of skilled individuals regardless of their disciplines, our environment would be more productive and, not incidentally, more pleasant.

On Working in the Present

Both Weiss and Stead have commented in writing that they worked always in the present, not worrying about the past nor fearing the future. Thus, each day became a work unto itself, and each day brought a fresh commitment to improvement. All three were, I believe, people who worked in the present. The philosophy is quite consonant with the popular concepts promoted by Professor W. Edward Deming and adopted by Japanese industry of seeking constant improvement in the quality of the product. Although these three leaders had long-term dreams, the dreams never prevented them from working hard and well each day.

The Importance of Heroes

Although it has been said that all our heroes have clay feet, I strongly believe that we need heroes to help model and shape our lives. For some people, religion may serve that purpose. For me, Weiss, Stead, and Beeson are among my pantheon of heroes, the medical branch. In politics, John Kennedy remains heroic (even if his feet are a bit dusty), along with Thomas Jefferson and Abraham Lincoln. In music, Marian Anderson surmounted prejudice and poverty, with her majestic voice and her magnanimous love for humanity. As she sings of "holding the whole world in my hands," she seems to me a true heroine.

Hard Work and Self-Discipline

Dr. Eugene Ferris, in his eulogy of Dr. Weiss, seems to have been bemusedly surprised that Weiss worked hard to accomplish his goals. A strong work ethic and sustained self-discipline characterized all three men, and is almost mandated by their accomplishments. Eugene Stead made those rounds on the Osler ward year after year. His residents arrived each morning for Report and found Stead and not some surrogate waiting. Paul Beeson made teaching rounds with students and housestaff in each of three hospitals, week after week with almost never even a short vacation. While keeping to his usual routine on the surface, those of us who knew him well would appreciate that he was often simultaneously editing the *Cecil Textbook*. Even in 1994, in their eighties, both Beeson and Stead were keeping up with events in medicine, corresponding with colleagues, writing editorials, and attending meetings.

Dr. Soma Weiss about 1940.

Dr. Eugene Stead
autographed this picture
for the author in 1952.

Dr. Paul Beeson as Chief Resident the Peter Bent Brigham Hospital under Dr. Weiss.

Dr. Beeson and the author in 1968.

Dr. Beeson, age 81, vacationing in La Jolla, California.

Appendix

Preface

SOMA WEISS became the second Physician-in-Chief of the Peter Bent Brigham Hospital September 1, 1939. He died January 31, 1942, from the rupture of a congenital intracranial aneurysm. In the intervening years, his generous spirit, his eager and able services for the Hospital, his great abilities as a physician, investigator, and teacher, left an indelible imprint on the Brigham Hospital. We, the Trustees, are powerless to do full justice and honor to his memory, but we are happy to take this method of letting others share with us these tributes to one who in a short professional career made a lasting contribution to the beneficent profession of medicine. Here is recorded the Curriculum Vitae of Soma Weiss and following this are the remarks presented at a memorial meeting in his honor at the Harvard Medical School, March 19, 1942.

CHARLES S. PIERCE, President
for the Board of Trustees

IN MEMORIAM

SOMA WEISS
1899 - 1942

Physician-in-Chief
Peter Bent Brigham Hospital

Hersey Professor of the Theory and Practice of Physic
Harvard University

Curriculum Vitae

Soma Weiss

Born January 27, 1899, at Bestercze, Hungary.*
A.B., Columbia University - 1921.
M.D., Cornell University - 1923.
Demonstrator, Institute of Physiology, Royal Hungarian
    University, Budapest, 1917-1918.
Demonstrator and Research Fellow, Institute of Biochem-
    istry, Royal Hungarian University, Budapest,
1918-1920. Assistant, Department of Pharmacology, Cor-
    nell University Medical School, 1920-1923.
Interne, Bellevue Hospital, New York City, 1923-1925.
Assistant, Thorndike Memorial Laboratory, Boston City
    Hospital, 1925-1929.
Research Fellow, Department of Medicine, Harvard Med-
    ical School, 1925-Jan. 11, 1926.
Assistant, Department of Medicine, Harvard Medical
    School, 1926-1927.
Instructor, Department of Medicine, Harvard Medical
    School, 1927-1928.
Faculty Instructor, Department of Medicine, Harvard
    Medical School, 1928-1929.

*He was the son of distinguished parents. His father was
an outstanding architect and engineer who was responsible for many of the bridges and roads of Hungary. For
this service he was knighted by Emperor Francis Joseph.

Assistant Physician, Boston City Hospital, 1927-1929.
Associate Physician, Thorndike Memorial Laboratory,
Boston City Hospital, 1929-1939.
Assistant Professor of Medicine, Harvard Medical School,
1929-1932.
Assistant Director, Thorndike Memorial Laboratory, Boston City Hospital, 1930-1932.
Associate Professor of Medicine, Harvard Medical School,
1932-1939.
Director of the Second and Fourth Medical Services (Harvard), Boston City Hospital, 1932-1939.
Physician-in-Chief, Peter Bent Brigham Hospital, 1939-1942.
Hersey Professor of the Theory and Practice of Physic,
Harvard University, 1939-1942.

Opening Remarks

We are here this afternoon because we knew Soma Weiss and looked upon him with enduring respect and affection. Also we are here because his glowing nature and his unselfish devotion to medical science and art touched the lives of all of us. Some of us were his pupils and learned from his wisdom; some were his patients and felt his gentleness and care; some of us were privileged to work with him, thus being disciplined by his insight, his judgment and his skill; some of us were his colleagues in the service of the University or the Hospital. All of us were his loyal friends.

We have gathered here to meditate together on his admirable qualities as we saw them unfold and win significance and power, and to bring back in memory the impressive stature and the deeds of Dr. Weiss, the man and the physician.

His early training in his native Hungary was followed by profitable years of initiation and adjustment in New York City. Then he moved to the Boston City Hospital. It was not long before he was revealed as a leader in medicine, bringing cheer to the sick and the miserable, engaging in illuminative studies of disease, and inspiring students and disciples to follow his ideals of eager helpfulness and love of learning. His exceptional ability was recognized in a signal manner when he was appointed Physician-in-Chief at the Peter Bent Brigham Hospital. There, in a term all too short, he left a standard of stimulating leadership which, through future years, will be looked upon as a model. In addition to performing duties in hospital wards and laboratories Soma Weiss was an earnest and faithful servant of Harvard University.

For all these manifold activities and achievements, as well as for his noble human qualities, we would revive our memories of him and for a while share with one another his ardent and generous spirit.

WALTER B. CANNON,
Presiding Officer.

The New York Years

During the last ten years legends about Soma Weiss have been growing at Cornell Medical College and Bellevue Hospital. Stories are told of his industry, his kindness, his skill in diagnosis. Some of these may be exaggerations but all show the profound effect that a young man may exert on a medical community.

Soma was born January 27, 1899 in the town of Bestercze, then a part of Hungary, later a part of Rumania. As a young man he worked in the laboratory of Hari in Buda-Peste and the protocols of his paper on the respiratory quotient published in 1919 show that he had started this difficult, exact technique when he was only seventeen. He realized in 1920 that the future was dark in Europe and after exciting adventures crossed the borders and came to New York. The morning he landed he secured his first papers for citizenship. That same day he came to Cornell Medical College to see Graham Lusk, a friend of Hari's and Graham Lusk brought him over to the Sage calorimeter room in Bellevue Hospital.

I remember well the first impression of a tall young man, bubbling with enthusiasm. I remember the card he presented because it read Weiss Soma after the custom of Hungary. I remember our surprise that so young a man knew so much about the respiratory metabolism, but we soon realized that he was the Weiss who had written the fine article on the respiratory quotient, a paper that is still quoted. Of course, we were sincerely glad when we learned he was planning to enter our medical school.

Soma Weiss was hoping to secure work in biochemistry and it was largely chance that he devoted his first years to pharmacology. Graham Lusk found for him a part-time research position in the laboratory of Dr. Robert A. Hatcher, Professor of Pharmacology at Cornell. This helped support Soma during his student days. In order to meet a requirement of the New York law, a year of English was necessary before entering medical school. In this year he obtained the degree of A.B. at Columbia and then started with the second year class at Cornell. In these first two years Dr. Hatcher and Weiss accomplished their classical work on the emetic action of digitalis and clarified the whole field of the emetic action of drugs. Dr. Hatcher gives the main credit to his young assistant without whose skill in planning and executing the careful strategy and difficult technique the work would have been impossible. Soma was fortunate in having such an experienced and wise and considerate leader. Hatcher's profound respect and admiration for Soma influenced both men greatly. In our profession the respect of pupil for master is no more important than respect of master for pupil.

Throughout his years as medical student and intern Soma continued his research in pharmacology and his twenty or more papers, most of them with Hatcher and others, are still good. It was during his internship that Soma revised the therapeutic use of physostigmine and demonstrated its value in the relief of abdominal distention.

We in the medical school have always considered Soma Weiss as our most brilliant student. It was therefore a great surprise to me when a few days ago I looked over his college record and discovered that his average for marks was not high and that he just squeezed through some of the specialties. There is a legend that he would have flunked one of these had it not been for timely influence exerted by the head of another department.

Thank goodness his college had sense enough to disregard low marks and give him the internship he wanted. One of his examiners for this internship says that at first he was not sure if the candidate knew very much less or very much more medicine than the examiner. He quickly decided on the latter.

As intern Soma led us a merry dance. He was always on the job, knew his patients thoroughly and was so accurate in his diagnoses that it would have been embarrassing for the attending staff had it not been for his great tact and tolerance. We expect a house physician who lives on the ward about fifteen hours a day to know the game thoroughly and we are accustomed to good diagnoses from house physicians but Soma stood out in a surprising manner. His medicine was always based on a solid fundamental training in physiology and pharmacology. He knew the literature so thoroughly that it was almost overwhelming. Once a patient was encountered with a rare disorder of the circulation, and in the history it was noted that about ten years previously he had been admitted to a hospital in Edinburgh. Soma knew that if he had been there at that particular time with that particular disease he must have been seen by a certain clinician who had written on this subject. Soma hurried to the library, put his hand on the right volume, and found a detailed study of his patient.

There was nothing of the impractical laboratory theorist in his hard work. As intern he remained a constant joy to the chief of the service. He was the only man I ever knew who made a diagnosis of intestinal perforation within a minute of the time it occurred. This was no accident. He realized that the supreme test of the house officer was the time interval between perforation of the gut and the arrival of the surgeon. It was his custom to warn every typhoid patient to report to him at once any sudden pain in the abdomen. One day a typhoid patient called to him as he was making rounds. The diagnosis was clear, the surgeon prompt, and the recovery uneventful.

There came to the wards of Bellevue all sorts and conditions of men, minor gangsters, major politicians, the black sheep of the best families, the humblest of hoboes. He treated them all with equal kindness and they all trusted him. Soma could become the friend and adviser of the stern hospital superintendent, the crusty medical examiner, the exasperating head nurse, and even the floor polisher whose buzz machine would nullify all efforts towards auscultation.

What are the lessons that we can learn from the

career of one man before he reached the age of 26?

Teaching at times is a most discouraging vocation. Students seem to be slow in their understanding. Our methods appear inefficient. We fail to strike sparks and doubt our flint and the student tinder. Then there appears a young man like Soma Weiss. His mind is so receptive that it absorbs the best, then races ahead and the older mind must put forth its full efforts to keep up with the pace maker. In such a student we can vicariously fulfill our own ambitions of younger days. We can see ourselves at what we hoped was our best. We can enjoy once more that approach to fresh and untrodden fields of knowledge. Then later when our student has attained his position and made his mark in the world we share some of his triumphs in the belief and hope that our teaching made its contribution. It only takes a student like Soma Weiss to prove that teaching is a good vocation.

Our medical profession at times is terribly discouraging. We find in our own city selfishness, prejudices, inefficiency. We wonder if our colleagues can be fair in their judgments. Then comes a young man with no family backing, no influential friends, and he succeeds purely through his own ability and character. I remember once when Fredrich von Muller was visiting our summer house on the coast of Connecticut and Soma drove down from Boston to spend the week-end. How proud I was to show to the best of the older generation of Europe the best of the younger generation of America! Let us remember that Soma Weiss, coming from a foreign country, won help and friendship and full recognition from the very start and was accepted throughout his career as a product of American medicine. Our profession may have its faults, but it can be generous. It is a good profession.

There are times like the present when the whole world seems heavy with badness. Forces of evil take the ascendancy, and we forget the vast stores of latent goodness. Then come the memories of young men that we have known, men whose idealism has lifted us to higher planes. Men like Soma who with deep sympathies, constant cheerfulness and unfailing kindness, have helped all with whom they come in contact. Men like Soma who, by their devoted labors, have helped physicians and patients in all civilized countries. Such men prove that, after all, this is a good world.

EUGENE F. DU BOIS

For the Boston City Hospital

One afternoon at Northeast Harbor, Maine, in late June of 1926, Francis W. Peabody introduced me to one of his assistants at the Thorndike Memorial Laboratory and shortly we three and several other individuals were walking up the hill behind Peabody's house. The man's Hungarian pronunciation of the English language fascinated me and it remained present, but with decreasing intensity, throughout his life. The man's keen interest in everything around him and his desire to learn more about everything he saw struck me even on first acquaintance. It was this inquisitiveness that drove Soma Weiss ahead and led him to the height of his profession. He was recognized by Dr. Eugene F. Du Bois when he recommended him to Dr. Peabody "as the outstanding Cornell University Medical School graduate of the last three or four years; in fact one of the most brilliant men they have ever had."

Soma was appointed assistant at the Thorndike Memorial Laboratory and Research Fellow in the Department of Medicine of the Harvard Medical School as of September 1, 1925. He rose rapidly, demonstrating his great ability as an investigator, a teacher, an administrator and a clinician. In addition to these qualities his diplomatic handling of difficult situations, the ease with which he got on with individuals of varying personalities and from different walks of life, led me to persuade the Trustees of the Boston City Hospital to appoint Soma Director of the Second and Fourth Medical Services in September, 1932. In this position he also took charge in large part of the fourth year medical students and won their admiration and affection. One of the important contributions he made to teaching was in his development, with Doctor Parker, of the Clinico-Pathological Conference at the City Hospital. His own bi-weekly Pharmacological-Therapeutic Conference gave the students unusual insight into the use of drugs.

Soma possessed all the qualifications necessary to the great clinician. He was a master of observation. His ward rounds were excellent and while conducting them he never neglected the patients, the students, or the visiting physicians; he kept them all in proper balance while he dominated the whole. He wisely always insisted that clinical work must be the basis for the study of disease. He was not swayed by the pressure of the moment and he never succumbed to the fads which agitate medicine. Indefatigable energy and enthusiasm contributed to every stroke he took. This was evident in his investigative work in clinical medicine and clinical pharmacology which received international recognition. At first when he came to the Thorndike he worked with Herrman L. Blumgart on problems concerning human hemodynamics. Three years later, or five years after graduation in medicine, he had an assistant resident physician assigned to him, and before long he had two such men each year and usually one or two foreign or American research fellows and occasionally a student working with him.

He was a prolific writer and during Soma's fourteen years at the Thorndike he published, usually with one of his junior associates, about one hundred and fifty papers. The cardiovascular system particularly commanded his attention but he studied and wrote on many aspects of medicine. His interests were so broad and his influence permeated so widely that the bounds of his work are hard to assess but with every study he made, the sick man was the central object. It is not possible to select his most important communication but the three subjects I will refer to certainly are distinctive. He was one of the leaders in the modern school of cardiovascular experts who looked upon the heart as but one part of a dynamically functioning system, that is of the entire circulation. He felt that the greatest opportunities for creative work, not only as concerns peripheral circulatory phenomena, but in heart disease as well, lay in the study of the pathological-physiology of the circulation. To this creative work he richly contributed, and was one of the first to expound in modern physiological terms backed by experiments and observations of his own and of other physicians, the nature of heart failure, and particularly of left ventricular failure.

Soma presented this subject before the American College of Physicians at Baltimore in 1931, and about two years later with George P. Robb he wrote as follows on this topic, "On the basis of joint clinical and laboratory evidence one can definitely state that the syndrome of acute or subacute left ventricular failure suggested and discarded by a number of clinicians during the past century exists and plays a fundamental role in a large group of patients with heart disease." The syndrome is characterized by relative or absolute insufficiency of the left coronary circulation.

The next phase of his so versatile, and yet well integrated, investigative interests, was the elucidation of the clinical nature of the hypersensitive carotid sinus syndrome. In two monographs published in *MEDICINE* in 1933 and in 1935, the first with James P. Baker and the second with Eugene B. Ferris, Jr. and Richard B. Capps, he and his collaborators demonstrated the frequency of this condition and discussed its clinical and physiological nature in the causation of fainting and convulsions and the treatment thereof. In the last short paragraph of the summary of the 1935 paper, they noted the "Manifestations of the hyperactive carotid sinus reflex are the result of abnormalities in portions of the automatic nervous system rather than in the entire system." From here his interest in syncope, shock and sudden death continued and broadened.

There are no sharp lines of demarcation between one medical interest and another, or for that matter between medicine and a variety of disciplines. Soma fully realized that cross fertilization at the borderlines of knowledge can serve to develop new information. Coincident with the advances in the field of nutrition he observed some patients believed to have vitamin B complex deficiency and others with poor diets, in whom disturbance of the cardiovascular system could not be explained on the basis of factors recognized as being of etiological significance in circulatory failure. In 1936, with Robert W. Wilkins, he presented before the Association of American Physicians a paper entitled "The Nature of the Cardiovascular Disturbances and Vitamin Deficiency States," in which from a study of 12 cases and 85 more collected from about 900 records of various types of nutritional deficiencies, they were able to state "that dysfunction of the cardiovascular system may develop because of unbalanced food particularly lacking in vitamin B." About a year later these two men published an article expanding this work which clarified the condition of cardiac beri-beri. As time passed, Soma made it clear that beri-beri both with nervous and cardiovascular manifestations was not rare in North America, and at the Boston City Hospital existed in an least mild form in one case in 160 medical admissions. In Oriental beri-beri, polished rice plays a significant predisposing role, and in the Occident alcohol is the calorigenic substance frequently associated with deficient vitamin intake. He clearly showed that the cardiovascular manifestations of beri-beri are related to thiamin (vitamin Bl) deficiency and that the administration of thiamin may rapidly give relief. His interest in nutritional deficiency states as affecting the cardiovascular system did not stop with this work but was continued after he left the Thorndike.

His ability to help young men was amazing. He was able to stimulate their interest along definite lines of work and to help each one to accomplish his special object.

Soma knew well the importance of the patient as a whole and the fact that psychological disturbances might be at the root of an illness. As Reginald Fitz has written, "To work and teach as he did required not only remarkable industry but also omnivorous reading." One of his greatest contributions was that of a person who gave freely of the love of mankind.

When he left the Boston City Hospital he was honored by being appointed Consulting Physician to the hospital and to the Thorndike Memorial Laboratory. Although he did not go far away, the removal of his vivid and gay personality as well as his intellectual stimulus caused a great sense of loss to all the staff.

No appraisal of his character would be complete without mention of his kindness and thoughtfulness for others and his agreeable and charming manner which endeared him to all. He had hosts of friends and was welcomed everywhere. Others no doubt will take up his tasks where he left them and carry them forward on the paths he pointed out. But, however able and worthy, they cannot replace Soma in the hearts of those who felt his influence.

GEORGE R. MINOT

For the Disciples

I shall always remember my initial problem with Soma which began the morning of my arrival at the Thorndike. The patient was an elderly gentleman who had become so discouraged over repeated and undiagnosed fainting attacks that he had attempted suicide. Soma discovered that the attacks of fainting were associated with the swallowing of food, and he immediately applied the practical test. Swallowing food caused the heart rate to slow and the patient to feel faint. Since food ingestion proved to be a variable and transitory stimulus in reproducing the attacks, Soma connected a small rubber balloon to the end of a Reyfus tube, which, after testing on himself, he allowed the patient to swallow. Inflation of the balloon when properly placed would regularly reproduce the fainting attacks. Thus, we were able to study the circulatory abnormalities during the actual attack and to assay the effectiveness and modes of action of various drugs in reflex Stokes-Adams disease. In the three short weeks required to complete the study, we learned that the attack was caused by a reflex heart block; that the block occurred in the A-V node; that atropine prevented the block; that epinephrin and ephredin prevented asystole by inducing an ectopic ventricular rhythm; that barium chloride had no beneficial effect; and that digitalis and acetyl-choline accentuated the block. I learned the importance of independent interpretation of the patient's story and the need for imagination and curiosity in the daily practice of medicine, and began to realize that many things can be learned if the clinical tools at hand are properly utilized. One may well wonder about the reaction of the patient to all these procedures. He had the utmost faith in Soma, and was, in fact, the most cheerful member of the research team. He felt that Soma was interested in him as well as in his disease, and I think that the patient was correct in this belief, for when I last reminisced with Soma about this case, the two of them were still corresponding.

Those of us who were fortunate enough to have worked with Soma have discussed the relative importance of his various accomplishments and teachings during many informal gatherings. I believe a summary of these expressions may throw some additional light on the influence which he exerted and the manner in which he accomplished it.

On first acquaintance, one immediately sensed Soma's dynamic nature, his physiologic approach to clinical research and his broad background of knowledge in all fields of medicine. The enthusiastic spirit with which he approached all problems and the obvious pleasure which he attained in their solution was most contagious. His ability to make interesting the dullest case or the most tedious technical problem was one of his most impressive traits.

As time passed, those who worked closely with

Soma began to recognize the finer qualities by which he exerted such a marked influence, and to realize that his many talents were not inborn, but were attained by the familiar process of hard work and self-discipline. It was a rare but pleasant day when his associates arrived for work before Soma did. He not only exhibited great physical energy, but great mental energy as well; and in his thinking, he was able to eliminate all extraneous influences and concentrate solely on the task at hand. His associates would struggle along for weeks in the preparation of a paper while Soma with an afternoon in the Boston Medical Library and a night at home, would return in the morning with the paper completely organized and clarified. The discipline of his mental processes was apparent in his approach to the solution of clinical problems, in spite of his vivid imagination and many ideas. One can scarcely think of Soma without visualizing the little black notebook that he carried with him on all occasions, and in which he would jot down his own observations and mistakes and those of others. After a "cooling off" period, he would review and digest these notes and then file them himself. This file was an active and growing one, and Soma could produce these records of his previous experiences on a moment's notice. Thus, he could often prove his familiar expression, "I have seen it again and again."

Soma greatly influenced his young helpers both by his philosophy toward medical research and by his practical and dynamic methods of approach. His interest in research was not limited to the laboratory, but was maintained just as intensely in all his human contacts. His concept of the human body was that of an integrated organism, in which one part could not be fully understood without a knowledge of the other parts. He exemplified the idea that clinical research is not a monastic privilege, but depends for its survival on its practical benefits to the practice and teaching of medicine and to mankind in general.

He approached every problem in a practical manner and weighed the time and energy to be spent against the helpful knowledge to be gained. Although his knowledge of medical literature was most phenomenal, it did not interfere with his independence of thought. He encouraged his helpers first to work out a problem before delving too deeply into the thoughts of other investigators in the same field. Likewise, he disregarded any statement of opinion until he had studied the facts on which it was based; nor did he let custom or tradition stand in his way when it seemed to retard progress.

He preferred to use direct methods of proof, but when none were available, he would approach the problem indirectly from as many angles as possible, believing if all pointed in the same direction, the inference to be drawn was more likely to be correct. Being capable of utilizing most fields of experimental medicine, he was able to focus great light on the problems to be solved. As one of his helpers so aptly said, "Difficulties which often seemed insurmountable would melt away when brought to him; or if they really could not be destroyed, could be by-passed by probing around them in the manner of infiltration by a tank column, perhaps to be dealt with later by the infantry." Even if the study was failing its original purpose, Soma preferred that it be completed, because as he put it, one can learn a great deal from any experiment whether the original point is proved or not.

The relationship which Soma maintained between himself and his young associates was one to develop in them both independence of thought and energy output. He accepted each as an equal partner in a search for knowledge and maintained a free interchange of opinions and criticisms without rancor. He was quick to admit it when we proved him in error and never failed to acclaim our contributions. His youthful and humorous spirit made him a delightful as well as inspiring companion. Thus he made us feel that we need not defer to his position as chief, but only to his attainments. He let us recognize his shortcomings and watch how, by the constant application of hard work and self-discipline, he overcame them to become a great physician. And withal, he maintained a great dignity, based on the example which he set, the visible growth of understanding which he attained thereby, and his ever active interest in the intellectual development and personal happiness of each one of us.

EUGENE B. FERRIS

For the Peter Bent Brigham Hospital

The Brigham Hospital brings to this gathering its particular sense of a grievous loss. Soma Weiss satisfied for that Institution the ideal considerations for a chief of staff. He had youth which offered the happy expectation of many years of fruitful service; he was a highly competent physician, an indispensable requirement of those who care for the sick; he was a stimulating teacher and gathered around him pupils of all ages and of all types. Physicians who had long practiced their art in rural communities and research students fresh from the laboratories of the medical sciences found with him knowledge and inspiration. And finally he was possessed of an imagination and a sense of inquiry which garnered interest everywhere, often from what seemed to others of little consequence.

These qualities are rarely found linked together in a single individual. But in Dr. Weiss they fomented and served a personality that made his abilities as a teacher, a physician, and an administrator seem legendary even as early as 1938. Some of this arose because of his personal charm and cosmopolitanism. His modesty and unselfishness led always to his putting others first; his gracious manner avoided all possibility of conflict. His interest in details made him an intimate friend of all he met daily, and his help was always present and in a very personal sense. And his wide reading, capacious memory, and natural abilities set him apart. Moreover, there was firmness when necessity arose. This was reflected in the smoothness and directness with which his medical service carried on its labors. Intellectually he combined to an extraordinary degree the analytical powers of the scientist with the integrative faculty of a philosopher. And with these powers were the attributes of a generous and compassionate nature free of any taint of egocentricity.

His larger scientific interests broadened his character, and his association with scientific colleagues whose fields were often distant from medicine was the source of much value to his Hospital service. He took the best from the outside world and domesticated it in the Brigham Hospital. Therapeutic research which had languished at the Brigham Hospital now became revivified through his interest in pharmacology. A biochemical laboratory for the Hospital as a whole sprang into being under his eager spirit which was anxious to utilize every advance in modern medicine. A physiological laboratory was rejuvenated in rooms appropriately first occupied by Walter Boothby, where the first clinical studies were made of alterations of the resting metabolic rate and where our modern "basal metabolism" machines had their inception.

Not the least of his gifts to the Brigham Hospital were those which flowed continuously from the warmth and charm of his personality. These personal qualifications aided but never hid the eager constructive drive towards his ideals. They served to draw many within the vortex of his interests. It was natural that his family should suffer chiefly under this spell. His charming wife, so dear to many here today, was soon as much a part of the Brigham family as was her husband. And willy-nilly his good mother-in-law and father-in-law found their way thither, each in a different capacity but all sharing in Soma's drive onwards. This cyclone was entirely beneficent. Professor Sachs began to decorate our wards and proved to us that the bare walls dictated by the aseptic era not only were not made dangerous by beautiful pictures but that the spiritual uplift added a beneficial factor. Thus an artist rededicated the old medical axiom "do not forget the mind in treating the body." And Mrs. Sachs took to the fields - flowers and bushes, transplanted and nurtured by her own hands, brightened the mathematical areas between our wards. Here is proof that Soma Weiss was not the sort to bring to the Hospital only his technical equipment - all that he had he gave.

This type of man was bound to benefit everything he touched. The Nursing Service, the Social Service Department, the amplification of the Out-Door Department, all had their turn under his aegis and all profited. The Hospital took on a new coat of paint even, and this came not from a simple case of neatness but because of the "lift" a nice environment might give to pupils.

A chief tradition of the infant Brigham Hospital is that each and every one does his best for the care and comfort of the patients within its walls. This means first sympathy, understanding and expert care of all the patients, and second stimulating friendships among the staff, from students to Chiefs, that all in the hive may be happy and radiate this to patients. This tradition so forcefully begun by Henry Christian and Harvey Cushing has now been strengthened, sharpened and tempered by Soma Weiss. One cannot measure the care of patients in kilograms or centimeters; this function comes from the soul and is above the gauges and gadgets of all who work in laboratories. Soma Weiss was equipped above others with this spiritual capacity. We all recognize that institutions are made up of personalities; the shell is but bricks and dust, and certainly the success of institutions has much to do with the perpetuation of traditions. The lessons Soma Weiss added to this and other traditions will be carefully guarded and perpetuated down the years to help all who enter the doors of the Institution for which he so ardently labored.

But not only was he appreciated by his own staff and pupils. The Hospital Trustees, whose interested and generous stewardship play no small part in the Hospital's reputation and usefulness, soon became his warmest friends. Dr. Weiss recognized the financial difficulties which had come to the Hospital and in an understanding of the Trustees; problems he never complained about the limitations which these might place upon his hopes and ambitions. For the feelings of his colleagues I cannot give adequate expression. Soma Weiss bound men to his side with hoops of steel. His frank, generous and cheerful spirit dissolved worries, set aside difficulties and pointed the new and possible way ahead. Always there was something new in store, perhaps an additional associate or an increase in our laboratory facilities; again it was some way of bringing the Hospital to the attention of the public that we might possess a greater foundation on which to build our future. And the Hospital shared as a whole in everything he undertook. Just as in his conception of medical practice he always saw the whole individual and not only the diseased part, so he visualized the Hospital he served.

All this is but sampling the man. His full record stands for all time. Though the Brigham Hospital knew him as its Chief Physician but a short two and one-half years, the imprint of his spirit is cut deep in the annals of that Institution. His cheerful, buoyant spirit will long echo down that long line of communication known as the "pike." And we who benefited so greatly from his presence shall remember him as always happy. He seemed fitted in every way to the place, and he appeared to glow with the response which he so affectionately provoked.

ELLIOTT C. CUTLER

For the Undergraduate Students

Many of us here are students. Day after day we have come to these same halls to listen. But today our very presence here speaks - speaks more forcefully than any words that we can say. For today we sit in tribute to Dr. Weiss.

We in the fourth year class have known Dr. Weiss since he came to the Peter Bent Brigham Hospital as our professor. We first met him as a lecturer in clinical pathology, in physical diagnosis, and later in medicine. During our second year when we split into small groups to take clinical courses at the various hospitals, those of us who went to the Brigham again met Dr. Weiss, this time in conferences and small teaching groups. Again in the third and fourth years, those of us going to Brigham for clinical work met Dr. Weiss in the lecture room or in teaching groups, on ward rounds, in extracurricular groups, or at his home.

During this time, while in one way or another we were coming to know Dr. Weiss, we would compare notes about the Professor, as students are so apt to do. We were impressed by his clinical acumen and his ability to grasp any situation. His tremendous clinical knowledge, firmly based on wide general knowledge, was to the

fledgling student most awe-inspiring, yet certainly challenging. In small clinical groups his ability to emphasize
his points and to hold each man's attention by drawing
each into the discussion was unexcelled. His lectures,
well-prepared and justly popular, led us always several
steps beyond our previous horizons. Delivered in his characteristic accent and marked by that sentence structure
which was peculiarly his own, these lectures were impressive for their lucid thinking and amusing in their
many little oddities of expression. Many a session in
Vanderbilt Hall was enlivened by repetition of his color-
ful phraseology and quick wit. Fortunate was the
narrator who could even approximately mimic him.

But we soon learned that Dr. Weiss had a real
interest in us, and that it went well beyond our formal
contacts, and that despite his busy program he could find
time for each student and his individual problems. In one
instance a few students were seeking help in improving
certain conditions at Vanderbilt Hall. Such problems
would appear to be of little interest to a busy Professor
of Medicine, but this group found Dr. Weiss sincerely and
whole-heartedly interested and of great help in their cru-
sade. Similarly other groups found him a valued advisor.
He was particularly interested in promoting student discussion groups and in furthering student research
programs. He often invited whole student sections to his
home, and his, and his family's generous and spirited
hospitality helped relax even the most tense of his respectful guests.

He gave expression to his active interest in student
problems, when with characteristic thoroughness he or-

ganized his thoughts into a lecture entitled "The Medical Student Before and After Graduation," which was later published in the J.A.M.A. The principles he emphasized in this lecture guided both his teaching and his own clinical attitude. I remember a certain patient on the wards last summer, a case of periarteritis nodosa. As this rare and chronic disease was one of a group which had particularly interested Dr. Weiss, it would have been natural for his clinical enthusiasm to have carried him into a prolonged discussion of its pathological physiology. Actually, however, having clarified the disease picture by a brief discussion of its salient points, he spent the majority of his time in advising the patient how to adjust his life to his disease and in helping him plan a trip to California for rest. I remember clearly that what we students absorbed from that discussion was an understanding of the patient with periarteritis, rather than an academic picture of the disease. It is true that this is a principle not forgotten in modern medical teaching, and in this isolated instance it may seem a small thing that the brilliant clinician should be more interested in the patient than in the disease itself; yet in a lifetime it may have been this attitude that made the brilliant clinician into a great teacher of medicine.

As befits a great teacher, he was able to gather around him a group of younger men, who although promising in their own right, had visibly expanded under his guidance. Many of these younger men taught our student sections, and thus the influence of the "Chief" upon the students was multiplied many times. Likewise we have felt the impact of this personality strong in intellect and courage, good human and kindliness; and we, in our turn, will reflect this influence - a living heritage for students to come.

These thoughts find expression in this sonnet written by a close friend of Dr. Weiss:

He has not gone from us! Not when these halls
Throb with his presence! When continually
We seem to breathe in from the very walls
The essence of his rich vitality!
Forever in our hearts he is "The Chief,"
The Great Physician, teacher, guide and friend,
A gay blithe Spirit poised in bright relief
Against a world of pain. He could transcend
The narrow bounds of earth in daring flight.
And give us wings for pathless space above
Where we might soar in searching for the light
Of greater learning through our greater love;
But, of all the gifts that crowned his healing art,
The rarest was his understanding heart.
(Mary Koues Sachs)

WILLIAM E. WATTS

For Harvard University

We native Americans like to retain the ideal of America as a land of rich and inviting opportunity, a land where persons with ability can assuredly rise to positions of useful influence. We cherish also as an ideal a democracy in which there is freedom for everyone to serve his fellow men according to his talents. When these ideals are realized, as they were realized to a striking degree in the career of Soma Weiss, we have sound reasons for rejoicing. He came to the United States only twenty-two years ago, a stranger here, without friends or relatives to greet him. He was unacquainted with our ways. His native background in Hungary was that of a semi-feudal civilization. Though confronted with conditions which were wholly novel the young immigrant quickly became adapted to the liberties of democratic surroundings and began to demonstrate his remarkable endowments of mind and heart.

His special discipline in pharmacology in New York was followed by stimulating association with the Thorndike Memorial Laboratory at the Boston City Hospital. That experience began in 1925. Within four years young Dr. Weiss was appointed Assistant Professor of Medicine in Harvard University; in another four years he was advanced to an Associate Professorship; and seven years later (in 1939) he was given the most ancient professorial post of the Medical School - he was made the Hersey Professor of the Theory and Practice of Physic. In this honored chair he was the successor of such former worthies of Boston medical history as Benjamin Waterhouse, James Jackson, John Ware, George Cheyne Shattuck, Francis Minot and Reginold Heber Fitz. That is truly an astounding example of what America offers to a man who has outstanding natural gifts and skill.

The remarkable rise of Dr. Weiss to a commanding position in the University was matched by a nation-wide recognition of his ability. He was elected to the most important medical organizations in the country; he became an active member of the Council on Pharmacy and Chemistry of the American Medical Association; he gave expert judgment on the Committee appointed to revise the United States Pharmacopoeia. Invitations came to him from near and far to address professional meetings - invitations which took him across the continent to Seattle, far south to Dallas, and to other cities less distant.

These extramural services to medicine were not permitted, however, to interfere with devotion to his duties in faculty meetings and in wards and clinics, as a professor and as a physician. These duties are onerous; indeed, the burden borne by the professor of medicine who is also physician-in-chief of a hospital is almost intolerable. He has insistent obligations to patients, to the families of patients, to hospital trustees, to the students whom he teaches, to the internes whom he disciplines, to clinical investigators whose researches he directs, to the medical school as an organized body and to its committees, besides being expected to keep abreast of progress in the medical sciences as they contribute to improvement of medical practice. Dr. Weiss met not only these multitudinous demands; he accepted also appointments on various committees of the Medical School when his knowledge and wise counsel were called for. He was Chairman of two important continuing committees which required thoughtful consideration of recurrent problems. When a friend remarked to him that he was a very busy man, he replied that he thought the tasks of the Dean were more numerous and heavier than his and that those of the President of the University were even more oppressive than the Dean's - a cheerful grading of burdens that appeared to leave him with a relatively light load.

One of the greatest responsibilities laid upon Dr. Weiss was the chairmanship of the Committee on Pharmacotherapy. By action of the University authorities a plan was initiated to bring into cooperation hospital clinics, the Department of Pharmacology of the Medical School and the efforts of organic chemists in Cambridge, all working toward advances in the treatment of disease. The hope was expressed that this enterprise would help to lift pharmacology up from the poverty into which it had fallen in the United States, that young men would be encouraged to engage in pharmacological investigation and become experts in a sadly slighted field of great medical value, and that contributions might result that would bring relief to the sick and the distressed. Dr. Weiss's early training in pharmacology in New York, added to his confident use of therapy in the treatment of patients during nearly a score of years, and the high reputation he had gained for wisdom and reliability, made his appointment as leader in this expectant undertaking most appropriate. As a consequence of the hope thus held forth the University received from interested parties the promise of generous support of the plan for a series of years. When, last autumn, the diverse interests concerned with pharmacotherapy met in conference the central figure was Soma Weiss; one could only look with admiration on his mastery of the occasion, for his extensive and varied experience permitted him to turn to every interest which was represented and offer suggestions and comments with appreciative insight and understanding.

It might be supposed that the numerous demands on his time would have left him with little chance to do more than carry on a routine of daily duties. That, however, was not true. During the short period of two and a half years, while he was responsible to the University as professor of medicine and to the Hospital as chief physician, he published more than thirty articles - reports of cases, editorials, summaries of bedside observations, addresses to medical societies, accounts of clinical researches - besides bringing out, in cooperation with one of his disciples, a book recording an elaborate investigation into the toxemia of pregnancy. For years his investigative concern had been directed towards learning as much as possible about disorders of the circulatory system. So well known were his contributions in this realm that when Professor Heymans, Nobel Laureate in Medicine for 1938, was here as Dunham Lecturer, he proposed to Dr. Weiss that they collaborate in writing a treatise on the normal and pathological aspects of control of the heart and blood vessels - a project rudely shattered by the outbreak of war.

In his attitude towards the conflict of ideologies now raging throughout the world there was no question as to Dr. Weiss's stand. He wholeheartedly supported the struggle for preservation of individual liberty. His own life had revealed the enticing possibilities which that liberty presents to the gifted and the eager. The United States was his chosen land and he was devoted to its purposes. When the opportunity arose for him to engage in conducting tests which were fundamentally important for providing on a large scale the means of giving to wounded men, in peril from shock or hemorrhage, a life-saving treatment, he gladly accepted it and was actively engaged in the work when death intervened.

A survey of Soma Weiss's brilliant career after his arrival in the United States proves that he rose to eminence in his profession and enjoyed the respect and affection of all who knew him, solely because of the golden qualities of his unique personality and his unselfish devotion to the highest standards of medical service. In making his own way upward he became accustomed to independence and self-reliance. An inner core of firmly established integrity and idealism in his character assured him steadiness and poise. In discussions - at faculty meetings, for example - he was frank and courageous in expressing his views, an attitude emerging directly from large experience, clear thinking and well-tried convictions. A quick appreciation of humor, and a readiness to use it on appropriate occasions, flashed moments of lightness into his remarks, whether in debate or in conversation.

Perhaps the most valuable of Soma Weiss's services in the Medical School was as a teacher. He never forgot that he was training young men to go forth to care for human beings afflicted in body and in mind - "there is a mental element," he wrote, "in every disease." He gave himself lavishly to making sure that students understood as clearly as he himself the nature of the disease and the proper treatment of the patient. And the students perceived his earnest wish that they should know and were gratefully appreciative. His unfailing kindness and cheerfulness, his sympathetic insight, his evident sincerity, and his generous spending of time and effort became known to a host of beginners in their medical careers.

What is the significance of a man's life? Surely not the number of years he has lived. The years are significant only as they are filled with worthy deeds - deeds which may have unlimited beneficent consequences. It has been said that a teacher affects eternity, for no one can ever tell where his influence will stop. When a great teacher is also a great physician he affects eternity to a magnified degree; his influences reach onward through his disciples whom he has inspired and also through the useful lives he has prolonged. The years of Soma Weiss reached scarcely beyond two score, only half of them spent with us in our land. But calmly estimating his career who would deny that in passing from us he is one of the immortal dead who lives again in the men and women who have felt the beauty and the strength of his spirit

and who will pass it on to others through unnumbered
years to come.

WALTER B. CANNON

Curriculum Vitae

Soma Weiss

Birthplace and date: Bestercze, **Hungary**; January 27, 1899

Education: A.B., 1921, Columbia University
              M.D., 1923, Cornell University

Experience:

1917-1918 -   Demonstrator, Institute of Physiology, Royal Hungarian University, Budapest

1918-1920 -   Demonstrator and Research Fellow, Institute of Biochemistry, Royal Hungarian University, Budapest

1920-1923 -   Assistant, Department of Pharmacology, Cornell University Medical School

1923-1925 -   Intern, Bellevue Hospital, New York City

1925-1929 -   Assistant, Thorndike Memorial Laboratory, Boston City Hospital

1925-1926 -   Research Fellow, Department of Medicine, Harvard Medical School

1926-1927 -   Assistant, Department of Medicine, Harvard Medical School

1927-1928 -   Instructor, Department of Medicine, Harvard Medical School

1928-1929 -   Faculty Instructor, Department of Medicine, Harvard Medical School

1927-1929 -   Assistant Physician, Boston City Hospital

1929-1939 - Associate Physician, Thorndike Memorial
            Laboratory, Boston City Hospital
1929-1932 - Assistant Professor of Medicine, Harvard
            Medical School
1930-1932 - Assistant Director, Thorndike Memorial
            Laboratory, Boston City Hospital
1932-1939 - Associate Professor of Medicine, Harvard
            Medical School
1932-1939 - Director of the Second and Fourth Medical
            Services (Harvard), Boston City Hospital
1939-1942 - Physician-in-Chief, Peter Bent Brigham
            Hospital
1939-1942 - Hersey Professor of the Theory and Practice
            of Physic, Harvard University

Publications

1.   Weiss, S. Ueber die Bedeutung des erhoehten
      respirationen Quotienten bei forcieter Atmung
      und erhoehter Muskelarbeit. Biochemische
      Zeitschrift 101:7, 1919.

2.   Weiss, S. Ueber die Bedeutung des erhoehten
      respirationen Quotienten bei forcieter Atmung
      und erhoehter Muskelarbeit. Biochemische
      Zeitschrift 121:40, 1921.

3.   Weiss, S. Uber Spontankontraktionen uberle-
      bender Arterien. Pflugers Archiv fur die gesamte
      Physiologie des Menchen und der Tiere 81:213,
      1920.

4.   Weiss, S., and Hatcher, R.A. Tincture of digitalis
      and the infustion in therapeutics. J.A.M.A. 76508,
      1921.

5.   Hatcher, R.A., and Weiss, S. The seat of the emet-
      ic action of the digitalis bodies. Arch. Int. Med.
      29:690, 1922.

6.   Weiss, S., and Hatcher, R.A. Studies on strychnin.
      J. Pharmacol. Exp. Therap. 19: 419, 1922.

7.   Hatcher, R.A., and Weiss, S. Studies on vomiting.
      J. Pharmacol. Exp. Therap. 22:139, 1923.

8.   Weiss, S. Some modifications of the Emil Fisher's
      micropolarimeter. Proc. Soc. Exp. Biol. Med.
      20:202, 1923.

9.   Weiss, S., and Hatcher, R.A. The mechanism of
      the vomiting induced by antimony and potassium
      tartrate (Tartar Emetic). J. Exp. Med. 37:97, 1923.

10.   Weiss, S., and Hatcher, R.A. Study of a digitalis
      body which is elminated rapidly after its intrave-
      nous injection in the cat. J. Am. Pharmaceutical
      Assoc. 12:26, 1923.

11.   Weiss, S. A study of the action of calcium in ex-
      perimental cocaine poisoning. J.A.M.A. 81:1282,
      1923.

12.   Morris, R.M., Witter, M.S., and Weiss, S. An un-
      usual sensitzing action of thyroid substance on the
      effect of epinephrine in man. Proc. Soc. Exp. Biol.
      Med. 21:149, 1923.

13.   Weiss, S. Ichtiol. J.A.M.A. 82:565, 1924.

14.   DeGraff, A.C., and Weiss, S. Observations on the
       mechanism of complete heart block in man. Proc.
       Soc. Exp. Biol. Med. 21:333, 1924.

15.   Weiss, S., and Kennedy, F. Clinical experiments in
       myotonia congenita (Thomsen) with especial ref-
       erence to the parasympathetic nervous system.
       Arch. Neurol. Psych. 11:543, 1924.

16.   Weiss, S. A clinical and experimental investigation
       of arsphenamine poisoning. J.A.M.A. 84:577,
       1925.

17.   Martin, H.E., and Weiss, S. The use of physostig-
       min in abdominal distention. J.A.M.A. 84:1407,
       1925.

18.   Weiss, S. Persistence of action of physostigmin and
       the atropine-physostigmin antagonism in animals
       and in man. J. Pharmacol. Exp. Therap. 27:181,
       1926.

19.   Weiss, S. Anesthesia induced by barbituric acid
       derivatives with special reference to associated
       blood sugar changes. Proc. Soc. Exp. Biol. Med.
       23:363, 1926.

20.   DeGraff, A.C., and Weiss, S. Observations on the
       extrinsic nervous control of the auricles and ven-
       tricles in complete auriculo-ventricular block in
       man. J. Clin. Invest. 2:227, 1926.

21.   Weiss, S., and Hatcher, R.A. A method for the
       quantitative determination of small amounts of

quinin and quinidin with bromin water. Proc. Soc. Exp. Biol. Med. 23:33, 1925.

22. Weiss, S., with Blumgart, H. The velocity of blood flow in health and disease. J. Clin. Invest. 2:600, 1926.

23. Weiss, S., with Blumgart, H Clinical observations on the velocity of blood flow in auricular fibrillation and in emphysema. Trans. Assoc. Am. Phys. 41:294, 1926.

24. Hatcher, R.A., and Weiss, S. Studies on quinin. J. Pharmacol. Exp. Therap. 29:279, 1926.

25. Weiss, S., and Hatcher, R.A. II. Studies on quinin. J. Pharmacol. Exp. Therap. 30:327, 1927.

26. Weiss, S., and Hatcher, R.A. III. Studies on quinidin. J. Pharmacol. Exp. Therap. 30:335, 1927.

27. Weiss, S. The action of atropin, quinin, quinidin, and ouabain on the fibrillation of skeletal muscles. Proc. Soc. Exp. Biol. Med. 23:567, 1926.

28. Blumgart, H.L., and Weiss, S. The velocity of venous blood to the right heart in man. Proc. Soc. Exp. Biol. Med. 23:694, 1926.

29. Norris, V.H., and Weiss, S. The pharmacological and therapeutic properties of alpha-lobelin. A comparison of its action on the respiratory center with that of other respiratory stimulants. J. Pharmacol. Exp. Therap. 31:43, 1927.

30. Blumgart, H.L., and Weiss, S. Studies on the veloc-

ity of blood flow. II. The velocity of blood flow in normal resting individuals and a critique of the method used. J. Clin. Invest. 4:15, 1927.

31.   Blumgart, H.L., and Weiss, S. Studies on the velocity of blood flow. III. The velocity of blood flow and its relation to other aspects of the circulation in patients with rheumatic and syphilitic heart disease. J. Clin. Invest. 4:149, 1927.

32.   Weiss, S. Acute hemorrhagic nephritis. Boston Med. Surg. J. 196:178, 1927.

33.   Blumgart, H.L., and Weiss, S. Studies on the velocity of blood flow. IV. The velocity of blood flow and its relation to other aspects of the circulation in patients with arteriosclerosis and in patients with arterial hypertension. J. Clin. Invest. 4:173, 1927.

34.   Blumgart, H.L., and Weiss, S. Studies on the velocity of blood flow. V. The physiological and the pathological significance of the velocity of blood flow. J. Clin. Invest. 4:199, 1927.

35.   Blumgart, H.L., and Weiss, S. Studies on the velocity of blood flow. VI. The method of collecting the active deposits of radium and its preparation for intravenous injection. J. Clin. Invest. 4:389, 1927.

36.   Blumgart, H.L., and Weiss, S. Studies on the velocity of blood flow. VII. The pulmonary circulation time in normal resting individuals. J. Clin. Invest. 4:399, 1927.

37.   Weiss, S., and Blumgart, H.L. Studies on the veloc-

ity of blood flow. VIII. The velocity of blood flow and its relation to other aspects of the circulation in patients with pulmonary emphysema. J. Clin. Invest. 4:555, 1927.

38.   Weiss, S. The clinical aspect of obstructive diseases of the common bile-duct. Med. Clinics No. America 10:1183, 1927.

39.   Ritvo, M., and Weiss, S. Physostigmine as an aid in gastrointestinal roentgen-ray diagnosis. Am. J. Roentg. Radium Therapy 18:301, 1927.

40.   Gettler, A.O., Rhoads, C.P., and Weiss, S. A contribution to the pathology of generalized argyria with a discussion of the fate of silver in the human body. Am. J. Pathol. 3:631, 1927.

41.   Hatcher, R.A., and Weiss, S. Reflex vomiting from the heart. The mechanism of vomiting induced by digitalis bodies. J.A.M.A. 89:429, 19.27.

42.   Blumgart, H.L., and Weiss, S. Clinical studies on the velocity of blood flow. IX. The pulmonary circulation time, the velocity of venous blood flow to the heart, and related aspects of the circulation in patients with cardiovascular disease. J. Clin. Invest. 5:343, 1928.

43.   Blumgart, H.L., and Weiss, S. Clinical studies on the velocity of blood flow. X. The relation between the velocity of blood flow, the venous pressure and the vital capacity of the lungs in fifty patients with cardiovascular disease compared with similar measurements in fifty normal persons. J. Clin. In-

vest. 5:379, 1928.

44.   Hatcher, R.A., and Weiss, S. The seat of the emetic
       action of the digitalis bodies. J. Pharmacol. Exp.
       Therap. 32:37, 1928.

45.   Weiss, S., and Rhoads, C.P. Healing and healed
       vegetative (subacute bacterial) endocarditis. New
       Engl. J. Med. 199:70, 1928.

46.   Weiss, S., and Davis, D. The significance of the
       afferent impulses from the skin in the mechanism
       of visceral pain. Am. J. Med. Sci. 176:517, 1928.

47.   Blumgart, H.L., and Weiss, S. Clinical studies on
       the velocity of blood flow. XI. The pulmonary cir-
       culation time, the minute volume blood flow
       through the lungs, and the quantity of blood in the
       lungs. J. Clin. Invest. 6:103, 1928.

48.   Weiss, S., and Blumgart, H.L. The effect of the
       digitalis bodies on the velocity of blood flow
       through the lungs and on other aspects of the cir-
       culation. A study of normal subjects and patients
       with cardiovascular disease. J. Clin. Invest. 7:11,
       1929.

49.   Weiss, S., Lennos, W.G., and Robb, G.P. The dila-
       tor effect of histamine on the cerebral vessels in
       man. Proc. Soc. Exp. Biol. Med. 26:706, 1929.

50.   Hochrein, M., and Weiss, S. The pneumotacho-
       graph in certain intrathoracic diseases. Its
       diagnostic value. Arch. Int. Med. 44:289, 1929.

51.   Weiss, S., Robb, G.P., and Blumgart, H.L. The ve-

locity of blood flow in health and disease as measured by the effect of histamine on the minute vessels. Am. Heart J. 4:664, 1929.

52.   Weiss, S. The nature and management of cerebral hemiplegia in patients with arterial hypertension. Med. Clinics No. America 13:111, 1929.

53.   Weiss, S. Therapeutic indications and the dangers of the intravenous administration of sodium-phenyl-ethyl barbiturate (sodium luminal) and other barbituric acid derivatives. Am. J. Med. Sci. 178:390, 1929.

54.   Mallory, G.K., and Weiss, S. Hemorrhages from lacerations of the cardiac orifice of the stomach due to vomiting. Am. J. Med. Sci. 178:506, 1929.

55.   Ellis, L.B., and Weiss, S. The measurement of capillary pressure under natural conditions and after arteriolar dilatation; in normal subjects and in patients with arterial hypertension and with arteriosclerosis. J. Clin. Invest. 8:47, 1929.

56.   Weiss, S., and (by invitation) Ellis, L.B. The dynamics of the circulation in hypertension, and its bearing on therapy. J. Clin. Invest. 7:490, 1929.

57.   Weiss, S., and Ellis, L.B. Circulatory measurements in patients with rheumatic heart disease before and after the administration of digitalis. J. Clin. Invest. 8:435, 1930.

58.   MacMahon, H.E., and Weiss, S. Carbon tetrachloride poisoning with macroscopic fat in the pul-

monary artery. Am. J. Pathol. 5:623, 1929.

59.   Riseman, J.E.F., and Weiss, S. The age and sex incidence of arterial hypertension. Am. Heart J. 5:172, 1929.

60.   Shaw, L.A., Messer, A.C., and Weiss, S. Cutaneous respiration in man. I. Factors affecting the rate of carbon dioxide elimination and oxygen absorption. Am. J. Physiol. 90:107, 1929.

61.   Weiss, S., and Frazier, W.R. The density of the surface capillary bed of the forearm in health, in arterial hypertension, and in arteriosclerosis. Am. Heart J. 5:511, 1930.

62.   Weiss, S. The development of the clinical concept of arterial hypertension. New Engl. J. Med. 202:891, 1930.

63.   Weiss, S., and Ellis, L.B. The quantitative aspects and dynamics of the circulatory mechanism in arterial hypertension. Am. Heart J. 5:448, 1930.

64.   Riseman, J.E.F., and Weiss, S. The symptomatology of arterial hypertension. Am. J. Med. Sci. 180:47, 1930.

65.   Ellis, L.B., and Weiss, S. The local and systemic effects of arterio-venous fistula on the circulation in man. Am. Heart J. 5:635, 1930.

66.   Weiss, S., and Ellis, L.B. The rational treatment of arterial hypertension. J.A.M.A. 95:846, 1930.

67.   Weiss, S., and Manary, J.W. The care of ambula-

tory patients and the teaching of undergraduate medical students in the medical Out-Patient Department of the Boston City Hospital. In Methods and Problems of Medical Education, 18th series, The Rockefeller Foundation, New York, 1930.

68.   Weiss, S. The normal arterial blood pressure and its measurement. New Engl. J. Med. 204:600, 1931.

69.   Ellis, L.B., and Weiss, S. Studies in complete heart block. I. The cardiac output and the peripheral circulatory mechanism. Am. J. Med. Sci. 182:195, 1931.

70.   Patek, A., and Weiss, S. The tonus of the autonomic nervous system in arterial hypertension. New Engl. J. Med. 205:330, 1931.

71.   Weiss, S. Circulatory adjustments in heart disease: A concept of circulatory failure. Ann. Int. Med. 5:100, 1931.

72.   Weinstein, A.A., and Weiss, S. The significance of the potassium-calcium ratio and of the inorganic phosphorus and cholesterol of the blood serum in arterial hypertension. Arch. Int. Med. 48:478, 1931.

73.   Weiss, S., and Lennox, W.G. The cerebral circulation. XVII. Cerebral blood flow and the vasomotor response of the minute vessels of the human brain to histamine. Arch. Neruol. Psych. 26:737, 1931.

74.   Weiss, S. The effects of the digitalis bodies on the

nervous system: An analysis of the mechanism of cardiac slowing, nausea, and vomiting, psychosis, and visual disturbance following digitalis therapy. Med. Clinics No. America 15:963, 1932.

75. Davis, D., and Weiss, S. Rheumatic heart disease: I. Incidence and role in the causation of death. A study of 5,215 consecutive necropsies. Am. Heart J. 7:146, 1931.

76. Ellis, L.B., and Weiss, S. A study of the cardiovascular responses in man to the intravenous and intra-arterial injection of acetylcholine. J. Pharmacol. Exp. Therap. 44:235, 1932.

77. Weiss, S., Robb, G.P., and Ellis, L.B. The systemic effects of histamine in man. With special reference to the responses of the cardiovascular system. Arch. Int. Med. 49:360, 1932.

78. Weiss, S., and Mallory, G.K. Lesions of the cardiac orifice of the stomach produced by vomiting. J.A.M.A. 98:1353, 1932.

79. Robb, G.P., and Weiss, S. Effect of digitalis and rest on pulmonary and peripheral circulation in patients with circulatory failure caused by heart disease. Proc. Soc. Exp. Biol. Med. 29:1231, 1932.

80. Weiss, S. The interpretation of syndromes associated with arterial hypertension. New Engl. J. Med. 207:165, 1932.

81. Weiss, S. The use of ephedra in Asiatic medicine and rituals. New Engl. J. Med. 207:494, 1932.

82.   Davis, D., Goode, E.U., and Weiss, S. Localization of afferent visceral impulses in the spinal cord. Arch. Int. Med. 50:470, 1932.

83.   Weiss, S. The interaction between emotional states and the cardiovascular system in health and in disease. Emanuel Libman Anniversary Volumes 3:1181, 1932.

84.   Davis, D., and Weiss, S. Rheumatic heart disease. II. Incidence and distribution of the age of death. Am. Heart J. 8:182, 1932.

85.   Weiss, S., and Robb, G.P. The treatment of cardiac asthma (paroxysmal cardiac dyspnea). Med. Clinics No. America 16:961, 1933.

86.   Weiss, S., and Baker, J.P. Dizziness, fainting and convulsions due to hyperactivity of the carotid sinus reflex. Proc. Soc. Exp. Biol. Med. 30:614, 1933.

87.   Ellis, L.B., and Weiss, S. Renal function in arterial hypertension. J.A.M.A. 100:875, 1933.

88.   Davis, D., and Weiss, S. The relation of subacute and acute bacterial endocarditis to rheumatic endocarditis. A study of 66 cases with necropsies. New Engl. J. Med. 208:619, 1933.

89.   Weiss, S., Parker, F. Jr., and Robb, G.P. A correlation of the hemodynamics, function, and histologic structure of the kidney in malignant arterial hypertension with malignant nephrosclerosis. Ann. Int. Med. 6:1599, 1933.

90.   Robb, G.P., and Weiss, S. A method for the mea-
       surement of the velocity of the pulmonary and
       peripheral venous blood flow in man. Am. Heart
       J. 8:650, 1933.

91.   Weiss, S., and Robb, G.P. Cardiac asthma (parox-
       ysmal cardiac dyspnea), and the syndrome of left
       ventricular failure. J.A.M.A. 100:1841, 1933.

92.   Weiss, S., and Minot, G.R. Nutrition in relation to
       arteriosclerosis. In Arteriosclerosis, A Survey of
       the Problem, Chapter 8, pg 233, 1933.

93.   Weiss, S., and Ellis, L.B. Influence of sodium nitrite
       on the cardiovascular system and on renal activi-
       ty, in health, in arterial hypertension and in renal
       disease. Arch. Int. Med. 52:105, 1933.

94.   Ellis, L.B., and Weiss, S. Normal variations in
       renal function tests with discussion of their phys-
       iologic significance. Am. J. Med. Sci. 186:233,
       1933.

95.   Ellis, L.B., and Weiss, S. The renal function in per-
       sons with one kidney. Am. J. Med. Sci. 186:242,
       1933.

96.   Weiss, S. Circulatory disturbances of the extrem-
       ities: Medical aspects. New Engl. J. Med. 209:267,
       1933.

97.   Weiss, S., and Ellis, L.B. Arterial hypertension and
       arteriosclerosis associated with Raynaud's syn-
       drome. Am. Heart J. 8:761, 1933.

98.   Weiss, S., and Baker, J.P. The carotid sinus reflex

in health and disease. Its role in the causation of fainting and convulsions. Medicine 12:297, 1933.

99. Weiss, S., and Davis, D. Rheumatic heart disease. III. Embolic manifestations. Am. Heart J. 9:45, 1933.

100. Weiss, S. Drugs used in the treatment of cardiovascular diseases: I. Epinephrine and ephedrine groups. Modern Concepts id. Dis. 3:   , 1934.

101. Weiss, S. Drugs used in the treatment of cardiovascular diseases: II. Caffeine, camphor, and strychnine groups. Modern Concepts id. Dis. 3:   , 1934.

102. Capps, R.B., Ferris, E.B., Taylor, F.H.L., and Weiss, S. Role of pressor substances in etiology of arterial hypertension. Proc. Soc. Exp. Biol. Med. 31:1106, 1934.

103. Robb, G.P., and Weiss, S. The velocity of pulmonary and peripheral venous blood flow and related aspects of the circulation in cardiovascular disease. Am. Heart J. 9:742, 1934.

104. Weiss, S. The etiology of arterial hypertension. Ann. Int. Med. 8:296, 1934.

105. Weiss, S., and Ellis, L.B. The comparative effects of the intravenous administration to man of acetylcholine and acetyl-b-methylcholine. J. Pharmacol. Exp. Therap. 52:113, 1934.

106. Weiss, S., and (by invitation) Ferris, E.B. Jr., and Capps, R.B. The influence of reflexes in the induc-

tion of intracardiac disturbances. Trans. Assoc. Am. Phys. 49:177, 1934.

107.   Weiss, S., and Ferris, E.B. Jr. Adams-Stokes syndrome with transient complete heart block of vasgovagal reflex origin. Mechanism and treatment. Arch. Int. Med. 54:931, 1934.

108.   Weiss, S. The clinical course of spontaneous dissecting aneurysm of the aorta. Med. Clincs No. America 18:117, 1935.

109.   Weiss, S., and Ellis, L.B. Oxygen utilization and lactic acid production in the extremities during rest and exercise. Arch. Int. Med. 55:665, 1935.

110.   Davis, D., and Weiss, S. Rheumatic heart disease. IV. The life history of the severe form of the disease. Am. Heart J. 10:486, 1935.

111.   Weiss, S. Diseases of the heart and blood vessels. Practitioners Library of Med. & Surg. 8:623, Chapter 7, D. Appleton, 1935.

112.   Schwab, R.S., and Weiss, S. The neurologic aspect of leukemia. Am. J. Med. Sci. 189:766, 1935.

113.   Weiss, S. Syncope and related syndromes. Oxford Medicine 2:250(9), Chapter 8-A, 1935.

114.   Capps, R.B., Ferris, E.B. Jr., Taylor, F.H.L., and Weiss, S. Role of pressor substances in arterial hypertension. Arch. Int. Med. 56:864, 1935.

115.   Ferris, E.B. Jr., Capps, R.B., and Weiss, S. Carotid sinus syncope and its bearing on the

mechanism of the unconscious state and convulsions. Medicine 14:377, 1935.

116. Weiss, S. The indications and dangers of sedatives and hypnotics with special reference to the barbituric acid derivatives. Intl. Clinics 1:39, 1936.

117. Weiss, S. Recent advances in the treatment of arterial hypertension. Med. Clinics No. America 19:1343, 1936.

118. Weiss, S. Surgical operation for high blood pressure. New Engl. J. Med. 214:543, 1936.

119. Walker, I.J., Weiss, S., and Nye, R.N. Salmonella suipestifer infection with surgical complications. New Engl. J. Med. 214:567, 1936.

120. Weiss, S., Clinical medicine as a university discipline. Harvard Med. Alumni Bull. 10:37, 1936.

121. Haynes, F.W., Ellis, L.B., and Weiss, S. Pulse wave velocity and arterial elasticity in arterial hypertension, arteriosclerosis, and related conditions. Am. Heart J. 11:385, 1936.

122. Weiss, S., Haynes, F.L., and Shore, R. The relation of arterial pulse pressure to the hemodynamics of arterial hypertension. Am. Heart J. 11:402, 1936.

123. Weiss, S. Case records of the Massachusetts General Hospital. Case 22151. Differential diagnosis. New Engl. J. Med. 214:733, 1936.

124. Ellis, L.B., and Weiss, S. Vasomotor disturbance and edema associated with cerebral hemiplegia.

Arch. Neurol. Psych. 36:362, 1936.

125. Weiss, S., Capps, R.B., Ferris, E.B. Jr., and Munro, D. Syncope and convulsions due to a hyperactive carotid sinus reflex. Diagnosis and treatment. Arch. Int. Med. 58:407, 1936.

126. Parker, F. Jr., and Weiss, S. The nature and significance of the structural changes in the lungs in mitral stenosis. Am. J. Pathol. 12:573, 1936.

127. Zoll, P.M., and Weiss, S. Electrocardiographic changes in rats deficient in vitamin B1. Proc. Soc. Exp. Biol. Med. 35:259, 1936.

128. Weiss, S., and Wilkins, R.W. The nature of the cardiovascular disturbances in vitamin deficiency states. Trans. Assoc. Am. Phys. 51:341, 1936.

129. Weiss, S. The relationship of vitamin deficiency and cardiovascular dysfunction. In the Minutes of the New England Heart Association. New Engl. J. Med. 215:1258, 1936.

130. Weiss, S. The clinical use and dangers of hypnotics. J.A.M.A. 107:2104, 1936.

131. Weiss, S., Wilkins, R.W., and Haynes, F.W. The nature of circulatory collapse induced by sodium nitrite. J. Clin. Invest. 16:73, 1937.

132. Wilkins, R.W., Haynes, F.W., and Weiss, S. The role of the venous system in circulatory collapse induced by sodium nitrite. J. Clin. Invest. 16:85, 1937.

133.   Weiss, S. Case records of the Massachusetts General Hospital. Case 23011. Differential diagnosis. New Engl. J. Med. 216:23, 1937.

134.   Wilkins, R.W., Taylor, F.H.L., and Weiss, S. Bisulphite binding substances in the blood in health and in disease, particularly vitamin B1 deficiency. Proc. Soc. Exp. Biol. Med. 35:584, 1937.

135; Ferris, E.B. Jr., Capps, R.B., and Weiss, S. Relation of the carotid sinus to the autonomic nervous system and the neuroses. Arch. Neurol. Psych. 37:365, 1937.

136.   Weiss, S., and Wilkins, R.W. Syncope, collapse and shock: their medical significance and their treatment. Med. Clinics No. America 1:481, 1937.

137.   Weiss, S., and Sprague, H.B. Vagal reflex irritability and the treatment of paroxysmal auricular tachycardia with Ipecac. Am. J. Med. Sci. 194:53, 1937.

138.   Weiss, S., and Wilkins, R.W. The nature of the cardiovascular disturbances in nutritional deficiency states (Beriberi.). Ann. Int. Med. 11:104, 1937.

139.   Weiss, S., and Wilkins, R.W. Myocardial abscess with perforation of the heart. Am. J. Med. Sci. 194:199, 1937.

140.   Weiss, S., and Wilkins, R.W. Disturbance of the cardiovascular system in nutritional deficiency. J.A.M.A. 109:786, 1937.

141. Taylor, F.H.L., Weiss, S., and Wilkins, R.W. The bisulphite binding power of the blood in health and in disease with special reference to vitamin B1 deficiency. J. Clin. Invest. 16:833, 1937.

142. Weiss, S. The intoxications. In Cecil's Textbook of Medicine, 4th Edition, Philadelphia, pg 556, 1937.

143. Wilkins, R.W., Weiss, S., and Haynes, F.W. The effect of epinephrin in circulatory collapse induced by sodium nitrite. J. Clin. Invest. 17:41, 1938.

144. Weiss, S. Cardiovascular manifestations of beriberi. Modern Concepts id. Dis. 7:   , 1938.

145. Weiss, S., Haynes, F.W., and Zoll, P.M. Electrocardiographic manifestations and the cardiac effect of drugs in vitamin B1 deficiency in rats. Am. Heart J. 15:206, 1938.

146. Wilkins, R.W., Weiss, S., and Taylor, F.H.L. Relationship of pyruvic acid to the bisulphite binding substances of the blood. Proc. Soc. Exp. Biol. Med. 38:296, 1938.

147. Weiss, S. Dissecting aneurysm of the aorta. Two cases with unusual features. New Engl. J. Med. 218:512, 1938.

148. Weiss, S. Case records of the Massachusetts General Hospital. Case 24201. Differential diagnosis. New Engl. J. Med. 218:838, 1938.

149. Weiss, S. The Application of Electrocardiography in the Detection of Avitaminosis B-1. In Nutrition: The Newer Diagnostic Methods. Proc. Round Ta-

ble on Nutrition and Public Health, 16th Annual Conference, Milbank Memorial Fund, March 29-31, 1938, New York, pg 82, 1938.

150. Weiss, S., and (by invitation) Parker, F. Jr. Vascular changes in pyelonephritis and their relation to arterial hypertension. Trans. Assoc. Am. Phys. 53:60, 1938.

151. Weiss, S. The regulation and disturbance of the cerebral circulation through extracerebral mechanisms. Proc. Assoc. Res. Nervous & Mental Dis. 18:571, 1938.

152. Wilkins, R.W., Weiss, S., and Taylor, F.H.L. The effect and rate of removal of pyruvic acid administered to normal persons and to patients with and without "vitamin B deficiency." Ann. Int. Med. 12:938, 1939.

153. Kunkel, P., Stead, E.A. Jr., and Weiss, S. Blood flow and vasomotor reactions in the hand, forearm, foot, and calf in response to physical and chemical stimuli. J. Clin. Invest. 18:225, 1939.

154. Weiss, S. Chemical structure: biological action: therapeutic effect. New Engl. J. Med. 220:906, 1939.

155. Muus, J., Weiss, S., and Hastings, A.B. Tissue metabolism in vitamin deficiencies. II. Effect of thiamine deficiency. J. Biol. Chem. 129:303, 1939.

156. Weiss, S. Diseases of the heart and the aorta which are not well recognized. Med. Clinics No.

America 23:1323, 1939.

157. Weiss, S., and Parker, F. Jr. Pyelonephritis: its relation to vascular lesions and to arterial hypertension. Medicine 18:221, 1939.

158. Stead, E.A. Jr., Kunkel, P., and Weiss, S. Effect of pitressin in circulatory collapse induced by sodium nitrite. J. Clin. Invest. 18:673, 1939.

159. Kunkel, P., E.A. Stead Jr., and Weiss, S. Effect of paredrinol (a-N-dimethyl-p-hydroxyphenethylamine) on sodium nitrite collapse and on clinical shock. J. Clin. Invest. 18:679, 1939.

160. Weiss, S.. Vascular diseases with particular reference to arterial hypertension. New Engl. J. Med. 221:939, 1939.

161. Weiss, S. Syncope, collapse, and shock. Proc. Inst. Med. (Chicago) 13:2, 1940.

162. Weiss, S. Pharmacotherapy. New Engl. J. Med. 222:237, 1940.

163. Weiss, S. Clinico-pathological conference. Bull. New Engl. Med. Center 2:27, 1940.

164. Weiss, S. Arterial hypertension and its complications. Modern Med. Therapy in Gen. Practice, pg. 2711, 1940.

165. Weiss, S. Geriatrics. New Engl. J. Med. 222689, 1940.

166. Weiss, S. The medical student before and after graduation. J.A.M.A. 114:1709, 1940.

167. Weiss, S. Report of the Physician-in-Chief. Peter
      Bent Brigham Hospital, 26th Annual Report for
      the Year 1939, pg 79, 1940.

168. Leary, T., and Weiss, S. Dissecting aneurysm of
      the aorta in experimental atherosclerosis. Arch.
      Pathol. 11:665, 1940.

169. Weiss, S. The clinical and physiologic characteris-
      tics of arterial hypertension. Am. Assoc. Adv. Sci.
      13:295, 1940.

170. Haynes, F.W., and Weiss, S. Responses of the nor-
      mal heart and the heart in experimental vitamin
      B1 deficiency to metabolites (pyruvic acid, lactic
      acid, methyl glyoxal, glyceraldehyde, and adenyl-
      ic acid) and to thiamin. Am. Heart J. 20:34, 1940.

171. Weiss, S., Kinney, T.D., and Maher, M.M. Dissect-
      ing aneurysm of the aorta with experimental
      atherosclerosis. Am. J. Med. Sci. 200:192, 1940.

172. Weiss, S. The Intoxications. In Cecil's Textbook of
      Medicine, 5th Edition, Philadelphia, pg 595, 1940.

173. Weiss, S. Heart and deficiency diseases. Diag.
      Treat. . Dis. 2:1252, 1940.

174. Weiss, S. Symptoms of patients with heart disease
      and their interpretation. Med. Clinics No. Ameri-
      ca 24:1295, 1940.

175. Weiss, S. Occidental beriberi with cardiovascular
      manifestations. J.A.M.A. 115:832, 1940.

176. Weiss, S. Instantaneous "physiologic" death. New

Engl. J. Med. 223:793, 1940.

177. Weiss, S., and (by invitation) Dexter, L., Parker, F. Jr., and Tenney, B. Jr. Arterial hypertension in pregnancy and the hypertensive toxemia syndrome of pregnancy (preeclampsia and eclampsia). Trans. Assoc. Am. Phys. 55:282, 1940.

178. Weiss, S., and Parker, F. Jr. Relation of pyelonephritis and other urinary-tract infections to arterial hypertension. New Engl. J. Med. 223:959, 1940.

179. Weiss, S. Arterial hypertension. New Engl. J. Med. 223:959, 1940.

180. Weiss, S. Treatment of cardiovascular syphilis. Bull. Genitoinfectious Dis. 4:1, 1941.

181. Weiss, S. Diet and Bright's disease. Conn. State Med. J. 5:496, 1941.

182. Weiss, S. Arteritis: diseases associated with inflammatory lesions of the peripheral arteries. New Engl. J. Med. 225:579, 1941.

183. Weiss, S. Preeclamptic and eclamptic toxemia of pregnancy. Proc. Inter-State Postgraduate Medical Assembly of North America, October 13-17, 1941.

184. Weiss, S. The interpretation and treatment of spells of unconsciousness in medical and surgical practice. Proc. Inter-State Postgraduate Medical Assembly of North America, 1941.

185. Weiss, S. Report of the Physician-in-Chief. Peter

Bent Brigham Hospital, 27th Annual Report, for the Year 1940, pg 91, 1941.

186. Dexter, L., and Weiss, S. Preeclamptic and Eclamptic Toxemia of Pregnancy. Little, Brown Co., Publishers, Boston, 1941.

187. Weiss, S. Pulmonary congestion and edema. Bull. N.Y. Acad. Med. 18:93, 1942.

188. Weiss, S. Self-observations and psychologic reactions of medical student A.S.R. to the onset and symptoms of subacute bacterial endocarditis. J. Mt. Sinai Hosp. 8:1079, 1942.

189. Weiss, S. The treatment of vertigo and syncope. J.A.M.A. 118:529, 1942.

190. Weiss, S. Report of the Physician-in-Chief. Peter Bent Brigham Hospital, 28th Annual Report, for the Year 1941, pg 83, 1942.

191. Gordon, W.H., Parker, F. Jr., and Weiss, S. Gummatous aortitis. Arch. Int. Med. 70:386, 1942.

192. Dexter, L., Weiss, S., Haynes, F., and Sise, H.S. Hypertensive toxemia of pregnancy. Preeclampsia and eclampsia. J.A.M.A. 122:145, 1943.

193. Weiss, S., Stead, E.A., Warren, J.V., and Bailey, O.T. Scleroderma heart disease. With a consideration of certain other visceral manifestations of scleroderma. Arch. Int. Med. 71:749, 1943.

194. Golden, A., Dexter, L., and Weiss, S. Vascular disease following toxemia of pregnancy (preec-

lampsia and eclampsia). Observations on its clinical course. Arch. Int. Med. 72:301, 1943.

195. Peters, J.H., Dexter, L., and Weiss, S. Clinical and theoretical considerations of infection of the left side of the heart with echinococci. Am. Heart J. 29:143, 1945.

196. Peacock, W.C., Evans, R.D., Gibson, J.G. II, Good, W.M., Kip, A.F., and Weiss, S. The use of two radioactive isotopes of iron in studies of erythrocytes. J. Clin. invest. 25:605, 1946.

197. Gibson, J.G. II, Weiss, S., Evans, R.D., Peacock, W.C., Irvine, J.W. Jr., Good, W.M., and Kip, A.F. The measurement of the circulating red cell by means of two radioactive isotopes of iron. J. Clin. Invest. 25:616, 1946.

CURRICULUM VITAE
Eugene Anson Stead, Jr.

Birthplace and date: Atlanta; October 6, 1908
Education: B.S., 1928, Emory University
                 M.D., 1932, Emory University

Experience:
1932-1933 -   Intern, Medicine, Peter Bent Brigham Hospital
1933-1934 -   Research Fellow, Medicine, Harvard
1934-1935 -   Intern, Surgery, Peter Bent Brigham Hospital
1935-1936 -   Assistant resident, Medicine, Cincinnati General Hospital
1936-1937 -   Resident, Medicine, Cincinnati General Hospital
1937-1939 -   Assistant in Medicine, Harvard and Boston City Hospital
1939-1941 -   Instructor in Medicine, Harvard
1939-1942 -   Associate in Medicine, Peter Bent Brigham Hospital
1941-1942 -   Associate in Medicine, Harvard
1942-1946 -   Professor of Medicine and Chairman, Department of Medicine, Emory University
1945-1946 -   Dean, Emory University School of Medicine
1947-1967 -   Florence McAlister Professor of Medicine and Chairman, Department of Medicine, Duke University; Physician-in-Chief, Duke Hospital
1967 -   Florence McAlister Professor Emeritus of

Medicine, Duke University
1978-1985 - Distinguished Physician of the Veterans
Administration

Other Activities

Past secretary and past president, American Society of Clinical Investigation.

Past secretary and past president, Association of American Physicians

Master, American College of Physicians

Honorary Fellow, American College of Cardiology

Member, Association of University Cardiologists

Member, American Medical Association

Past member, Research Allocation Committee, American Heart Association

Past chairman, Ethics Committee, American Heart Association

Founding member, National Academy of Sciences Institute of Medicine

Past member, Panel on Space Science and Technology (NASA) of the President's Science Advisory Committee

Member, American Heart Association

Past member, Council of the National Heart Institute

Past member, Council of the National Institute of Arthritis and Metabolic Diseases

Past consultant to the National Heart Institute, Artificial Heart and Myocardial Infarction Program

Past member, Advisory Council, Life Insurance Medical Research Fund

Past director, Regenstrief Foundation for Research in

Health Care
Past editor, MEDICAL TIMES, 1966-1970
Past editor, CIRCULATION, 1973-1978
Medical Director, Durham Methodist Retirement Home, 1975-1978 Established training program for physician's assistants at Duke University, 1965
Editor, NORTH CAROLINA MEDICAL JOURNAL, 1983-
Board of Regents, National Library of Medicine, 1984-1988

Honors and Awards
Phi Beta Kappa
Alpha Omega Alpha
Distinguished Professor, Duke University, 1947
Honorary Fellow, American College of Cardiology
Citation for Distinguished Service to Research, American Heart Association, 1959
The John M. Russell Award, Markle Foundation, 1968
Distinguished Teacher Award, American College of Physicians, 1969
The Robert H. Williams Award, Association of Professors of Medicine, 1970
James B. Herrick Award, American Heart Association, 1970 Abraham Flexner Award for Distinguished Service to Medical Education, Association of American Medical Colleges, 1970
Founder's Award, Southern Society for Clinical Investigation, 1973
Honorary degree: Doctor of Science, Emory University, 1968 Honorary degree: Doctor of Science, Yale University, 1971

Georgia Heart Association, Symposium in Honor of Eugene Stead, 1976

Distinguished Teaching Award, Duke Medical Alumni Association, 1974

Gold Heart Award, American Heart Association, 1976

Honorary degree: doctor of Science, Medical College of Ohio, 1978

Kober Medal, Association of American Physicians, 1980

Rodman E. & Thomas G. Sheen Award, 1983

Publications

1. Bryan, A.H., Evans, W.A., Fulton, M.N., and Stead, E.A. Diuresis following the administration of salyrgan. Arch. Int. Med. 55:735-744, 1935.

2. Gregersen, M.I., Gibson, J.J., and Stead, E.A. Plasma volume determination with dyes: errors in colorimetry; use of blue dye T-1824. Am. J. Physiol. 113:No. 1, September 1935.

3. Stead, E.A., and Kunkel, P. A plethysmographic method for the quantitative measurement of the blood flow in the foot. J.   Clin. Invest. 17:711, 1938.

4. Kunkel, P., and Stead, E.A. Blood flow and vasomotor reactions in the foot in health, in arteriosclerosis, and in thrombo-angiitis obliterans. J. Clin. Invest. 17:715, 1938.

5. Kunkel, P., Stead, E.A., and Weiss, S. Blood flow and vasomotor reactions in the hand, forearm, foot and calf in response to physical and chemical stimuli. J. Clin. Invest. 18:225, 1939.

6. Stead, E.A., and Kunkel, P. Influence of the peripheral circulation in the upper extremity on the circulation time as measured by the sodium cyanide method. Am. J. Med. Sci. 198:49, 1939.
7. Stead, E.A., and Kunkel, P. Mechanism of the arterial hypertension induced by paredrinol. J. Clin. Invest. 18:439, 1939.
8. Stead, E.A., and Kunkel, P. Factors influencing the auricular murmur and the intensity of the first heart sound. Am. Heart J. 18:261, 1939.
9. Stead, E.A., Kunkel, P., and Weiss, S. Effect of pitressin in circulatory collapse induced by sodium nitrite. J. Clin. Invest. 18:673, 1939.
10. Stead, E.A., and Weiss, S. Effect of paredrinol on sodium nitrite collapse and on clinical shock. J. Clin. Invest. 18:679, 1939.
11. Stead, E.A., and Kunkel, P. Nature of peripheral resistance in arterial hypertension. J. Clin. Invest. 19:25, 1940.
12. Stead, E.A., and Kunkel, P. Absorption of sulphanilamide as an index of the blood flow in the intestine of man. Am. J. Med. Sci. 199:680, 1940.
13. Ebert, R.V., and Stead, E.A. The effect of the application of tourniquets on the hemodynamics of the circulation. J. Clin. Invest. 19:561, 1940.
14. Stead, E.A., and Ebert, R.V. The peripheral circulation in acute infectious diseases. Med. Clin. North America 24:1387, 1940.
15. Stead, E.A. Changes in the circulation produced by poor postural adaptation. Bull. New England Med. Center 2:290, 1940.

16.   Romano, J., Stead, E.A., and Taylor, Z.E. Clinical and electroencephalographic changes produced by a sensitive carotid sinus of the cerebral type. New Engl. J. Med. 223:708, 1940.

17.   Ebert, R.V., and Stead, R.A. An error in measuring changes in plasma volume after exercise. Proc. Soc. Exper. Biol. & Med. 46:139, 1941.

18.   Stead, E.A., and Ebert, R.V. Relationship of the plasma volume and the cell plasma ratio to the total red cell volume. Am. J. Physiol. 132:411, 1941.

19.   Stead, E.A., and Ebert, R.V. The action of paredrinol after induction of hemorrhage and circulatory collapse. Am. J. Med. Sci. 201:396, 1941.

20.   Stead, E.A., and Ebert, R.V. Postural hypotension; a disease of the sympathetic nervous system. Arch. Int. Med. 67:546, 1941.

21.   Ebert, R.V., and Stead, E.A. Demonstration that in normal man no reserves of blood are mobilized by exercise, epinephrine and hemorrhage. Am. J. Med. Sci. 201:655, 1941.

22.   Ebert, R.V., and Stead, E.A. Demonstration that the cell plasma ratio of blood contained in minute vessels is lower than that of venous blood. J. Clin. Invest. 20:317, 1941.

23.   Stead, E.A. The treatment of circulatory collapse and shock. Am. J. Med. Sci. 201:775, 1941.

24.   Ebert, R.V., and Stead, E.A. Circulatory failure in acute infections. J. Clin. Invest. 20:671, 1941.

25.   Ebert, R.V., Stead, E.A., and Gibson, J.G. Response

of normal subjects to acute blood loss. Arch. Int.
Med. 68:578, 1941.

26. Schales, O., Ebert, R.V., and Stead, E.A. Capillary
tube Kjeldahl method for determining protein content of 5 to 20 milligrams of Tussie fluid. Proc.
Soc. Exper. Biol. & Med. 490:1, 1942.

27. Stead, E.A., and Ebert, R.V. Shock syndrome produced by failure of the heart. Arch. Int. Med.
69:369, 1942.

28. Ebert, R.V., Stead, E.A., Warren, J.V., and Watts,
W.S. Plasma protein replacement after hemor-
rhage in dogs with and without shock. Am. J.
Physiol. 136:299, 1942.

29. Stead, E.A., Ebert, R.V., Romano, J., and Warren,
J.V. Central autonomic paralysis. Arch. Neurol.
Psychiat. 48:92, 1942.

30. Warren, J.V., Walter, C.W., Romano, J., and Stead,
E.A. Blood flow in the hand and forearm after
paravertebral block of the sympathetic ganglia.
Evidence against sympathetic vasodilator nerves
in the extremities of man. J. Clin. Invest. 21:665,
1942.

31. Schales, O., Stead, E.A., and Warren, J.V. Nonspe-
cific effect of certain kidney extracts in lowering
blood pressure. Am. J. Med. Sci. 204:797, 1942.

32. Warren, J.V., and Stead, E.A. The effect of the
accumulation of blood in the extremities on the
venous pressure of normal subjects. Am. J. Med.
Sci. 205:501, 1943.

33. Weiss, S., Stead, E.A., Warren, J.V., and Bailey,
O.T. Scleroderma heart disease. Arch. Int. Med.

71:749, 1943.

34.   Stead, E.A., and Warren, J.V. Clinical significance
      of hyperventilation: the role of hyperventilation in
      the production, diagnosis and treatment of certain
      anxiety symptoms. Am. J. Med. Sci. 206:108,
      1943.

35.   Warren, J.V., Merrill, A.J., and Stead, E.A. The
      role of the extracellular fluid in the maintenance
      of a normal plasma volume. J. Clin. Invest. 22:635,
      1943.

36.   Stead, E.A. The Pathologic Physiology of General-
      ized Circulatory Failure and of Cardiac Pain. In A
      Textbook of Medicine. Ed: Cecil, 6th ed., W.B.
      Saunders Co., Phila., 1943, pp 1017-1030.

37.   Stead, E.A. Circulatory Collapse and Shock. In A
      Textbook of Medicine. Ed: Cecil, 6th ed., W.B.
      Saunders Co., Phila., 1943, pp 1199-1202.

38.   Warren, J.V., and Stead, E.A. Fluid dynamics in
      chronic congestive heart failure. Arch. Int. Med.
      73:138, 1944.

39.   Stead, E.A., and Warren, J.V. The effect of the
      injection of histamine into the brachial artery on
      the permeability of the capillaries of the forearm
      and hand. J. Clin. Invest. 23:283, 1944.

40.   Stead, E.A., and Warren, J.V. The protein content
      of the extracellular fluid in normal subjects after
      venous congestion and in patients with cardiac
      failure, anoxemia and fever. J. Clin. Invest.
      23:283, 1944.

41.   Stead, E.A., and Warren, J.V. Care of the patient
      with chronic heart disease. Med. Clin. North

America 28:381, 1944.

42.   Stead, E.A. Shock. Kentucky Med. J., May 1944.
43.   Warren, J.V., Stead, E.A., Merrill, A.J., and Brannon, E.S. Chemical, clinical and immunological studies on the products of human plasma fractionation. IX. The treatment of shock with concentrated human serum albumin: a preliminary report. J. Clin. Invest. 23:506, 1944.
44.   Warren, J.V., and Stead, E.A. The protein content of edema fluid in patients with acute glomerulonephritis. Am. J. Med. Sci. 208:618, 1944.
45.   Cooper, F.W., Stead, E.A., and Warren, J.V. The beneficial effect of intravenous infusions in acute pericardial tamponade. Ann. Surg. 120:822, 1944.
46.   Stead, E.A., and Warren, J.V. Orientation to the mechanisms of clinical shock. Arch. Surg. 50:1, 1945.
47.   Stead, E.A., Warren, J.V., Merrill, A.J., and Brannon, E.S. The cardiac output in male subjects as measured by the technique of right atrial catheterization. J. Clin. Invest. 44:326, 1945.
48.   Brannon, E.S., Merrill, A.J., Warren, J.V., and Stead, E.A. The cardiac output in patients with chronic anemia as measured by the technique of right atrial catheterization. J. Clin. Invest. 44:332, 1945.
49.   Warren, J.V., Brannon, E.S., Stead, E.A., and Merrill, A.J. The effect of venesection and the pooling of blood in the extremities on the atrial pressure and cardiac output in normal subjects with observations on acute circulatory collapse in three

instances. J. Clin. Invest. 44:337, 1945.

50. Stead, E.A. Shock syndrome in internal medicine.
     Oxford Medicine 2:133, 1945.

51. Warren, J.V., Stead, E.A., and Brannon, E.S. The
     cardiac output in man: a study of some of the er-
     rors in the method of right heart catheterization.
     Am. J. Physiol. 145:458, 1946.

52. Brannon, E.S., Stead, E.A., Warren, J.V., and Mer-
     rill, A.J. Hemodynamics of acute hemorrhage in
     man. Am. Heart J. 31:407, 1946.

53. Merrill, A.J., Warren, J.V., Stead, E.A., and Bran-
     non, E.S. The circulation in penetrating wounds of
     the chest: a study by the methods of right heart
     catheterization. Am. Heart J. 31:413, 1946.

54. Warren, J.V., Brannon, E.S., Stead, E.A., and Mer-
     rill, A.J. Pericardial tamponade from stab wound
     of the heart and pericardial effusion of empyema:
     a study utilizing the method of right heart cathe-
     terization. Am. Heart J. 31:418, 1946.

55. Stead, E.A., Brannon, E.S., Merrill, A.J., and War-
     ren, J.V. Concentrated human albumin in the
     treatment of shock. Arch. Int. Med. 77:564, 1946.

56. Stead, E.A., Hickam, J.B., and Warren, J.V. Mech-
     anism for changing the cardiac output in man.
     Trans. Assoc. Am. Phys. 60:74, 1947.

57. Stead, E.A., and Warren, J.V. Cardiac output in
     man. An analysis of the mechanisms varying the
     cardiac output based on recent clinical studies.
     Arch. Int. Med. 80:237, 1947.

58. Stead, E.A. Fainting. In Signs and Symptoms. Ed:
     MacBryde. J.B. Lippincott, Phila., 1947, pp 179-

187.

59.   Stead, E.A. Relation of the cardiac output to the symptoms and signs of congestive heart failure. Modern Concepts of Cardiovasc. Dis. 16:No. 12, 1947.

60.   Warren, J.V., Brannon, E.S., Weens, H.S., and Stead, E.A. Effect of increasing the blood volume and right atrial pressure on the circulation of normal subjects by intravenous infusions. Am. J. Med. 4:192, 1948.

61.   Scheinberg, P., Dennis, E.W., Robertson, R.L., and Stead, E.A. The relation between arterial pressure and blood flow in the foot. Am. Heart J. 35:409, 1948.

62.   Stead, E.A., Warren, J.V., and Brannon, E.S. Cardiac output in congestive heart failure. Am. heart J. 35:529, 1948.

63.   Stead, E.A., Warren, J.V., and Brannon, E.S. Effect of lanatoside C on the circulation of patients with congestive heart failure. Arch. Int. Med. 81:282, 1948.

64.   Scheinberg, P., and Stead, E.A. The cerebral blood flow in male subjects as measured by the nitrous oxide technique. Normal values for blood flow, oxygen utilization, glucose utilization and peripheral resistance, with observations on the effect of tilting and anxiety. J. Clin. Invest. 28:1163, 1949.

65.   Stead, E.A. Edema of heart failure. Bull. New York Acad. Med. 24:607, 1948.

66.   Stead, E.A. The role of the cardiac output in the mechanisms of congestive heart failure. Am. J.

Med. 6:232, 1949.

67. Stead, E.A. Circulatory factors in congestive heart
     failure. Trans. 3rd Conf., Josiah Macy, Jr. Founda-
     tion 178, May 1949.

68. Stead, E.A. Dietary and diuretic management of
     congestive failure. North Carolina Med. J. 2:54,
     1950.

69. Stead, E.A. Heart failure. Proc. lst Natl. Conf. Car-
     diovascular Diseases. Am. Heart Assoc., New
     York, 157-160, 1950.

70. Scheinberg, P., Stead, E.A., Brannon, E.S., and
     Warren, J.V. Correlative observations on cerebral
     metabolism and cardiac output in myxedema. J.
     Clin. Invest. 29:1139, 1950.

71. Stead, E.A., Myers, J.D., Scheinberg, P., Cargill,
     W.H., Hickam, J.B., and Levitan, B.A. Studies of
     cardiac output and of blood flow and metabolism
     of splanchnic area, brain and kidney. Trans. Asso.
     Am. Phys. 63:241, 1950.

72. Stead, E.A. Circulatory Collapse and Shock. In
     Textbook of Medicine. Ed: Cecil & Loeb. W.B.
     Saunders Co., Phila., 1951, pp 1211-1214.

73. Stead, E.A. Pathologic Physiology of Generalized
     Circulatory Failure. The Treatment of Congestive
     Heart Failure, Cardiac Dilatation and Hypertro-
     phy. In Textbook of Medicine. Ed: Cecil & Loeb.
     W.B. Saunders Co., Phila., 1951, pp 1051-1066.

74. Stead, E.A. Renal factor in congestive heart fail-
     ure. Circulation 3:294, 1951.

75. Stead, E.A. Cerebral blood flow and metabolism.
     Am. J. Med. 9:415, 1950.

76.   Murphy, R.J., and Stead, E.A. Effects of exogenous and endogenous posterior pituitary antidiuretic hormone on water and electrolyte excretion. J. Clin. Invest. 30:1055, 1951.

77.   Stead, E.A. Edema and dyspnea of heart failure. Bull, New York Acad. Med. 28:159, 1952.

78.   Holland, B.C., and Stead, E.A. Effect of vasopressin (pitressin)-induced water retention on sodium excretion. A.M.A. Arch. Int. Med. 88:571, 1951.

79.   Bell, D.M., and Stead, E.A. Effects of epinephrine on the vessels of the calf. Observations on the period of initial vasodilatation. J. Appl. Physiol. 5:228, 1952.

80.   Stead, E.A. Fainting. Am. J. Med. 13:387, 1952.

81.   Stead, E.A. Presidential Address: Proc. 45th Annual Meeting, American Society for Clinical Investigation, May 1953. J. Clin. Invest. 32:548, 1953.

82.   Stead, E.A. Treatment of chronic and undiagnosed illness. GP 8:73, 1953.

83.   Stead, E.A. Peripheral Vascular Disease. In Textbook of Medicine. Ed: Cecil & Loeb. Blakiston, New York, 1954, pp 1437-1448.

84.   Stead, E.A. General Considerations of Pain. In Principles of Internal Medicine. Ed: Harrison. McGraw-Hill, New York, 1954, pp 17-20.

85.   Holland, B.C., and Stead, E.A. Electrolyte excretion after single doses of ACTH, cortisone, desoxycorticosterone glucoside and motionless standing. J. Clin. Invest. 33:132, 1954.

86.   Stead, E.A. Circulatory Collapse and Shock. In
       Textbook of Medicine. Ed: Cecil & Loeb. W.B.
       Saunders Co., Phila., 9th ed., 1955, pp 1261-1264.
87.   Stead, E.A. Diseases of the Cardiovascular System.
       In Textbook of Medicine. Ed: Cecil & Loeb. W.B.
       Saunders Co., Phila., 9th ed., 1955, pp 1230-1246.
88.   Stead, E.A., and Hickam, J.B. Heart Failure.
       Disease-a-Month. Year Book Publishers, Inc.,
       Chicago, 1955, pp 3-32.
89.   Burnum, J.F., Hickam, J.B., and Stead, E.A. Hy-
       perventilation in postural hypotension. Circulation
       10:362, 1954.
90.   Stead, E.A., and Warren, J.V. Controlling obesity
       with low fat cookery. Am. Acad. Gen. Pract. 15:98,
       1957.
91.   Stead, E.A. Fainting (Syncope). In Signs and Symp-
       toms. Ed: MacBryde. J.P. Lippincott, 3rd ed.,
       1957, pp 665-678.
92.   Stead, E.A., and Wallace, J.M. Reactivity of small
       blood vessels. Trans. Assoc. Am. Phys. 70:275,
       1957.
93.   Orgain, E.S., and Stead, E.A. Congestive heart fail-
       ure. Circulation 16:291, 1957.
94.   Wallace, J.M., and Stead, E.A. Spontaneous pres-
       sure elevations in small veins and effects of
       norepinephrine and cold. Circul. Res. 5:650, 1957.
95.   Stead, E.A. Peripheral Vascular Disease. In
       Principles of Internal Medicine. Ed: Harrison.
       Blakiston, New York, 1958, pp 1339-1348.
96.   Stead, E.A. Diagnosis and Treatment of Congestive
       Heart Failure. Interview. Modern Medicine, Au-

gust 1958, pp 164-182.

97. Stead, E.A. Pathological Physiology of Generalized Circulatory Failure. In A Textbook of Medicine. Eds: Cecil & Loeb. W.B. Saunders Co., Phila., 1959, 19th ed., pp 1172-1187.

98. Stead, E.A. Circulation Collapse and Shock. In A Textbook of Medicine. Eds: Cecil & Loeb. W.B. Saunders Co., Phila., 1959, 19th ed., pp 1199-1202.

99. Stead, E.A. Pain in the Extremities. In Principles of Internal Medicine. Ed: Harrison. Blakiston, New York, 1958, 3rd ed., pp 64-67.

100. Wallace, J.M., and Stead, E.A. Fall in pressure in radial artery during reactive hyperemia. Circul. Res. 7:876, 1959.

101. Stead, E.A. Hyperventilation. Disease-a-Month, February 1960. Year Book Publishers, Inc., Chicago.

102. Wallace, J.M., Garcia, H., and Stead, E.A. Arteriovenous differences of the norepinephrine-like material from normal plasma and infused norepinephrine. J. Clin. Invest. 40:1387, 1961.

103. Gorten, R., Gunnells, J.C., Weissler, A.M., and Stead, E.A. Effects of atropine and isoproterenol on cardiac output, central venous pressure, and mean transit time with indicators placed at three different sites in the venous system. Circul. Res. 9:979, 1961.

104. Stead, E.A., and Kinney, T.D. Clinicopathologic Conferences, Duke University School of Medicine. Ed: A.G. Smith. So. Med. J. 55:410, 1962.

105. Stead, E.A. Pain in the Extremities. In Principles of Internal Medicine. Ed: Harrison. McGraw-Hill, New York, 1962, pp 56-60.
106. Stead, E.A. Meaning of human behavior to the physician of tomorrow. Arch. Int. Med. 110:409, 1962.
107. Stead, E.A. Medical care: its social and organization aspects. Postgraduate medical education in the hospital. New England J. Med. 269:240, 1963.
108. Stead, E.A. The evolution of the medical university. J. Med. Educ. 39:368, 1964.
109. Stead, E.A., and Greenfield, i.C. Pressures and pulses. Physiology for Physicians 2:March 1964.
110. Stead, E.A., and Greenfield, J.C. Pressures and pulses. Trans. Assoc. Life Insurance Med. Directors of American 48:164, 1964.
111. Stead, E.A. An internist looks at behavior. JAMA 195:565, 1965.
112. Stead, E.A. Hyperbaric oxygenation. Editorial. Circulation 34:361, 1966.
113. Stead, E.A. Preparation for practice. Pharos 29:70, 1966.
114. Stead, E.A. Vascular Disease of the Extremities. In Principles of Internal Medicine. Ed: Harrison. McGrawHill, 5th ed., New York, 1966, pp 719-728.
115. Stead, E.A. Challenge and opportunity. Editorial. Med. Times 94:70, 1966.
116. Stead, E.A. Your National Library of Medicine. Editorial. Med. Times 94:507, 1966.
117. Stead, E.A. The many facets of asbestosis. Edito-

rial. Med. Times 94:633, 1966.

118. Stead, E.A. Hypertension—highways and byways. Editorial. Med. Times 94:766, 1966.

119. Stead, E.A. Looking at the heart in 1966. Editorial. Med. Times 94:884, 1966.

120. Stead, E.A. Intern and residency training. Editorial. Med. Times 94:1001, 1966.

121. Stead, E.A. Hyperbaria. Editorial. Med. Times 94:1128, 1 9 6 6 .

122. Stead, E.A. On bacterial endocarditis. Editorial. Med. Times 94:1250, 1966.

123. Stead, E.A. Reversible "madness". Editorial. Med. Times 94:1403, 1966.

124. Stead, E.A. "Good will toward men". Editorial. Med. Times 14:1535, 1966.

125. Stead, E.A. Training and use of paramedical personnel. New England J. Med. 277:800, 1967.

126. Stead, E.A. Pathologic Physiology of Heart Failure. In A Textbook of Medicine. Eds: Cecil & Loeb. W.B. Saunders Co., Phila., 1967, pp 577-590.

127. Stead, E.A. Treatment of Congestive Heart Failure. In A Textbook of Medicine. Eds: Cecil & Loeb. W.B. Saunders Co., Phila., 1967, pp 590-593.

128. Stead, E.A. Health manpower. Editorial. Med. Times 95:116, 1967.

129. Stead, E.A. The lung. Editorial. Med. Times 95:235, 1967.

130. Stead, E.A. Quality of medical care. Editorial. Med. Times 95:356, 1967.

131. Stead, E.A. Traps and stratagems of diagnosis. Editorial. Med. Times 95:588, 1967.

132. Stead, E.A. Thinking ward rounds. Editorial. Med. Times 95:706, 1967.

133. Stead, E.A. Patients that recover. Editorial. Med. Times 95:802, 1967.

134. Stead, E.A. The Duke plan for physician's assistants. Editorial. Med. Times, January 1978.

135. Stead, E.A. Prevention of myocardial reinfarction. Editorial. Med. Times 95:899, 1967.

136. Stead, E.A. Postural hypotension. Editorial. Med. Times 95:1120, 1967.

137. Cleland, J., Aitken, P., Bryson, E., Hohman, L., Jones, T., Menefee, Peete, W., and Stead, E.A. The right to live and the right to die. Med. Times 95:1171, 1967.

138. Stead, E.A. The rights of the foetus. Editorial. Med. Times 95:2226, 1967.

139. Stead, E.A. The birth of a new educational venture — the association of schools of allied health professions. Editorial. Med. Times 96:99, 1968.

140. Stead, E.A. The delivery of health care. Editorial. Med. Times 96:216, 1968.

141. Stead, E.A. Educational programs and manpower. Bull. New York Acad. Med. 44:204, 1968.

142. Stead, E.A. More knowledge about the renal factors influencing sodium excretion. Editorial. Med. Times 96:665, 1968.

143. Stead, E.A. Myocardial infarction: the first 15 minutes. Editorial. Med. Times 96:665, 1968.

144. Stead, E.A. Health and illness. Editorial. Med. Times 96:753, 1968.

145. Stead, E.A. A college-based physician's assistant

program. Editorial. Med. Times 96:847, 1968.

146. Stead, E.A. Cost conscious doctors. Editorial. Med. Times 96:947, 1968.

147. Stead, E.A. The need for a machine processable medical data base. Editorial. Med. Times 96:1154, 1968.

148. Stead, E.A. Words make pictures. Editorial. Med. Times 96:1249, 1968.

149. Stead, E.A. The limitations of teaching. Pharos 32:54, 1 9 6 9

150. Stead, E.A. What we have learned about myocardial infarction from epidemiologic and dietary studies. Circulation 40:IV-85, 1969.

151. Stead, E.A. The role of the university in graduate training. J. Med. Educ. 44:739, 1969.

152. Stead, E.A. The assets of a community hospital. Editorial. Med. Times 97:225, 1969.

153. Stead, E.A. Picking other people's brains. Editorial. Med. Times 97:264, 1969.

154. Stead, E.A. To manage or not to manage. Editorial. Med. Times 97:241, 1969.

155. Stead, E.A. A National Academy of Medicine. Editorial. Med. Times 97:234, 1969.

156. Stead, E.A. Space biology and medicine — an unmet challenge. Editorial. Med. Times 97:228, 1969.

157. Stead, E.A. The physician's assistant — job description and licensing. Editorial. Med. Times 97:246, 1969.

158. Stead, E.A. Public assistance and society. Editorial. Med. Times 97:231, 1969.

159. Stead, E.A. The white bear syndrome. Editorial. Med. Times 97:256, 1969.
160. Stead, E.A. Why moon walking is simpler than social progress. Editorial. Med. Times 97:248, 1969.
161. Stead, E.A. "Clinical trials" for proposed legislation? Editorial. Med. Times 97:187, 1969.
162. Stead, E.A. Pain in the Extremities. In Principles of internal Medicine. Ed: Wintrobe. McGraw-Hill, New York, 1970, pp 1265-1274.
164. Stead, E.A. Medical education and practice. Ann. Int. Med. 72:271, 1970.
165. Stead, E.A. Congestive heart failure revisited. Editorial. Med. Times 98:200, 1970.
166. Stead, E.A. Angina pectoris teaches. Editorial. Med. Times 98:201, 1970.
167 - Stead, E.A. "Origin of the species". Editorial. Med. Times 98:223, 1970.
168. Stead, E.A. Dialogue in California. Editorial. Med. Times 98:204, 1970.
169. Stead, E.A. Universal service — a necessity and an opportunity. Editorial. Med. Times 98:217, 1970.
170. Stead, E.A. "If I become ill and unable to manage my own affairs..." Editorial. Med. Times 98:191, 1970.
171. Stead, E.A. Up the health staircase. Editorial. Med. Times 98:213, 1970.
172. Stead, E.A. Fainting (Syncope). In Signs and Symptoms. Ed: MacBryde. J.P. Lippincott, Phila., 1970, pp 712-721.
173. Stead, E.A. A proposal for the creation of a com-

pulsory national service corps. Arch. Int. Med. 127:89, 1971.

174. Stead, E.A. Why moon walking is simpler than social progress. Pharos 34:3, 1971.

175. Stead, E.A. Physicians — past and future. Arch. Int. Med. 127:703, 1971.

176. Stead, E.A. Use of physicians, assistants in the delivery of medical care. Ann. Rev. Med. 22:273, 1971.

177. Stead, E.A., Editor: with C.M. Smythe, C.G. Gunn, M.H. Littlemeyer. Educational technology for medicine: roles for the Lister Hill Center. J. Med. Educ. 46:11-93, 1971.

178. Stead, E.A. The way of the future. Presidential Address. Trans. Assoc. Am. Phys. 85:1-5, 1972.

179. Stead, E.A. Building a school. Am. J. Dis. Children 124:343, 1972.

180. Rosati, R.A., Wallace, A.G., and Stead, E.A. The way of the future. Arch. Int. Med. 131:285, 1973.

181. Stead, E.A. Information and chronic illness. Editorial. J. Intn. Research Communications, November 1973.

182. Anlyan, W.G., Austen, W.G., Beck, J.C., Bradford, W.D., Brown, R.E., Cherkasky, M., Elam, L.C., Kinney, T.D., London, I.M., Medearis, D.N., vander Kooot, W.G., and Stead, E.A. The Future of Medical Education. Duke University Press, 1973, pp 192.

183. Stead, E.A. Medical care policy rounds: physician's assistants. Ed: Robbins. CMA Journal 197:439, 1972.

184. Stead, E.A. Philosophy and Practice. In Hippocrates Revisited. Ed: R.J. Bulger. Medcom Press, New York, 1973, pp 283.

185. Stead, E.A. Walter Kempner: a perspective. Arch. Int. Med. 133:755, 1974.

186. Stead, E.A. New roles for personnel in hospitals: physician extenders. Bull. New York Acad. Med. 55:41, 1979.

187. Stead, E.A., and Stead, N.W. Problems and challenges in the treatment of the aging patient. Disease-a-Month 26:No. 11, 3-41, 1980.

188. Stead, E.A. The physician's assistant and internal medicine. Am. J. Med. 70:1161, 1981.

189. Stead, E.A. The biological basis for career changes. The Internist, October 1981, Vol. 22, pg 6.

190. Stead, E.A. Heart Disease in the Elderly. In The Heart. Ed: Hurst. McGraw-Hill, 5th ed., 1981, pp 1545-1546.

191. Stead, E.A. Unsolved issues in medicine: geriatrics as a case in point. Editorial. J. Am. Geriatrics Soc. 30:231, 1982.

192. Stead, E.A. Where one stands determines what one sees. Pharos 45:27, 1982.

193. Stead, E.A. Management of Common Problems in the Elderly. In Cecil Textbook of Medicine. Ed: J.B. Wyngaarden and L.H. Smith. W.B. Saunders Co., Phila., 16th ed., 1982, pp 39-44.

194. Stead, E.A. Organization of departments and divisions of dermatology in a time of change. Editorial. J. Am. Acad. Dermatology 9:785, 1983.

195. Stead, E.A. The Editor's philosophy. Editorial. N.C.

Med. J. 44:209, 1983.

196. Stead, E.A. The need for social preventive medicine. Editorial. N.C. Med. J. 44:278, 1983.

197. Stead, E.A. Joint Conference Committee on Medical Care, Inc. Editorial. N.C. Med. J. 44:348, 1983.

198. Stead, E.A. What you cannot learn from your own practice. Editorial. N.C. Med. J. 44:349, 1983.

199. Stead, E.A. Requirements for successful coalitions. Editorial. N.C. Med. J. 44:469, 1983.

200. Stead, E.A. The use of the fundus to demonstrate the complexity of communications. Editorial. N.C. Med. J. 44:617, 1983.

201. Stead, E.A. NCMJ advertising revenues. Editorial. N.C. Med. J. 44:771, 1983.

202. Stead, E.A. How the handle fit in 1960. Editorial. N.C. Med. J. 45:766, 1984.

203. Stead, E.A. Time will tell. Editorial. N.C. Med. J. 45:178, 1984.

204. Stead, E.A. Why dependency is increasing. Editor. N.C. Med. J. 45:178, 1984.

205. Stead, E.A. A curious, interested doctor at peace with the complexities of biology. Editorial. N.C. Med. J. 45:251, 1984.

206. Stead, E.A. Training is no substitute for education. Editorial. N.C. Med. J. 45:579, 1984.

207. Stead, E.A. How the handle fit in 1960. Editorial. N.C. Med. J. 45:766, 1984.

CURRICULUM VITAE
Paul Bruce Beeson

Birthplace and date: Livingston, Montana; October 18, 1908

Education: 1925-1928, University of Washington
M.D., C.M., 1933, McGill University
Hon. D.Sc., 1968, Emory University
D.M., 1969, Oxford University
Hon. D.Sc., 1971, McGill University
Hon. D.Sc., 1975, Yale University
Hon. D.Sc., 1975, Albany Medical College
Hon. D.Sc., 1979, Medical College of Ohio

Experience:
1933-1935 - Intern, Hospital of the University of Pennsylvania
1935-1937 - General Practice, Wooster, Ohio
1937-1939 - Resident, Rockefeller Institute Hospital
1939-1940 - Resident in Medicine, Peter Bent Brigham Hospital
1940-1942 - Chief Physician, American Red Cross - Harvard Field Hospital Unit, Salisbury, England
1942-1944 - Assistant Professor of Medicine, Emory University
1944-1946 - Associate Professor of Medicine, Emory University
1946-1952 - Professor and Chairman, Department of Medicine, Emory University

1952-1965 - Professor and Chairman, Department of Medicine, Yale University

1965-1974 - Nuffield Professor of Clinical Medicine, Oxford University

1974-1981 - Distinguished Physician, Veterans Administration

1974-1981 - Professor of Medicine, University of Washington (Emeritus, 1981-present)

Honors and Awards

1962 - Member, American Academy Arts & Sciences

1963 - Co-Editor, Cecil Textbook of Medicine (to 1979)

1963 - Fiftieth Anniversary Gold Medal, Peter Bent Brigham Hospital

1966 - Fellow, Royal College of Physicians

1967 - President, Association of American Physicians

1968 - Alumnus Summa Laude Dignatus, University of Washington

1968 - Member, National Academy of Sciences

1970 - Master, American College of Physicians

1972 - Bristol Award, Infectious Diseases Society of America

1973 - Kober Medal, Association of American Physicians

1973 - Honorary Knight Commander of the British Empire

1975 - Honorary Fellow, Royal Society of Medicine

197 - Honorary Fellow, Magdalen College, Oxford

1976 - Phillips Award, American College of Physicians

1977 - Flexner Award, Association of American Medical Colleges

1980 - Honorary Member, Reticuloendothelial Society
1981 - Paul B. Beeson Professorship created, Yale University
1981 - Honorary Fellow, Green College, Oxford
1981 - Gold-Headed Cane Award, University of California, San Francisco
1982 - Founders Award, Southern Society for Clinical Research
1984 - Willard Thompson Award, American Geriatrics Society
1984 - Honorary Member, Canadian Society of Internal Medicine
1986 - Co-Editor, Oxford Companion to Medicine
1990 - Distinguished Teacher Award, American College of Physicians

Publications
1.   Beeson, P.B., and Hoagland, C.L. Use of calcium chloride in relief of chills following serum administration. Proc. Soc. Exp. Biol. (N.Y.), 38:160, 1938.
2.   Hoagland, C.L., Beeson, P.B., and Goebel, W.F. The capsular polysaccharide of the Type XIV pneumococcus and its relationship to the specific substances of human blood. Science 88:261, 1938.
3.   MacLeod, C.M., Hoagland, C.L., and Beeson, P.B. The use of the skin test with the type specific polysaccharides in the control of serum dosage in pneumococcal pneumonia. J. Clin. Invest. 17:739, 1938.
4.   Goebel, W.F., Beeson, P.B., and Hoagland, C.L.

Chemoimmunological studies on the soluble specific substance of pneumococcus, IV. The capsular polysaccharide of Type XIV pneumococcus and its relationship to the blood group A specific substance. J. Biol. Chem. 129:455, 1939.

5.   Beeson, P.B., and Goebel, W.F. The immunological relationship of the capsular polysaccharide of Type XIV pneumococcus to the blood Group A specific substance. J. Exp. Med. 70:239, 1939.

6.   Beeson, P.B., and Hoagland, C.L. The use of calcium chloride in the treatment of chills. N.Y. St. J. Med. 40:803, 1940.

7.   Beeson, P.B., and Janeway, C.A. The antipyretic action of sulfapyridine. Am. J. Med. Sci. 200:632, 1940.

8.   Beeson, P.B., and Goebel, W.F. Immunological crossreactions of Type B Friedlander bacillus in Type 2 antipneumococcal horse and rabbit serum. J. Immunol. 38:231, 1940.

9.   Janeway, C.A., and Beeson, P.B. The treatment of pneumococcal pneumonia; with special reference to the use of sulfathiazole, intramuscular serum, the Francis test and histaminase. New Engl. J. Med. 244:592, 1941.

10. Beeson, P.B. Factors influencing the prevalence of trichinosis in man. Proc. Roy. Soc. Med. 34:585, 1941.

11. Beeson, P.B. Trichinosis. Clinical manifestations and diagnosis. Lancet 2:67, 1941.

12. Levine, S.A., and Beeson, P.B. The Wolff-Parkinson-White syndrome,.with paroxysms of ven-

tricular tachycardia. Am. Heart J. 22:401, 1941.

13. Beeson, P.B., and Scott, T.F. McN. An epidemic myalgia distinct from Bornholm disease, which chiefly affected the muscles of the neck. Ann. Rheum. Dis. 2:1, 1941.

14. Beeson, P.B., and Scott, T.F. McN. Clinical, epidemiological and experimental observations on an acute myalgia of the neck and shoulders; its possible relation to certain cases of generalized fibrositis. Proc. Roy. Soc. Med. 35:733, 1942.

15. Scott, T.F. McN., Beeson, P.B., and Hawley, W.L. Paratyphoid B infection. The ineffectiveness of sulphaguanadine. Lancet 1:487, 1943.

16. Beeson, P.B. Jaundice occurring one to four months after transfusion of blood or plasma. Report of seven cases. J.A.M.A. 121:1332, 1943.

17. Beeson, P.B., and Westerman, E. Cerebrospinal fever. Analysis of 3,575 case reports, with special reference to sulphonamide therapy. Brit. Med. J. 1:497, 1943.

18. Beeson, P.B. The problem of the etiology of rat bite fever. Report of two cases due to Spirillum minus. J.A.M.A. 123:332, 1943.

19. Beeson, P.B. Fever. Clinics 2:1361, 1944.

20. Beeson, P.B., and Miller, E.S. Relationship of lymphogranuloma venereum infection to the incidence of hyperglobulinemia. Am. J. Med. Sc. 297:643, 1944.

21. Beeson, P.B., Chesney, G., and McFarlan, A.M. Hepatitis following injection of mumps convalescent plasma. I. Use of plasma in the mumps

epidemic. Lancet 1:814, 1944.
22. Beeson, P.B., and Miller, E.S. Epidemiological study of lymphogranulama venereum, employing the complement-fixation test. Am. J. Publ. Health 34:1076, 1944.
23. Beeson, P.B., Brannon, E.S., and Warren, J.V. observations on the sites of removal of bacteria from the blood in patients with bacterial endocarditis. J. Exp. Med. 81:9, 1945.
24. Beeson, P.B., and Heyman, A. Studies on chancroid, II. Efficiency of the cultural method of diagnosis. Am. J. Syph. 29:633, 1945.
25. Heyman, A., Beeson, P.B., and Sheldon, W.H. Diagnosis of chancroid. The relative efficiency of biopsies, cultures, smears, auto-inoculations and skin tests. J.A.M.A. 129:935, 1945.
26. Beeson, P.B., and Miller, E.S. Murine typhus fever. Medicine (Baltimore) 25:1, 1946.
27. Heyman, A., and Beeson, P.B. Studies on chancroid. III. Ducrey skin reactions in Negro hospital patients. J. Vener. Dis. Inform. 27:104, 1946.
28. Beeson, P.B. Studies on chancroid. IV. The Ducrey bacillus: growth requirements and inhibition by antibiotic agents. Proc. Soc. Exp. Biol. (N.Y.) 61:81, 1946.
29. Beeson, P.B. Development of tolerance to typhoid bacterial pyrogen and its abolition by reticulo-endothelial blockade. Proc. Soc. Exp. Biol. (N.Y.) 61:248, 1946.
30. Beeson, P.B., Wall, M.J., and Heyman, A. Isolation of virus of lymphogranuloma venereum from

blood and spinal fluid of a human being. Proc. Soc. Exp. Biol. (N.Y.) 62:306, 1946.

31.   Heyman, A., Wall, M.J., and Beeson, P.B. The effect of sulfonamide therapy on the persistence of the virus of lymphogranuloma venereum in buboes. Am. J. Syph. 31:81, 1947.

32.   Beeson, P.B. Effect of reticulo-endothelial blockade on immunity to the Shwartzman phenomenon. Proc. Soc. Exp. Biol. (N.Y.) 64:146, 1947.

33.   Wall, M.J., Heyman, A., and Beeson, P.B. Studies on the complement fixation reaction in lymphogranuloma venereum. Am. J. Syph. 31:289, 1947.

34.   Beeson, P.B. Tolerance to bacterial pyrogens. I. Factors influencing its development. J. Exp. Med. 86:29, 1947.

35.   Beeson, P.B. Tolerance to bacterial pyrogens. II. Role of the reticuloendothelial system. J. Exp. Med. 86:39, 1947.

36.   Cargill, W.H., and Beeson, P.B. The value of spinal fluid examination as a diagnostic procedure in Weills disease. Ann. Int. Med. 27:396, 1947.

37.   Heyman, A., and Beeson, P.B. Influence of various disease states upon the febrile response to intravenous injection of typhoid bacterial pyrogen; with particular reference to malaria and cirrhosis of the liver. J. Lab. Clin. Med. 34:1400, 1949.

38.   Michael, M. Jr., Cole, R.M., Beeson, P.B., and Olson, B.J. Sarcoidosis. Preliminary report on a study of 350 cases with special reference to epidemiology. Am. Rev. Tuberc. 62:403, 1950.

39. Bennett, I.L. Jr., and Beeson, P.B. The properties and biologic effects of bacterial pyrogens. Medicine 29:365, 1950.

40. Beeson, P.B., and Hankey, D.D. "Benign aseptic meningitis" as a manifestation of leptospiral infection. Trans. Assoc. Am. Phys. 63:130, 1950.

41. Beeson, P.B. Fever of obscure origin. Veterans Adm. Med. Bull., pg 10, 1951.

42. Beeson, P.B., Hankey, D.D., and Cooper, C.F. Leptospiral iridocyclitis. Evidence of human infection with leptospira pomona in the United States. J.A.M.A. 145:229, 1951.

43. Beeson, P.B., and Hankey, D.D. Leptospiral meningitis. Arch. Int. Med. 89:575, 1952.

44. Beeson, P.B. Cryptococcic meningitis of nearly sixteen years' duration. Arch. Int. Med. 89:797, 1952.

45. Beeson, P.B. Leptospiral infections of man (editorial). Am. J. Med. 15:591, 1953.

46. Bennett, I.L. Jr., and Beeson, P.B. Studies on the pathogenesis of fever. I. The effect of injection of extracts and suspensions of uninfected rabbit tissues upon the body temperature of normal rabbits. J. Exp. Med. 98:477, 1953.

47. Bennett, I.L. Jr., and Beeson, P.B. Studies on the pathogenesis of fever. II. Characterization of fever-producing substances from polymorphonuclear leukocytes and from the fluid of sterile exudates. J. Exp. Med. 98:493, 1953.

48. Bennett, I.L. Jr., and Beeson, P.B. The effect of cortisone upon reactions of rabbits to bacterial

endotoxins with particular reference to acquired resistance. Bull. Johns Hopkins Hosp. 93:290, 1953.

49.   Bennett, I.L. Jr., and Beeson, P.B. Bacteremia: a consideration of some experimental and clinical aspects. Yale J. Biol. Med. 26:241, 1954.

50.   Beeson, P.B. Subacute bacterial endocarditis: optimal duration of treatment (editorial). Am. J. Med. 19:1, 1955.

51.   Hollingsworth, J.W., and Beeson, P.B. Experimental bacteremia in normal and irradiated rats. Yale J. Biol. Med. 28:56, 1955.

52.   Beeson, P.B. Factors in the pathogenesis of pyelonephritis. Yale J. Biol. Med. 28:81, 1955.

53.   Hollingsworth, J.W., Finch, S.C., and Beeson, P.B. The role of transfused leukocytes in experimental bacteremia of irradiated rats. J. Lab. Clin. Med. 48:227, 1956.

54.   Guze, L.B., and Beeson, P.B. Observations on the reliability and safety of bladder catheterization for bacteriologic study of the urine. New Engl. J. Med. 255:474, 1956.

55.   Guze, L.B., and Beeson, P.B. Experimental pyelonephritis. I Effect of ureteral ligation on the course of bacterial infection in the kidney of the rat. J. Exp. Med. 104:803, 1956.

56.   Guze, L.B., and Beeson, P.B. The effect of cortisone on experimental hydronephrosis following ureteral ligation. J. Urol. (Baltimore) 78:337, 1957.

57.   Beeson, P.B., Rocha, H., and Guze, L.B. Experi-

mental pyelonephritis: influence of localized injury in different parts of the kidney on susceptibility to hematogenous infection. Trans. Assoc. Am. Phys. 70:120, 1957.

58. Beeson, P.B. The case against the catheter (editorial). Am. J. Med. 24:1, 1958.

59. Guze, L.B., and Beeson, P.B. Experimental pyelonephritis. II. Effect of partial ureteral obstruction on the course of bacterial infection in the kidney of the rat and the rabbit. Yale J. Biol. Med. 30:315, 1958.

60. Rocha, H., Guze, L.B., Freedman, L.R., and Beeson, P.B. Experimental pyelonephritis. III. The influence of localized injury in different parts of the kidney on susceptibility to bacillary infection. Yale J. Biol. Med. 30:341, 1958.

61. Freedman, L.R., and Beeson, P.B. Experimental pyelonephritis. IV. Observations on infections resulting from direct inoculation of bacteria in different zones of the kidney. Yale J. Biol. Med. 30:406, 1958.

62. Beeson, P.B., and Rowley, D. The anticomplementary effect of kidney tissue. Its association with ammonia production. J. Exp. Med. 110:685, 1959.

63. Rocha, H., Guze, L.B., and Beeson, P.B. Experimental pyelonephritis. V. Susceptibility of rats to hematogenous pyelonephritis following chemical injury of the kidneys. Yale J. Biol. Med. 32:120, 1959.

64. Freedman, L.R., Kaminskas, E., and Beeson, P.B. Experimental pyelonephritis. VII. Evidence on the

mechanisms by which obstruction of urine flow enhances susceptibility to pyelonehphritis. Yale J. Biol. Med. 33:65, 1960.

65. Beeson, P.B. Clinical medicine and the future. Yale J. Biol. Med. 33:235, 1960.

66. Freedman, L.R., and Beeson, P.B. Experimental pyelonephritis. VIII. Effect of acidifying agents on susceptibility to infection. Yale J. Biol. Med. 33:318, 1961.

67. Petersdorf, R.G., and Beeson, P.B. Fever of unexplained origin. Report of 100 cases. Medicine 40:1, 1961.

68. Beeson, P.B., and McDermott, W. (editors) The Cecil-Loeb Textbook of Medicine, 11th Edition, Philadelphia, W.B. Saunders Co., 1963.

69. Beeson, P.B. Nocardiosis as a complication of pulmonary alveolar proteinosis (editorial). Ann. Int. Med. 60: 1964.

70. Beeson, P.B., Bondy, P.K., Donnelly, R.C., and Smith, J.E. Panel discussion: moral issues in clinical research. Yale J. Biol. Med. 36:455, 1964.

71. Beeson, P.B. The Academic Doctor. Presidential Address, Transactions of the Association of American Physicians, lxxx, 1967.

72. Beeson, P.B., and McDermott, W. (editors) The Cecil-Loeb Textbook of Medicine, 12th Edition, Philadelphia, W.B. Saunders Co., 1967.

73. Beeson, P.B. Special Book Review of "Sickness and Society" by Duff and Hollingshead. Yale J. Biol. Med. 41:226, 1968.

74. Beeson, P.B. Eugene A. Stead, Jr.: A biographical

note. Ann. Int. Med. 69:986, 1968.

75. Basten, A., Boyer, M.H., and Beeson, P.B. Mechanism of eosinophilia. I. Factors affecting the eosinophil response of rats to Trichinella spiralis. J. Exp. Med. 131:1271, 1970.

76. Basten, A., and Beeson, P.B. Mechanism of eosinophilia. II. Role of the lymphocyte. J. Exp. Med. 131:1288, 1970.

77. Boyer, M.H., Basten, A., and Beeson, P.B. Mechanism of eosinophilia. III. Suppression of eosinophilia by agents known to modify immune responses. Blood 36(No-4):458, 1970,

78. Beeson, P.B., and McDermott, W. (editors) The Cecil-Loeb Textbook of Medicine, 13th Edition, Philadelphia, W.B. Saunders Co., 1971.

79. Morgan, J.E., and Beeson, P.B. Experimental observations on the eosinopenia induced by acute infection. Br. J. Exp. Path. 52:214, 1971.

80. Beeson, P.B. Medical education for the future. Montreal General Hospital 1921-1971. C.M.A. Journal 105:1253, 1971.

81. Beeson, P.B. "Quality of Survival". Reprinted from Patient, Doctor, Society. Published for the Nuffield Provincial Hospitals Trust by the Oxford University Press, 1972.

82. Boyer, M.H., Spry, C.J.F., Beeson, P.B., and Sheldon, W.H. Mechanism of eosinophilia. IV. The pulmonary lesion resulting from intravenous injection of Trichinella spiralis.. Yale J. Biol. Med. 43:351, 1971.

83.   Durack, D.T., and Beeson, P.B. Experimental bacterial endocarditis. I. Colonization of a sterile vegetation. Brit. J. Exp. Path. 53:44, 1972.
84.   Durack, D.T., and Beeson, P.B. Experimental bacterial endocarditis. II. Survival of bacteria in endocardial vegetations. Brit. J. Exp. Path. 53:50, 1972.
85.   Walls, R.S., and Beeson, P.B. Mechanism of eosinophilia. VIII. Importance of local cellular reactions in stimulating eosinophil production. Clin. Exp. Immunol. 12:111, 1972.
86.   Walls, R.S., and Beeson, P.B. Mechanism of eosinophilia. IX. Induction of eosinophilia in rats by certain forms of dextran. Proc. Soc. Exp. Biol. Med. 140:689, 1972.
87.   Durack, D.T., Beeson, P.B., and Petersdorf, R.G. Experimental bacterial endocarditis. III. Production and progress of the disease in rabbits. Br. J. Exp. path. 54:142, 1973.
88.   Durack, D.T., Petersdorf, R.G., and Beeson, P.B. Penicillin prophylaxis of experimental S.Viridans endocarditis. Reprinted from Transactions of the Association of American Physicians, Vol. lxxx, pg 222, 1972.
89.   Walls, R.S., Bass, D.A., and Beeson, P.B. Mechanism of eosinophilia. X. Evidence for immunologic specificity of the stimulus (37989). Proc. Soc. Exp. Biol. Med. 145:1240, 1974.
90.   Beeson, P.B. Some good features of the British National Health Service. J. Med. Ed. 49:42, 1974.

91. Beeson, P.B., and McDermott, W. (editors) Textbook of Medicine, 14th Edition, Philadelphia, W.B. Saunders Co., 1975.
92. Beeson, P.B. The ways of academic clinical medicine in American since World War II. Man and Medicine 1:65, 1975.
93. Horstmann, D., and Beeson, P.B. John Rodman Paul. Biographical memoirs. Natl. Acad. Sci. (U.S.) 47:323, 1975.
94. Beeson, P.B. Infectious Diseases (Microbiology). In Advances in American Medicine. Essays at the Bicentennial. Eds: Bowers, J.Z., and Purcell, E.F., Macy Foundation, New York, 1976.
95. Starkebaum, M., Durack, D., and Beeson, P.B. The "Incubation Period" of subacute bacterial endocarditis. Yale J. Biol. Med. 50:49, 1977.
96. Beeson, P.B. Role of the Eosinophil. In Immunology of the Gut. (Ciba Foundation Symposium 46 - new series). Elsevier Excerpta Medica, North-Holland, pg 203, 1977.
97. Beeson, P.B. The development of clinical knowledge. J.A.M.A. 237:2209, 1977.
98. Durack, D.T., and Beeson, P.B. Protective role of complement in experimental Escherichia coli endocarditis. Infect. Immun. 16:213, 1977.
99. Beeson, P.B., and Bass, D.A. The Eosinophil. W.B. Saunders Co., Philadelphia, 1977.
100. Beeson, P.B. McKeown's The Role of Medicine: A Clinician's Reaction. Milbank Memorial Fund Quarterly, Summer 1971, pg 365.

101. Durack, D.T., and Beeson, P.B. Pathogenesis of Infective Endocarditis. In Infective Endocarditis. Ed: Rahimtoola, S.H., Grune & Stratton, New York, 1978.

102. Beeson, P.B. Training doctors to care for old people. Ann. Int. Med. 90:262, 1979.

103. Beeson, P.B. The growth of knowledge about a disease: hepatitis. Am. J. Med. 67:366, 1979.

104. Beeson, P.B., and McDermott, w. (editors) Textbook of Medicine, 15th Edition, Philadelphia, W.B. Saunders Co., 1979.

105. Beeson, P.B. Book Review of "Infectious Diseases: Prevention and Treatment in the Nineteenth and Twentieth Centuries", by Wesley W. Spink. J. Hist. Med. 34:370, 1979.

106. Beeson, P.B. Changes in medical therapy during the past half century. Medicine 59:79, 1980.

107. Beeson, P.B. How to foster the gain of knowledge about disease. Perspect. Biol. Med. 23:59, 1980.

108. Beeson, P.B. Some diseases that have disappeared. Am. J. Med. 68:806, 1980.

109. Beeson, P.B. The natural history of medical subspecialties. Ann. Int. Med. 93:624, 1980.

110. Beeson, P.B. The Clinical Significance of Eosinophilia. In The Eosinophil in Health and Disease. Eds: Mahmoud, A.A.F., and Austen, K.F., Grune & Stratton, New York, 1980.

111. Beeson, P.B. Withering revisited. New Engl. J. Med. 303:1475, 1980.

112. Beeson, P.B. Priorities in medical education. Perspect. Biol. Med. 25:673-687, 1982.

113. Beeson, P.B. Lessons learned from editing a geriatrics journal. J. Am. Geriat. Soc. 32:849, 1984.

114. Beeson, P.B. Geriatrics. J.A.M.A. 252:2209, 1984.

115. Beeson, P.B. Alleged susceptibility of the elderly to infection. Yale J. Biol. Med. 58:71, 1985.

116. Beeson, P.B. The Institute of Medicine report on aging and medical education - 1984 update. Bull. N.Y. Acad. Med. 61:478, 1985.

117. Beeson, P.B. Classics in infectious diseases: Observations on the sites of removal of bacteria from the blood of patients with bacterial endocarditis. Retrospective commentary. Rev. Infect. Dis. 7:574, 1985.

118. Beeson, P.B. One hundred years of American internal medicine. Ann. Int. Med. 105:436, 1986.

119. Beeson, P.B. The changing role model, and the shift in power. In Americals Doctors, Medical Science, Medical Care, Daedalus, pg 83, 1986.

120. Beeson, P.B. Making medicine a more attractive profession. J. Med. Education 62:116, 1987.

121. Beeson, P.B. Walsh McDermott. In Biographical Memoirs. Natl. Acad. Sci., in press.

122. Beeson, P.B. Too many specialists, too few generalists. Daedalus, pg. 2-6, Spring, 1991.